Practical Carp Fishing

PRACTICAL CARP
Fishing

Julian Cundiff

The Crowood Press

First published in 1993 by
The Crowood Press Ltd
Ramsbury, Marlborough
Wiltshire SN8 2HR

British Library Cataloguing in Publication Data

A catalogue record for this book is available from the British Library.

ISBN 1 85223 733 3

Dedication
This book is dedicated to Tim Paisley, Eric Hodson and Eric Taylor. Particular thanks are also due to my family, workmates and special lady, without whose patience I could never have completed it.

Designed by:
D & N Publishing
DTP & Editorial Services
The Old Surgery
Lambourn
Berkshire RG16 7NR

Throughout this book the pronouns 'he', 'his' and 'him' have been used to refer to both men and women.

All photographs by the author.
Line drawings by Brian Atkins.

Phototypeset by FIDO Imagesetting, Witney, Oxon.
Printed and bound in Great Britain by
BPCC Hazell Books Ltd
Member of BPCC Ltd

CONTENTS

ACKNOWLEDGEMENTS

I know that this book could not have been completed without the advice, help and friendship of my friends in carp fishing. A large part of carp fishing is spent in the company of others, and for me this has meant both good friends and good fishing. There have been odd clashes of personalities, but to all those I have met on the bank I wish the best of luck in the coming years. However, to leave it at that would be most unfair to the special friends I have, and to the following people in particular I owe a debt of gratitude.

For Special Friendship
Tim and Mary Paisley, Andy Little and family, Chris Ball and family, Zenon Bojko, Mike Wilson, Eric Hodson and family, Pete Curtis, Brian Atkins, Rob Heald, Tony Hamshaw, Pete Fidling, Kevin Nash, Richard Skidmore, Bill Cottam, John Raison and crew, Ritchie Macdonald, Kevin Clifford, Dave Cooper, and Fran and Ian Dain.

For Friendship
John Harry, Peter Broxup, Peter Wright, Roger Hawkins, Keith Selleck, Mark Nichols, Frank Warwick, Mark Lawson, Dave Colledge, Geoff Thompson, Brian Skoyles, Andy Pratt and Ray Marshall.

For Inspiration
Kevin Maddocks, Rob Maylin, Rod Hutchinson, Mathew Black, Mike Wilson, Geoff Kemp, Lee Jackson, Alan Smith, Zenon Bojko, Andy Little, Ritchie Macdonald, Tim Paisley, Roger Smith, Bob Jones, Harry Haskell, Peter Springate, Eric Hodson, Clive and Malcolm, Kevin Nash, Chris Ball and Paul Selman.

For Help with Products
Bill Cottam and Richard Skidmore at Nutrabaits, John Middleton at Daiwa Ltd, Gary Barclay at Drennan Tackle, Keith Selleck at Middlesex Angling Centre, Kevin Nash at Kevin Nash Tackle, Bryan Jarrett at Hinder's of Swindon, Bob Baker at Streamselect Ltd, Dave Chilton at Kryston Products, Richard Gardner at Gardner Tackle, Cliff Fox at Fox Tackle, Len Gurd at Original Video Co Ltd, Brian Parker at Cotswold Baits, Martin Kowal at SBS, Roger Sherwood at Crafty Catcher, Eddie Turner at E. T. Products, Chris Brown at C. B. Developments, Nina Sansome at Cobra Products, Albert Romp and Jim Martinez at Romart, Dave Fletcher at Obelisk Stainless, and Alan Bramley at Partridge Hooks.

For Good Service
Rob Heald at Rotherham Carp Baits, Kevin Crawley at Leslie's of Luton, Shaun Harrison at Walker's of Trowell, all the lads at Tackle Box, and Keith Selleck at Middlesex Angling Centre.

For Publishing
Tim Paisley at Angling Publications, Simon Roff at *Coarse Fisherman*, David Hall at *Coarse Fishing*, Rob Maylin at *Big Carp*, Richard Howard at *Anglers' Mail*, John Bailey at Crowood, and Alec Welland at *Carp Catcher*.

For the Future
John Patterson, Colin Davidson, Neil Budd, Scott Kempton, Lee Nash, Duncan Putman, Andy Price, Darren Kade and Jamie Holt.

FOREWORD

Having been involved in the compilation of over fifty carp fishing magazines, I have handled numerous first efforts at writing about carp. As a rule, first efforts are inspired by the capture of an exceptional fish. Some are very good and others not so good, but nine times out of ten the article turns out to be the would-be-writer's only article and you don't hear of them again – not as a writer, anyway.

Out of literally hundreds of first efforts, I remember Julian Cundiff's first submission to *Carp Fisher* magazine quite vividly. It was called 'Who's Kidding Who?' and I had to write back to query the grammar of the title, and ask for further pictures with the angler *and* the fish in focus. The pictures were immediately submitted, with a note suggesting that there were plenty more where those came from!

Six or seven years on, 'The Selby Flier', as Jules is affectionately known, has flown. His photographs cannot be faulted in their variety or quality, and he has developed into a publisher's dream. You want an article? He'll write you an article and have it to you on time – if not sooner – and it will be prolifically illustrated. You want a book? He'll write a book – and here's his first major work to prove it. He has already compiled *Carp Waters* in the Carp in Depth series and I would venture to guess that there are many more books to come from his talented pen. But to Jules this one will always be special, and this will make it special to those of us who are fortunate enough to befriend this remarkable young man.

Julian's first book; my first foreword. Being asked to write it makes me feel very old – which I suppose I am. It also makes me feel flattered and proud. I know that an enormous amount of hard work has gone into the writing and illustrating of the pages that follow. The end result is a book that cannot fail to help all of us catch carp. Well done Jules.

Tim Paisley

Tim Paisley and the author with Tim's first Crowood book in 1988.

INTRODUCTION

I suppose the thought of writing a book about carp fishing must go through most carp angling writers' minds and, to be fair, it is something I have thought about since early 1990 but hadn't constructively worked at until John Bailey contacted me in May 1992. Although I have written many articles since the mid-1980s which have gradually become more technical and informative, it was only recently that I felt I could put forward a book that would be a worthwhile addition to the carp angler's bookshelf and hopefully would help people catch carp.

Since 1983 I have been an avid collector of all types of carp angling literature from bait catalogues to magazines to leather-bound classics on our favourite species. Every single article or piece I have ever read has had something I could draw from, even if that usage has been subconscious rather than copying a specific rig or bait recipe. All literature can be useful; my task is to convince you, the reader, that this book will be more than merely interesting, rather it will help you catch carp, and catch carp consistently.

Initially, I was approached to write a smaller book, an A–Z of carping for carp anglers. However, as I sat down and talked to John, it was clear to us that a space was there in the market – in fact a glaring space – which ought to be filled by an up-to-date book on practical carp fishing.

There are a number of basic 'how to do it' books on carp fishing which I am sure you are more than well aware of. I shall not go into too much detail, but David Batten's *Introduction to Carp Fishing*, Peter Mohan's *Basic Carp Fishing* books and many more all provide a good starting block for the budding carp angler. Similarly, at the top end of carp fishing, books like *Big Carp* by Tim Paisley and *Big Water Carp* by Jim Gibbinson have been written for those experienced carp anglers who have been relatively successful over the years and wish to move on to larger fish and bigger waters. Yet few books are aimed at the ninety per cent of anglers in the carp world who have only been fishing for carp a few years, or have been fishing for carp a number of years.

From my series in *Coarse Fisherman*, which started way back in 1990 and still continues in 1993, it is clear that many of you have progressed beyond the basics but need good, common-sense advice in carp angler's language from which you can draw your own conclusions. I hope this book is for you.

I won't pretend I could ever become as accomplished as the Tim Paisleys and Rod Hutchinsons of this world, but what I feel I do have is the ability to put on to paper advice from which a large percentage of you will be able to gain something. If this book is aimed at anybody, it is aimed at those who have caught carp but wish to be more proficient at it. As I have sat and written the book, I have tried to write what I should have liked to have read when I needed help.

As you sit and read this I truly hope it will provide all of you with some help with your carp fishing. Whilst there are always some who will proclaim to have learnt nothing, I am confident that somewhere in this book and – it is hoped – throughout this book, you will be informed and inspired to catch carp as I have been over the last ten years.

Julian Cundiff

1

THE CARP

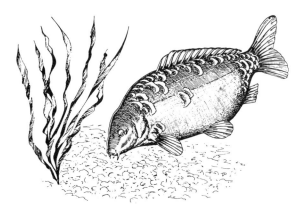

Ask a football manager how he plans to beat an opposing team, or a prize fighter how he intends to pulverize the opposition and he will say, aside from the usual patter, that you should know your opponent. Fishing for carp should not be any different, and if you really want to catch carp on a regular basis it is vital that you know at least a little of how they tick, what attracts and repels them, and what you can do to decrease the odds which are stacked in the carp's favour. Many carp anglers, especially today, seem to forget this point altogether and are so wound up in baits, rigs and all the hype that they forget that the quarry they are seeking to catch hasn't got hands, hasn't read *Carp Fever* or *Fox Pool* and certainly isn't impressed with expensive bedchairs. If you really want to catch those carp, as I know you do, leave the sheep to their endless rig and bait discussions and think carp!

I am not going to make this section too heavy because I know many of you will be more interested in bait, rigs and the like, and a couple of thousand heavy words on the carp is only likely to have you flicking past the chapter at great speed. Well, please don't do that – I'll keep it

basic and practical, and whilst more detailed carp studies are available I'm sure that what I'm about to lay down will more than satisfy your needs. As I say throughout the book, a successful carp angler will be a person who has a good working knowledge of all carp fishing matters and not just baits, rigs or even the anatomy of a carp!

ANATOMY OF A CARP

I have included a diagram of the carp (*see* Fig. 1) at this stage with two main purposes in mind. Firstly, you need to be aware of what a carp has and has not got compared with a human, and secondly how the position of its vital organs should affect the way you hold a carp when you catch it (be positive!).

HANDLING CARP

Although it may appear that this section looks out of sequence, because carp seem to be caught so regularly nowadays and people are catching them even if they don't really understand why, I think it is vital that you are at least aware of how the vital organs in a carp can be damaged if it is not held properly when the inevitable trophy shot is taken. As Fig. 1 shows, the carp's vital organs such as the heart, liver and kidneys are localized towards the area where most carp anglers hold a fish when wishing to emphasize its size. This area is soft and unprotected, and when a carp's weight out of water rests directly on hands placed under this area real problems can occur (*see* Fig. 2). The results may be pain to the carp or in some cases death, so please get this important process right

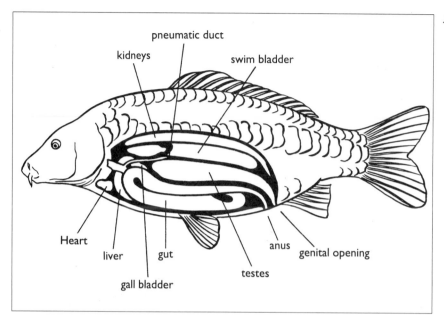

Fig. 1 Anatomy of a carp.

kidneys

pneumatic duct

swim bladder

Heart

liver   gut

gall bladder

testes

anus   genital opening

before you read any further. Simply spread your hands a little more apart, keep the fish low and over the unhooking mat and smile (*see* Fig. 3).

CARP SENSES

Sight

In most animals sight is the primary sense, but with carp and other bottom-feeding fish the ability to feed using this sense alone is extremely limited. There is no evidence as far as I am aware that carp have any special form of eyesight to allow feeding to continue in low light conditions. Most waters we fish are full of suspended solids of all sorts: grit, decomposed vegetable matter, algae and so on that live in what at times is almost a thin soup. If the water is particularly clear and it is daylight, visibility may be as much as 20ft, but in typical waters it can be down to 3ft or less. In such conditions it is not the blue end of the spectrum that penetrates the furthest but the red colour. Even when they are faint, it is fair to say that red colours show up best. However, the colour you see may not be the colour the carp will recognize; because we are humans and not carp it is impossible to say for sure. What we can say with a

degree of certainty is that there is no way a carp can see a bait when there is no light by which to see. So if all your action is coming in darkness your bait colour is not the deciding factor – or is it? Perhaps your baits are too visible in the day, so deterring carp, and it is only when the light fades that they are prepared to pick them up?

Touch

The sense of touch is vital in a carp as it is one of the primary survival mechanisms which can cause it to bolt or to investigate further. This sense of touch is contained within the four sensitive barbules which probe for live organisms contained in the river or lake bed. By pushing its head into the silt or weed, a carp is able to extend the range of these barbules and so increase its chances of finding food.

Hearing

Carp have two forms of hearing: the first is the inner ear which is connected via the swim bladder and which is receptive to low- to mid-range frequencies; the second is the lateral line which many anglers are aware of even if they do choose to ignore its effectiveness. This lateral line is responsive to waves caused by vibration and other movements in the carp's environment, and as sound travels well in water you should realize that shouting, banging rod rests and so on all go towards decreasing your chances of success rather than increasing them!

Smell

Carp have a particularly well developed sense of smell and can detect minute traces of food even at a distance. However well this sense is tuned in it is far superior to a human's and far different. Just because you may like or dislike the smell of a boily as you perceive it, don't think a carp is in any way like you – this is a common mistake many of us make. Providing your particular bait is attractive enough to the carp via its sense of smell it will then move on to taste that bait.

Taste

As with our sense of smell, our taste awareness is very different from that of the carp, and again don't confuse your preferences with those of the carp. I can't stand spicy foods but I know carp like Robin Red so I use it! Providing the bait or food tastes correctly (in other words, like food!) to the carp it will continue feeding until satisfied. If not, it will reject the food and sample other items instead.

Knowledge of the five main senses of a carp can dictate how successful or otherwise you are as a carp angler. I could have gone into a lot more detail on these, but as long as you are aware of these senses and how they differ from a human's, then we have made progress.

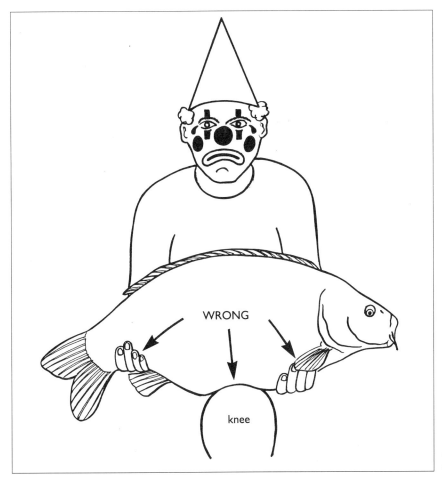

WRONG

knee

Fig. 2 The incorrect way to hold a carp.

HOW DOES A CARP FEED?

First of all – and I'm not trying to be clever here – carp do not have hands to use to pick food items up like we do, so never confuse your feeding habits with those of a carp. What may look like a good or bad rig to you may well appear or act quite differently when tried on carp in their natural environment.

A carp will adapt to feed in whatever way its environment or body shape dictates. Hence, even fish with terribly torn mouths or those carrying fixed rigs sometimes continue to feed and grow. Whilst it is impossible to say definitely how a carp feeds on all waters, I have found them to feed in two particular ways; ways in which they can seek out rogue baits from free offerings when subjected to constant recapture on a certain bait and certain method.

The first and probably most common way is where the carp sucks in its food from a distance of between ¼in to 3in from its mouth. Whilst I have heard talk of carp sucking in baits from up to 12in away, I have never seen this and have difficulty in accepting that it can be possible. Certainly a carp may move a bait at distance by releasing water through its gills, but I doubt it could suck a bait in at that range! Normally, the carp will approach a food item which it has located by sight, smell or other means and, at a certain distance from the bait as the carp sees fit, it will seek to take that bait in.

First, it will raise its pharyngeal cap and close its mouth and gullet to create a partial vacuum inside. The mouth will then open, there will be an inrush of water which draws all sorts of sediment and food items into the mouth. The mouth will then close, the food items will be held by the tongue and, as the mouth contracts, water will be

RIGHT

fish held low over mat

Fig. 3 *The correct way to hold a carp.*

pushed out of the gills and hopefully your carp will be hooked. However, it is not quite as easy as that and if your food item hasn't made it into the carp's mouth it will obviously not be hooked. If the fish has taken the food but decides to reject it then it will release the tongue pressure and instead of taking the bait in will spit it out. If your hooking arrangement is good enough you may hook the carp, if not you won't. Carp can follow this process either when stationary or whilst on the move and have the ability to do it many times in just a few seconds, dependent on how big the fish is and how many food items it is taking in.

The second method of feeding is where carp simply purse their lips over the food item and gently take it in, almost sucking it in. This is not the only way of feeding on all carp waters and, whilst everybody seems to think carp are extremely wary and feed in this way while feeling for hooks and such like, I'm sure it doesn't happen on half the waters you might think it does. Some carp suck and blow, some pick up and some do a combination of both. The successful carp angler will vary and change his hooking arrangements until he gets it right. The unsuccessful ones will not even think about it! Of course, you will only hook the carp if it moves and pulls the hook into itself.

THE EFFECT OF THE SEASONS ON CARP

If you intend to fish for carp all year round then it is vital that as the seasons change you adapt your fishing to suit the carp's feeding requirements at that time of year. To follow exactly the same baiting and angling methods from summer through to winter may ruin your chances in winter, and may mean you are not making the most of it when the going is good in summer. Big beds of fishmeal may well work well in summer, but try them in winter and it can and probably will be the kiss of death. Similarly, if you just use one or two baits and a stringer you may well catch fish in winter but in the summer those carp may well pass you by. Adapt and catch – don't stagnate!

The business end of our quarry.

Spring

In the spring, water temperatures will generally have been low for some time and then will start to rise. As the temperature rises so will a carp's need to feed in order to grow and repair damage, and, providing you are sensible, the spring can be an excellent time to catch carp. The carp will be looking for food again and as long as you don't overface them you have every chance of catching numbers of fish rather than just the odd one. How much the carp will eat will be determined by water temperature, quality of water and so on, but at this time of year when it is neither too hot nor too cold you do have an excellent chance of early success.

Summer

Once the temperature reaches a certain level, carp will feed and feed strongly. I have been told that the optimum feeding water temperature is 66°F, so in summer when the daytime temperature can exceed this it may be that dawn and dusk are your most productive times, providing you can locate the carp. At the correct temperature a carp will feed more and need more food (protein) to grow. Use your common sense and, if possible, tailor your fishing time and bait introduction to the times and places where a carp is most likely to feed the strongest. Prolonged hot summer weather and subsequent decreases in oxygen levels will limit these feeding spells so that your need to hit it spot-on and with the correct amount of bait becomes even more important.

Autumn

As in the spring, the autumn can produce bonanza catches because temperatures may be at the correct level for longer periods. Unlike the summer when dawn and dusk offer your best chances, or winter when temperatures are struggling to rise, autumn produces constant temperatures that are also often close to the optimum. However, if it is still very hot or there has been a drastic fall in temperature, regulate your bait introduction to the needs of the carp and not your personal whims and fancies.

Winter

Because carp are cold-blooded creatures their body temperature will fluctuate as the water temperature fluctuates. In winter when water temperatures drop so will the carp's body temperature (to within 10 per cent of the water temperature), and when its body temperature is low so will be its ability to digest and utilize food. So in winter cut right back on food and also make sure the food you use is digestible. This may mean that high-fat fishmeals are out and protein or attractor baits should be looked at if you wish to use boiled baits.

Hopefully, this chapter will have given you some sort of an insight into the world of the carp and exactly what makes it tick. Carp have only survived for all these years because they have become masters of their own environment. In a changing environment survival means the ability to recognize, pick up and utilize the carp anglers' baits, but also to reject those food items which spell danger. Blanking is not necessarily just down to you not having the right rig or bait; it can be down to the carp's need to feed balanced against your behaviour on the bank, so think on!

A thing of beauty, but do you know what makes it tick?

2 LOCATION IN THE 1990s

If you pick up any book on carp fishing you will find that one of the author's main priorities seems to be trying to stress how important location is. From walking around a fishery and looking for fish to plumbing as many swims as possible, authors have rightly suggested that location is very important in carp fishing – after all, you can't catch a carp if you don't put a bait where it will pick it up, can you? Now if this was a perfect world where you could go down to your fishery each and every time and have your 'choice' of swims, then those who get location right should catch most of the fish. However, on many waters it's a case of getting in where you can, if you can get in at all. Carp fishing is a boom business and everybody seems to want to catch one. Each person who goes fishing takes up another swim and even if they've dropped into the best swim by accident, there's nothing you can do about it and you have to make do with what's available. This chapter is aimed not only at trying to locate carp in a fishery but also at how to make the best of the swim that you may find yourself in by default rather than by choice.

JUST HOW IMPORTANT IS LOCATION?

You will catch carp only if you place your bait where they are prepared to feed – there is no getting away from this fact. However, just getting your location right is not an automatic guarantee that you will catch carp. This is because of what we call hot spots.

Hot Spots

Even if you think you are in the right spot it is very easy not to position your bait in the right place. Fish jumping out in front of you, signs of fish feeding or an acknowledged 'hot swim' are all indicators that you may be in the right area – but is your baited tackle in the right spot? Anybody who has ever fished to a weedbed or to snags will know how important it is to be in the right gap or directly next to a certain branch. Cast too far away from it and you don't get a pick-up, get it right and you may catch a number of fish.

This isn't limited only to visible features, and even if you are fishing to underwater features such as bars, shelves, plateaux or gulleys it can be vitally important to be in *the* correct spot. This might be a slight depression in a bar which carp use to pass over, or perhaps a concentration of bloodworm or whatever, but there are certain areas within a lake from which carp are more likely to be caught. Finding them is the problem and no amount of literature can tell you their placement as it varies from water to water. These hot spots can be the key to making your results spectacular rather than mediocre. Don't think that just because you are in a good swim you will catch or in a bad one that you won't, because that's just not true; it is the correct areas in that swim that are the key to success.

As I said, nobody can tell you where these hot spots are; it's a case of finding them through educated guesswork and luck. My usual way is to find an area of water I think will contain carp and then try to work that area as best as I can. Fish only the swim you are in and not across everybody elses'. Whilst some people don't agree with me, I usually place all three rods to an area and try to find *the* hot spot in that area. That could mean for a session or two I have all my rods to the first bar or weedbed until I find a spot I'm happy with. Then I'll leave one rod on it and try another area and so on. It works for me and I think it can work for you, too. However, to make sure you are in the correct spot each and every time it is essential to remember to keep a record of where the exact spot is. I cover this in the next chapter, so read on.

EFFECTS ON LOCATION

Angler Pressure

As I have said, there are certain areas which are more prolific than others on a fishery. Your aim is to find these areas and catch from them before everybody else does. Areas can become fished out, so even if a certain bar or weedbed has been good to you and still screams carp, you should be aware that angler pressure may have forced carp away from it, or at least made them very wary when feeding in such an area. Don't flog a once-good swim for no reason other than memories – make some new ones instead!

The Seasons

Do be aware that as the seasons change so do a carp's feeding habits and therefore its location. In winter you may well find carp grouped tightly together but, once warmer weather is upon us, they may well disperse and feed in a variety of places. Whilst they may well feed avidly in the shallows in the summer, if you fish there all year round you may not even get a take from November to March.

Below is a list of areas in which I would expect to find carp at different times of the year. It's now up to you to use your common sense and see if it agrees with what you've found on your local waters:

Spring Dead weedbeds, secluded but fairly deep bays, island margins, dead lily pads, snags.
Summer Weedbeds, shallows, plateaux, tops of bars, baited areas.
Autumn Open areas of water, sides of bars, drop-offs, baited areas.
Winter Snags, dead weedbeds, between bars, silty areas, dead lily pads, under trees.

The Weather

You should also be aware that certain swims which are productive at a certain time of year can sometimes die on you just because of a change of weather. Mind you, they can also come alive if you've dropped in lucky! In summer the shallows may be a good place to fish, but a cold northerly wind blowing down into them could move fish out and into deeper water. Conversely, a warm south-westerly which churns those shallows up in the autumn may encourage numbers of carp to move in to feed – difficult isn't it? It's a case of playing it by ear and, if you do have a change in the weather, play it very cautiously before bowling in all your bait. Remember that you can't take it out!

Below are listed just some of the effects that weather change, or constant weather, can have on carp's feeding habits and, as a consequence, location. It's up to you to decide where you are most likely to find feeding carp and then fish the correct spot in that swim.

Wind A warm wind from the south or south-west should improve your chances and drive oxygenated water into shallow areas, so increasing the likelihood of carp feeding more avidly. A cold wind from the north or the east has the opposite effect and can turn a water off for days.
Rain A warm, light drizzle may lead to increased feeding, especially in summer when it has been hot for long periods. Prolonged rain or rain in winter can decrease your chances.
Drop in temperature A clear sky after a warm

day will cool areas very quickly and can decrease a carp's desire to feed.

Rise in temperature This increases appetite and improves your chances of feeding from carp.

Prolonged hot weather This can lead to feeding spells being limited in length and possibly restrict them to after dark and before first light. However, if you can find time when the carp are feeding strongly, you can really make your fishing time effective.

Prolonged cold weather Whilst a cold snap can turn carp right off, once it settles down you may find they do start to feed again, albeit for short, limited spells.

Time of Day

Just as a change in the weather will dictate where a carp may decide to locate and feed, the carp may also move between features at different times of day. Obviously this is more apparent in summer when fish can spend time moving all over the water rather than in winter when they sometimes locate themselves in certain areas and do not move for days, weeks or even months. So in winter it's a case of finding the swim with the carp in it and finding the spot from which the carp will pick up the bait, whilst in summer you may have to move between swims, or maybe even just move your rods to locate the carp during the limited feeding period.

Spring I have found that carp feed most avidly at first light up until 9 a.m., and then from late afternoon to, say, 8 p.m. or 9 p.m. My rods are usually left to fish the same spots as I think it's a case of waiting for the carp to feed rather than moving your bait constantly to them.

Summer Carp feed at all sorts of times but I've found night time brings an increase in feeding. In the day I look towards the shallows whilst at night I look to water that is a little deeper. Locate natural feeding areas for most consistent results.

Autumn Most action comes from early afternoon to early evening (2 p.m. 7 p.m.), providing the weather is autumnal and not like high summer. I would definitely be tempted to move myself or my rods around to find fish on the move at this time of year.

Winter Carp can be very localized, and can feed morning, noon or night. I tend to have my baits to the same spots, hoping for just one pick-up but also watching for signs of fish feeding elsewhere. Try to find that spot and keep working at it.

Do be aware how the time of day can affect the carp's location, and with a little common sense you can fish the correct spots at the productive times. At certain times by fishing only evenings or nights you can identify the better feeding times, whilst if you decide to fish through the day

There are 27 acres of water, but where are the carp?

you may need to either move your rods or use floater tactics. Don't just sit it out for the sake of it; use your own brain and move on to fish or arrange your fishing round the fishes' prime feeding times. You have to fit in with their habits and not vice versa!

As I said earlier, it's often a case in today's carp scene of setting up where you can, or picking the best of what is available. Don't be too concerned that you may not get what you either think is or what is commonly accepted as *the* swim, because it has been my experience that most swims will produce carp if you fish them correctly, and even the best swims won't produce fish if you fish like an idiot. Just hope that the person in *the* swim hasn't got a clue and make the best of what is available in front of you. Always fish your own swim and fish it hard; don't be tempted to just chuck your baits out and sit waiting for the day you can get what you think is a better swim. You will be wasting a lot of time, and by the time you get that swim you probably wcn't catch from it anyway – and that will serve you right and may teach you a lesson.

So, even presuming that you have had to make the best of a bad job, what sort of features do hold carp, which are worth fishing to and more importantly, *why*?

CARP-HOLDING FEATURES

Weedbeds

For anybody who has fished anywhere other than a gravel pit or mere, weedbeds are an obvious choice to put a bait to. They seem to act as a magnet to both carp and carp anglers, so do be aware that although carp may well be present, they may be wary of feeding confidently in such areas and you may have to have everything perfect to catch fish. It's no good just chucking a bait against or towards a weedbed and hoping – you may have to do a little more to earn a fish.

Usually, I put a bait as close as possible to the weed providing it is possible to extract the carp from it before it snags me up. With care and

patience you may be able to extract a carp from such a position, but don't try to pull its head off and, if possible, don't let it get in there in the first place! In summer you can certainly expect to find carp in a weedbed all day, but I have found that even though some fish may well move away at night there are still usually one or two present which can be tempted. Come winter when the weed drops but doesn't disappear carp do still hole up in them, and they can be excellent winter features to try.

Lily Pads

Not present on all fisheries, lily pads are like the ever-popular weedbed as a magnet for carp and carp anglers alike. In summer I can sometimes be tempted to place a bait straight up off the lead (say 3–10in) against them because I've found carp to lay up in them while seemingly taking in the sun. A bait on the bottom can be ignored until the hours of darkness, so don't waste those daylight hours and try one popped up instead. At night you always have a chance of fishing to them, but do be aware that fish that do get in them can be impossible to free and inevitably transfer the hook from mouth to lily stalk. In winter dead lily-pad beds are brilliant places in which to find carp and I have caught a lot of winter fish from such places. Don't be afraid of the fact that it's not a lovely clean bottom; it needn't be. Carp love to hang around such features in winter, and providing you know where they are you are in with a chance.

Snags

As I devote a whole chapter to snag fishing later on in the book (*see* Chapter 8) I won't go on at length in this section, save to say that you really shouldn't ignore them, even if you don't like snag fishing. Between September and March or April each year I would place money on carp being around snags all the time, and the smaller number of snags there are the easier your location will be. Even in summer I'm sure you will find resident fish present in snags day in and day out. The only time that snags seem to be a waste of time is during spawning time, when carp have more than food on their mind! Do read and try to draw something from the chapter on snag fishing as they are such a good feature to fish to all year round. From single tree stumps to a full-scale 'orchard', carp love them.

Plateaux

A plateau such as the one you can see illustrated in Fig. 4 is a large area of fairly constant depth, usually quite noticeably shallower than the rest of the lake. Obviously, the smaller the plateau the easier the location of carp is, but the harder it is to find that plateau – try to find a 6ft square plateau at range and you will see what I mean. However, such as plateau might be a hell of a hot spot and, providing you can find it, would certainly be worth fishing to. Look for carp head and shouldering over certain spots time and time again. That may be indicative of a shallower spot in the lake and, if you are patient and methodical, you should be able to find it.

Personally, I have always done better in summer than in winter on such areas because I have noticed that as temperatures drop and the weed starts to fall back, fish move off plateaux to slightly deeper water, even if the odd fish does still visit them. However, a good warm wind may push fish on to them, so don't ignore them just because there are not any leaves on the trees!

Bays

There is an old saying which states that when carp are in bays they are brilliant areas to fish, and when they are not you might as well go home – well, I would have to agree with that. On quite a number of waters I fish there are small bays which carp do move into – especially at spawning time – and you can do really well. However, once those activities are over, weeks can go by without you seeing a fish in that area again. Although there may be one or two resident fish in these

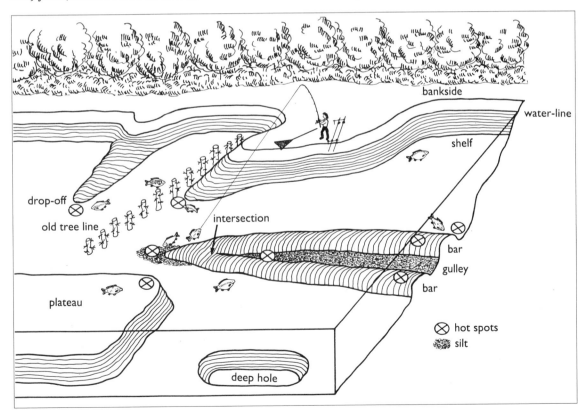

Fig. 4 Underwater features.

bays, the bulk of the catchable carp will be else-where. Providing you see fish in them, or you are 110 per cent convinced they will move into them, give them a try. However, if you are not, then look elsewhere.

Safe Areas

Anywhere that carp anglers cannot normally get a bait to but which can still be reached by legal methods (for example, long casting, using a model boat and so on) is always worth a try. Carp do learn by experience, and if the carp have learned that at times it is safer to stay in the middle then you may do well if you can get a bait to these areas.

This tactic is not just limited to range fishing as carp in weedbeds are very catchable as well. All that weed may lead them to believe they are safe, but if you are quick enough and have the right tackle, it is possible to take fish quite regularly in such areas. However, if your safe area is one in which you will lose the majority of carp you hook then don't even think about it. You shouldn't need fish that badly I hope!

The Margins

You would be amazed how many carp do visit the marginal areas even on busy waters, and providing you can keep quiet (and can keep others quiet) such areas are well worth putting baits to. As with fishing to weedbeds and snags, it is no use at all just dropping a bait in the margin – you have to do a lot more than that. Plumb about instead, and ask yourself if your bait should be on the marginal slope or at the bottom of the slope – only time and fishing the spot will tell you the answer. Leading about will always prove to be a good use of your time as you can feel clear spots and so on. Don't put too much bait in the margins as you don't need to. A solitary bait in the right place is often all that is needed to pick up a fish in such areas. Do remember that you are not trying to attract them into such areas, but are trying to catch them unawares.

Even better than the margins close to you are island margins at range which have the added advantage of decreased angler disturbance. Providing you can keep the lead and bait tight to the margin you should have a good chance in such spots.

Shaded Areas

Areas which are not easy to cast to often get ignored by carp anglers, so if you can find such spots and cast accurately to them they are also worth putting an end tackle to. Because of the difficulty in casting accurately under overhanging trees and bushes, many carp anglers leave them alone or cast too far away. However, if you do have the accuracy and patience to do it properly then you have an edge worth exploiting.

Once a bait is placed in such an area and you are perfectly happy with it, don't wind it in every couple of hours. The casting may well have

If it hadn't been for the swans, would you have known of this bar?

moved the carp away but he will come back and you must ensure your trap is baited when he does so. Again, keep freebies to a minimum to avoid spooking or overfacing the carp.

Silt

Anglers tend to fish in silt a great deal more than they imagine. This is a feature that is present on all sorts of waters from gravel pits to ponds, and from pools to meres. Whilst I am not convinced it is a hugely attractive feature to carp (although the food it contains may be), I do fish to such areas providing the silt is not the deep, black, horrible smelly stuff you do get in some lakes. The trick is to place your bait in the silt – if the carp want it, they will have it; if they don't then try elsewhere.

Deep Holes

In most people's minds deep holes are more a feature for winter fishing than summer, but I am not convinced this feature is really worth looking for at all. Obviously, a 7ft deep spot in an otherwise shallow water would have to be worth investigating, but when the feature is a 14ft hole with 12ft of water elsewhere it wouldn't automatically hold carp. However, if you find it is a good spot in your water, then try it.

Natural Food Areas

If you are able to locate areas of natural food like bloodworm beds and so on, then these are definitely worth putting a bait to. The larder is there and all you need to do is put your baited trap in it. However, in reality the ability to find such spots is very limited and you are more likely to drop on such a spot by accident rather than by design. Consistent carp activity in a specific area signposts a natural feeding spot. Carp continuously find new natural larders, so watch for them showing in new spots.

Drop-Offs

Areas where shallow water meets deep water can be brilliant little interception points, and it is often easy to catch carp moving round such areas. Bars and large plateau areas are like motorways and roads to the carp, and if you can place a bait in front of that fish – even if it's on the move – it may take it. Such fish are 'picking' at baits out of curiosity rather than looking for food, so do keep your baiting to sensible proportions.

Gravel Bars

Gravel bars seem to be more talked about, more fished to and more misunderstood than any other feature I can think of, and as a consequence everybody has their favourite position on which to place an end tackle. Some swear that this has to be on top of the bar, others the sides or bottoms, whilst I have found most of my action has come to areas where gravel bars meet. There is, of course, no definite answer about what position to fish and what not to fish, so all I can tell you of is my findings.

In summer, especially during the day, I have found the tops of bars the best point to place a bait to, whilst at night the best position has been at the bottom of bars. In winter I have had very little success on top of the bars, and action I have had has been at the silt areas at each end of the bars and between them where bars run close together. However, in both winter and summer, I have found intersection points of bars better than any other places, so what do you make of that? My own opinion is that very few people have an idea exactly where their baited tackle is lying, so for many it is a case of 'chuck it and chance it'. What I suggest is that you find your bar and, as I do, put all your eggs in one basket and experiment on top, on the side and in the gulleys – if you can find them. Find out what works best and when. My guess is that if you change waters you will find quite the opposite results from what you are used to. Still, that's carp fishing!

The big thing with location is that there are spots and then there is *the* spot. However, you should never think that you are automatically going to bag up just because you are in the going swim, or not catch because you aren't in that particular swim. A swim is what you make of it and, providing you do use your common sense, I bet most swims will produce on most waters.

3 APPROACHING A WATER

While I certainly wouldn't argue that location must play a major part in your success (or otherwise) in carp fishing, it is naive to think that you have to be in a particular swim to catch the fish, and that if you are not you will blank. Although in winter the fish may well be localized in just a couple of areas, it has been my experience that between May and November you will find carp all over the water. In the height of the season (June to August) carp may cover most spots in a lake in a day or two, so most anglers should theoretically be in with a chance of catching carp. However, it is not as easy as all that – how many times has somebody been in a swim for days and caught nothing, then somebody else has moved in and caught literally straight away?

Many would put this down to luck or just a fluke, and although this may be true, if you do work hard at your carp fishing and approach your swim methodically and patiently you can increase your chances of a take significantly. This is the reason why some people are so successful on certain waters and others fail dismally on that same water. Those who are consistent have a good knowledge of the water as a whole and have the ability to place a bait in a likely spot in many swims where they set up.

In this chapter I will follow the advice I gave on location in Chapter 2 by telling you how to approach a water, how to map it out, successful plumbing techniques you can use, and how to find the likely spots in each swim you pick. You should be confident in all swims and not just the one or two you may have had success in before.

INITIAL APPROACH

Before you decide even to fish a water you must be clear in your own mind why you want to choose that particular water. I suppose the reasons for choice of water are endless, and range from proximity to your home, to the look of the lake or whatever. As you become more experienced in carp fishing your reasons may change – that I can assure you. Some anglers desire big fish at any cost, whilst others want the chance of big fish but want to balance this with family commitments, time, scenery and so on. Whilst it is very easy to look in the angling press and see anglers like Maylin and Maddocks with big carp, you must ask yourself if you really want to endure all the blanks, backbiting and stress they have had to endure to catch those carp. If you do then good luck to you, but if you don't then don't set your targets at their high standards.

Having decided what you want from your carp fishing, you now have to decide if the water, or waters, you are thinking of will meet your requirements. I'm sure a number of you won't agree with me here, but I have found the only way to be successful is to stick to one water at a time – only when I'm totally happy with my results do I move on. I'm quite sure there are some of you who do fish around quite a bit, but it has been my experience that to be truly successful and catch numbers of big fish rather than just one or two, you really have to put all your time, money and effort into one water. By concentrating on this one water you will get to know it in all its moods, how weather affects its carp population, what does and doesn't work and, probably most importantly, the spots to put your end tackle to.

If you feel that you are not succeeding as you would like on a regular basis it may be worth trying this method, because I know it wasn't until I started working hard at each water I picked that I managed to catch consistently. It doesn't mean that you have to stick with one water for the rest of your life – that can be very self-limiting – or that you have to fish there in winter as well, but it does mean that from March through to November you should give one water your best shot rather than some half-hearted efforts in several places.

If you have picked a water purely and simply because you want a pretty lake to fish or one which is close to your home, you need to visit it only once or twice to see if it has what you want. However, many people nowadays pick lakes because of the size of the fish present in them. I'm sure a good number of you reading this book will never have caught a 20lb carp. Don't worry about it. You can only catch them if they are there and those anglers who have taken a lot of twenty-pounders have done so only because they have fished waters that contain a lot of carp of this weight. I could take anybody to two of my local syndicate lakes and would guarantee that if they fished competently all year they would catch at least half a dozen twenty-pounders, if not more.

Choosing the right water is important because you can't catch what isn't in that water. Year in and year out I hear so many people moaning about not catching doubles, twenties or thirties, yet they won't fish waters which contain those

Never underestimate the usefulness of watching the water.

fish. If you want to catch at all or be in with the chance of catching a certain size of carp, you have to fish a venue that contains that size of carp. Now let's see how we can find such a water for you.

By Luck

It may be that by chance you are fishing a water which contains doubles, or twenty- or thirty-pounders and it's just a case of working hard enough to catch those fish.

By Application

You may know of waters which have the required size of fish and, providing you are satisfied that these fish are there, the only way to catch them is to fish those waters. Some waters are open where anybody can join, so that is no problem. However, others are syndicated and the only way to join is to get your name down on their membership lists. If you want to join a syndicate you must not just sit thinking about it, you must write off now. To catch carp you have to work hard and that also includes working at getting on the right waters in the first place.

Write to the fishery owners or syndicate leader and enclose a stamped addressed envelope. Make your writing legible and make a polite but obviously enthusiastic enquiry. If you don't get a reply, write again and keep chasing it up until you do get one. What have you got to lose? Think of all those carp you are missing out on purely and simply because you can't be bothered to write a letter or two, so if you haven't done so, do it now.

Don't forget to enclose that stamped addressed envelope and, as I said, if you don't receive a reply within a month then write again. A very important point to note is that you should make a fresh application each year because it has been my experience that unless you apply each year, your original application goes to the bottom of the list.

Having decided which water to fish and, hopefully, at least been able to get into it, we now look at how much work you can put in in advance to make the actual fishing easier.

GETTING TO KNOW YOUR WATER

If you intend to fish a new water this year or are just trying to improve on last year's results, nothing should be too much trouble. Every little thing you do before you start will save you time when you are fishing and, if my experience and thoughts are anything to go by, they will also improve your confidence. No matter what anybody may tell you, new waters can be very intimidating – even now I look at a new water and ask myself how on earth I am going to come to grips with it. This is not a thought you want running through your mind when you've got all your tackle on your back and a water full of new faces smiling smugly to themselves. It can be intimidating, and I have seen many new anglers give up after just one or two trips when a little bit of pre-planning would have given them all the confidence they needed.

There are lots of ways to build up knowledge and confidence in a water, so I shall list the ones I resort to when I change waters.

Literature

What has been written about the lake in the past? As Features Editor for *Carp Fisher* and a collector of all types of angling literature, it has been obvious to me for some time that more and more people are writing about their fishing and how they have succeeded on certain waters. The old maxim of never naming the water seems to have gone by the board, and nowadays a large number of waters have been written about – and in detail too. Bait publications, monthly magazines and specialist carp magazines all pump out carp literature left, right and centre, so there is certainly a good chance that your water will have been written about at some time. Look in *Anglers' Mail* and *Angling Times* each week – there are always lots of pictures of smiling carp anglers and usually the name of the lake as well. Both Beekay and Angling Publications have published books which detail over 1,000 carp waters, so try these also (*see* Useful Addresses on pages 186–188 if you want more information on them).

Local Tackle Shops

If my local tackle shops are anything to go by then these establishments are a hive of information on waters. What may be new to you is probably common knowledge to the proprietors, staff or customers, and one or two afternoons spent in such places can prove to be very useful. Most shops have pictures of local carp anglers on the wall, and a subtle word here and there can reveal which fish were caught when. Remember that it's in the shops' interests that you catch fish and keep coming back, so if it has anything of a carp buzz to it, give it a try.

Carp Society Meetings

As I detail later in the book, the Carp Society does have local meetings all over the country and if you do go to these you may find out how the local water is fishing, who's catching and on what. I have included the Carp Society's address in the Useful Addresses section, and for this feature alone it has got to be worth joining. Just write to the Society and enclose a large stamped, addressed envelope, please.

Visiting the Water

No matter how much literature you do read on a fishery, or how much waffle you are told about it, there is simply no substitute for getting down to the water and looking at it yourself. Providing you are allowed to do this, it is vital that you visit the water at least once or twice in advance so you can get some idea of what you are up against. For example, 17 acres may not sound large, but if the lake is an open, featureless reservoir it will look huge. Similarly, 30 acres sounds a lot but if it's full of little islands, bays and inlets, it won't look half as big. So get down there now if you can.

The best time to visit is during the season when the water has anglers on it so that you are able to talk to people and get a general idea of just how prolific or otherwise a water is. It's all well and good traipsing round a water in winter or during the close season, but unless some keen anglers are there you will not make any earth-shattering discoveries straight away. Even if you are reading this book in the main part of the season and are thinking about a new water for next season, *now* is the time to look at it and not when everybody has pulled off in the winter. Remember that carp don't tend to show themselves much or get caught often in winter, so although it will be very quiet you won't get much feedback from the anglers on the bank. However, the one advantage gained from walking or trying to read a water in winter is that the weed will usually have died back in quantities so that plumbing is a lot lot easier. Mind you, you must not start sticking plumbing rods in here, there and everywhere unless you have permission to do so or have a water ticket for that year. After all, you don't want to get banned before you have even started to fish do you?

If you do visit a water when other anglers are present, it is best to adopt a courteous and interested attitude rather than the 'right, I'm here and what can you tell me?' one some anglers seem to have. When I am fishing I don't mind helping people providing that they do respect the fact that I am fishing and that I don't want any interference.

Similarly, don't walk round in groups of two or three even if you intend to fish in a group. It can be quite intimidating to have a gang standing behind you when you are fishing, and a person on their own is far more likely to be given help than a group of anglers. Don't ask specific questions like 'What bait?', 'What swim?', 'What rig?' or, even worse, 'Caught anything?' If the angler wants to tell you anything he will; if he doesn't he won't. You are far better off making some friends on the water rather than putting people's backs up and annoying them. Nobody wants to listen to a smart alec who is convinced he will empty their water. Even if you do feel quietly confident, don't force it down anyone's throat. Also, give a little as well as taking. Offering a cigarette, a piece of chocolate or details of your own water will go a long way to breaking the ice, and if somebody has caught one or two compliment him or at least his tackle. You don't have to grovel to get on, but you certainly ought to attempt to make a friend or two.

If I am visiting a water for the first time, I will draw a map of it on which I will mark every little

A small hole in a dense weedbed produced this lovely winter carp.

bit of information I am given. It may be wrong or it may be right, but at least it's something to go on. Each little bit you learn is another piece in the jigsaw puzzle and a step nearer to success. Once you have drawn your map and noted down anything you have been told, it's an idea to put it all in a folder complete with any literature that may have been written about that water. Whilst this may seem rather high tech, it's a method that I know works and one which could work for you as well.

APPROACH WHILST FISHING

Providing you've done some work in advance you should have an idea of the lake you are fishing and its carp stocking. Now it's time to get down to the lake to try and put theory into practice. To be fair, first sessions on fisheries usually fall into one of two main areas – either a total anticlimax as you blank gloriously, or a stupendous success as you drop on fish straight away. There is no way I can guarantee you success straight away, and all I can do is give you one or two pointers towards improving your chances.

Don't start on a weekend Weekends tend to be very crowded on most waters, and if you turn up for your first session on a Friday night in early June it's quite likely you will end up having no choice of swim at all, never mind being able to walk round the fishery to pick the best available one. My idea would be to take the Thursday and Friday off work and arrange a session from, say, Thursday to Saturday. Hopefully you will miss the main body of pressure and, providing it's not the first week of the season and it's Darenth, you will have at least some chance of a decent swim.

Don't start too early Unless you are used to, or enjoy getting up at ridiculously early hours, I would suggest you get down to the water at first light and not in darkness. You will have a lot of work to do that first day, and you will want to be fresh and not so tired that you just want to chuck the baits out and climb in your bag. That might

be all right if you know your water intimately, but it's not if you don't! First light is ideal because it is a perfect time to spot the fish, but if I had a choice between getting down very early and feeling totally exhausted, or getting down at say 9 or 10 a.m. and feeling fresh, I would definitely choose the latter.

Don't be in a hurry to get your rods out Don't expect to bag up automatically during your first session because this may not happen. If you know the water well and know where to put your baits then making assumptions is fine, but if you don't then take your time. Even if it is mid-afternoon before your baits are in, that's acceptable. It is a long season nowadays and if I am on a water I am not over familiar with I have to be very sure I am on fish straight away before I put any baited rods out. You should plumb and lead about before you put your baited rods out no matter what kind of fishery it is.

Don't set your bivvy up first I must admit that I don't use a bivvy in summer and only use one in winter because conditions can change so quickly. If you have set up your bivvy before your rods and find you are not in quite the right spot it can be a real pain having to pack it down and move swims in the midday heat. It is far better to do your leading and plumbing first before you set up home.

Don't be in a rush Even though it is nice to catch straight away, you shouldn't feel under any pressure to do so, so take your time and make a proper job of things. If it takes two hours to find a clear spot then that's how long it takes. Don't be in a rush to get your end tackle tied up, bivvy up and tea on. It's not a race – he who gets the bivvy set up first does not automatically catch the most.

The above points are some of the golden rules I use when approaching a water, and which I also try to adopt even when I am fishing a water I know a great deal about. However, no matter what water I do fish and no matter how well I feel I know it, I would not fish it without using my plumbing and leading rods to some extent. Ten minutes work can save hours of wasted time.

PLUMBING AND LEADING A WATER

Plumbing is the use of a marker float to find out changes of depth in a lake, with the aim of locating carp. Leading is the use of a lead to feel the nature of the bottom and its attractiveness (or otherwise) to carp.

Plumbing

Unless I have an accurate map of depths in a water I will always use a marker float to find out where the bars, plateaux and shelves in a water are. Even if I am aware where all these features are I will always use a marker float to cast to (range permitting). A marker float is essential for those two purposes: it shows you changes in depth which can be attractive to carp; and, unless you are fishing to visible features like snags and weedbeds, it gives you something at which to cast.

Plumbing in Gravel Pits

Compared to weedy waters, gravel pits are a joy to plumb as you can use a simplistic form of plumbing device and map out a swim in minutes rather than hours. I have included a diagram here (*see* Fig. 5) of the set-up I use in plumbing gravel pits or weedless waters and, although it is fairly self-explanatory, I will explain briefly how I use it.

1. The marker float in question is one of Drennan's large Piker floats and it is attached directly to the 12lb Berkley Big Game main line via a link clip. I don't tie the line directly to the float bottom as constant casting wears the float's eye out through chafing. This link swivel is clipped to a large Berkley swivel which acts as the stop for the large swivel attached to the lead. Next to the swivel is a large rubber shock bead, and next to that is a large swivel which is clipped to the lead. Use a large swivel here because it is essential that the line runs smoothly through it; a small swivel would clog up but a large one allows your float to pop up more easily. If you are plumbing a true gravel pit I would advise you to coat your leads in rubber to stop them becoming chipped on the gravel. A pitted lead is more likely to fray your main line, and such a frayed main line can lead to crack offs.

2. Pick your aiming point opposite you and cast directly at it (*see* Fig. 6). Don't give the cast too much force as you will have to get your free offerings to that spot as well and be able to cast a hookbait with accuracy to within a yard or two of it.

3. Once your line has sunk, wind down until the

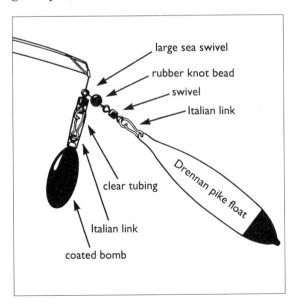

Fig. 5 Gravel pit set-up.

large sea swivel

rubber knot bead

swivel

Italian link

Drennan pike float

clear tubing

Italian link

coated bomb

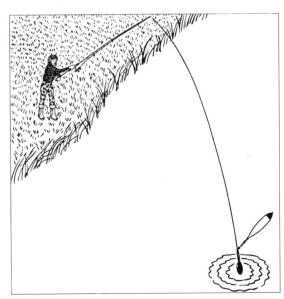

Fig. 6 Cast out.

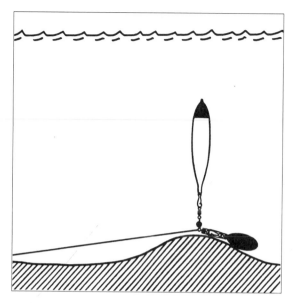

Fig. 7 *Pull tight.*

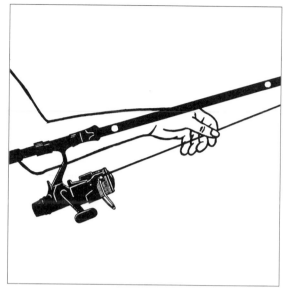

Fig. 8 *Pay off.*

float is tight against the lead (*see* Fig. 7). Your line will now almost be bowstring tight with your float bottom touching the bed of the lake. Because you have to pull the line tight to get the float right down it is essential that you use a good sized lead, say 2½oz plus to tighten up to.

4. Once your line is tight, open your bale arm whilst still holding the line tight in your other hand (*see* Fig. 8). Pay off the line, and in turn this will allow your float to rise. I have marked on my plumbing rod two marks which are 12in apart. That way I know each pay-off of the line marks the float coming up 12in.

5. Once the float reaches the surface you simply multiply the number of 'pay-offs' you did by 12in (*see* Fig. 9). That will give you the depth of the lake where the float popped up. It is essential to use a largish bright float so you can see it and it can rise through the water powerfully.

6. Record the information on your map, wind in, say, a couple of yards more and repeat steps 3, 4 and 5 again (*see* Fig. 10). This will give you another depth reading, and so on. Once you've marked out depths along that one line, cast a little to the left or right and continue doing so until you feel you have an accurate recording of the depths in front of you. Your plan should also

have a silhouette line to it so you know what you are casting to, as well as how deep it is.

Using a plumbing method like this will show you the depth of the water in front of you and at what distance out those depths are. Once you are satisfied that you know where you want to place a

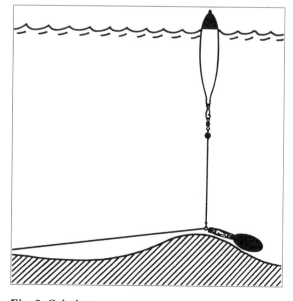

Fig. 9 *Calculate.*

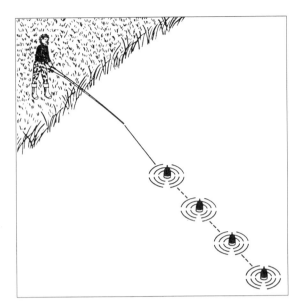

Fig. 10 *Wind in.*

baited tackle (in other words, on top of a bar, on a plateau and so on), cast your marker rod out, let it pop up in the right spot and cast your baited end tackle to it. If you are more than a foot or two away, do it again until you are spot-on and happy. Remember that baited end tackle may be out there for up to twenty-four hours, so it is essential that it is right in the first place.

Plumbing in Weedy Waters

Whilst plumbing in gravel pits is fairly easy (providing you do record all the information), plumbing in weedy waters is a little more difficult. The problem is that you cannot wind your float right down because it gets stuck in the weed, the consequences being that you have to use a different set-up.

1. Because bottom weed would normally clog your swivel and stop your float popping up, you have to use this alternative set-up (*see* Fig. 11). Furthest away from the reel is a 2–3oz bomb which is tied to a 12in piece of thick Terylene or heavy sea Dacron. Attached to the other end of this is a swivel. This length is the length which goes into the bottom weed or silt and, because it is a 1in length and has a swivel on it, the float can't go past the swivel and get caught in the weed. That swivel is tied to your main line which has a large rubber shock bead, a large Drennan Piker float with line through the middle, a second small bead and an 11lb power gum stop knot.
2. As with the gravel pit plumbing advice, cast your float at the required distance in the required line out when it is set to what you think is the depth at that point (*see* Fig. 12). Don't forget to mark down what you are casting at –

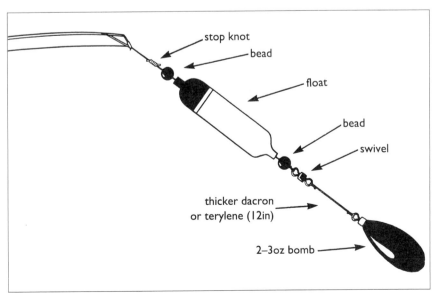

stop knot
bead
float
bead
swivel
thicker dacron or terylene (12in)
2–3oz bomb

Fig. 11 *Weedy water set-up.*

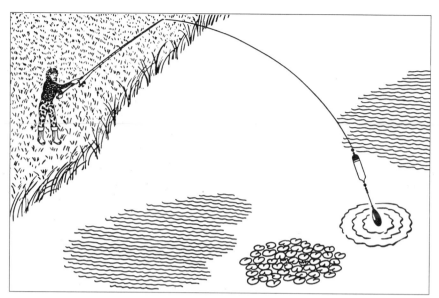

Fig. 12 Cast out.

unless weedbeds, lily pads and the like make it obvious.

3. If the float doesn't pop up, you have set it too shallow and you will need to move the stop knot, say, 6in at a time towards you to increase the depth (*see* Fig. 13). Obviously, to do this you have to wind in each time.

4. If the float stays on its side on the surface and your line is relatively slack, your float is set too deep and your stop knot will have to be moved towards the lead at, say, 6in a time to decrease

the depth (*see* Fig. 14). Again, as with Step 3, you will have to wind in each time.

When your float is at the correct depth it will sit proudly at the water-line. Wind in, record the depth and do it all over again, and again, and again . . . As you can see, this method takes a lot longer than the gravel pit plumbing method, but it is essential when you have any sort of bottom weed. Mind you, if something is hard to do it often pays off in the long run.

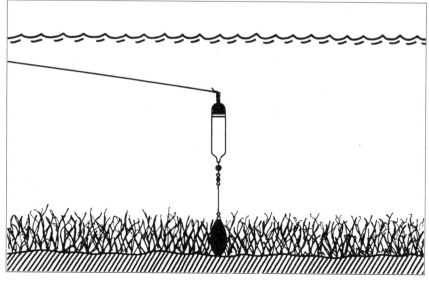

Fig. 13 The float is set too shallow.

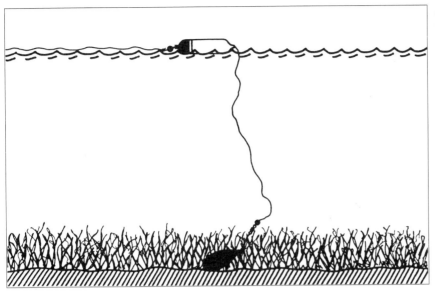

Fig. 14 *The float is set too deep.*

Leading

Leading about and feeling the bottom is something which I would advise all anglers to do even if plumbing has been done already. Whilst plumbing will tell you the depth of water and a *little* about the nature of what you are fishing on, it is the leading or feeling that will tell you exactly what kind of bottom your end tackle will be laying in.

To lead about all you need do is tie a 2oz or 3oz lead to a spare rod and cast it out to the areas you are intending to fish. By standing sideways to the water as I've illustrated in Fig. 15, and moving your rod in that arc, your line will tighten, move the lead and the feel of the lake's bottom will be transmitted down the line into your hands and, hopefully, to your brain.

Various bottoms feel different and give their own tell-tale plucks, knocks and tightening of the line. In time you will be able to tell exactly what your lead has landed on and is being pulled through. At first this is a little difficult, but with experience you will just 'know', believe me. Always use as heavy a weight as possible to pick up the features and don't use too sloppy a rod or you will lose the feel through your floppy rod tip. Below are a few tips as to how different features will show up on your rod and through your line.

Bottom weed Your lead will be a bit difficult to move at first and will keep plucking as it rasps through the weed. When you bring it in, strands will be caught around the lead and swivel.

Thick weed Your lead will feel solidly embedded and will be almost immovable. Your rod tip will bend right round and your line will feel like it is attached to a dead weight. You may have to point the rod at the lead to wind it in.

Snags Your lead will be coming in smoothly but will then stop suddenly with the rod tip banging right round. Your lead will jar against the snag and, if it is a particularly bad one, you may have to pull for a break.

Gravel Patches of gravel will feel like you are running your knuckles over billiard balls. You will feel the tremors through your line and your rod tip will keep flicking back and forward. Larger pieces of gravel and stones will give your rod tip an even more pronounced kick.

Pulling up gravel bars Your line will start to tighten and your rod tip will bend round gently as the lead creeps up the slope of the bar.

On top of the bar Your line will still be fairly tight but your rod tip will start to move back to its original shape.

Pulling off the bar Your line will go slack and your rod tip will flick straight back as if a fish has just dropped off. Your lead will have just fallen down the side of the bar. The more slack you have to wind in the higher the top of the bar in the water and the steeper its sides.

Silt Your lead will feel as though it's being pulled through cotton wool and, although there are no kicks in the rod tip, it feels as though you have an extra ounce or two on your lead. It will feel hard to pull out of and then smooth on a steady draw-back.

Clear spots in weed After a period of plucking the rod tip will flick straight back to the norm and it will feel like you are dragging it over smooth concrete. No kicks, plucks or tremors will be felt and the longer this lasts, the larger the clear spot is. No matter what I write down your best aid will be experience, and the more you lead about the easier it becomes. So many people use only a plumbing float *or* only a leading rod when both really go hand in hand. When you've found the correct feature use your leading rod to find the clear spots. All you need to do is cast half a dozen times round your popped-up float, and once you've found the exact distance from your float that *the* spot is, pop your end tackle and bait to it.

So there you have a practical look at how you can approach a water before and during your fishing. Location in itself is no guarantee of success; this is more likely to be a combination of the correct swim and the correct place in that swim which can only be found if you are prepared to work at it rather than just trust in luck.

arc of rod to feel the nature of the lake bed

Fig. 15 Leading.

4 MODERN CARP TACKLE

Whilst it really shouldn't be the prime consideration in carp fishing to have up-to-date carp tackle, many carp anglers seem to be obsessed with purchasing every piece of new carp tackle that comes on to the market. In the 1980s this wasn't such a bad thing as anglers such as Kevin Nash and Richard Gardner were producing items which were necessities rather than niceties. These items, such as quality bivvies, banksticks, buzzers and so on, were designed with the carp angler's needs in mind, unlike the tackle of the 1990s which often seems to be produced just for a fast buck. While the top producers of the 1980s would come to your aid with quality gear at a reasonable price if you weren't practically minded, the fact that carp fishing has become the in thing has meant that prices have risen astronomically and quality has dropped in some instances.

Unfortunately many of the products now available to carp anglers are shabby, ill-thought-out and aimed to catch the carp angler rather than the carp.

This chapter will look at sensibly priced items which do the job for which they were intended, and which are items me or my friends can personally confirm as reliable and useful. Undoubtedly, new items – which may or may not be useful – will appear on the market before this book goes to print.

FINDING GOOD TACKLE

While there is absolutely nothing wrong in possessing the best rods, reels, buzzers, landing nets and tackle carriers, these must not be purchased to the detriment of good quality and sufficient bait, good hooks and line, quality water tickets and so on. When you are planning on buying new tackle, you should consider whether or not the item you already have needs replacing, whether the new item justifies the outlay and whether the outlay on this new item would not be best directed to other areas of your fishing. For many of you reading this book, I would advise you to spend a reasonable amount of money on tackle but to make sure you purchase good bait, enough bait, good hooks, good line and choose a prolific water before you start spending astronomical sums on rods, reels, buzzers, landing nets and bivvies.

Do think very carefully before you decide to part with your money – it is all very well looking the part, but at the end of the season when you take stock of your results, do you honestly believe you couldn't have done better if you had purchased higher quality bait, more bait or a good syndicate place, or changed your hooks instead of losing that lunker due to a rusty hook or frayed hooklength? Please don't fall into the trap of seeing all those nice set-ups and thinking that that is what carp fishing is all about – it isn't, so don't be swayed that way. To a large extent carp fishing is about catching carp on a regular basis; to do this you must be on the right water, have a good enough bait on a reliable presentation, and be there enough times to catch that carp.

Tackle Reviews

Most monthly carp magazines carry reviews of carp tackle which is new to the market. Other than the odd long-term appraisal, by their very nature these reviews can be of a superficial nature only. A manufacturer who has a new product and who wishes to promote it in the market will mail it out to magazine editors and to some anglers of above-average ability. As most reviews are carried out within a month of receipt of the product, the review you see in your magazine can only be a short-term appraisal at best.

Products which are poor from day one, and I mean poor, are not generally reviewed, so they will not trouble you. However, other products which are good but whose deficiencies only show up when used regularly may not match up to their review after time passes or if conditions are different. I have been provided with buzzers which have worked for a month or so, but once subjected to heavy rain were not worth the postage, never mind the price. Had I reviewed those buzzers in the first three weeks or so I would have raved about them; as it is I'm raving at them. What I am saying is that you should be very careful when you read reviews as the product may not have shown its true colours or the reviewer may be being over-cautious.

To conclude, don't be led into parting with your money on reviews alone. If possible, let a product stand the test of time for three to six months, speak to the other anglers on the bank who are using them, and use your own common sense. Remember the old expression 'Fools rush in where angels fear to tread', and don't be a fool but be practical and sensible.

This chapter looks at the important items of tackle for general carp fishing, along with their strengths, weaknesses and value to you. Specialized items for winter fishing, snag fishing and so on will be covered in their relevant chapters.

Keep tackle to a minimum for overnight sessions.

RODS

There's no doubt about it, these are the most discussed items of a carp angler's kit year in, year out. One of the most talked-about aspects of rods is their price, which seems to go up and up each year. As time marches on new materials will be used, current materials will be modified and improved and prices will creep up again. However, do think back to what I said earlier in the chapter: what are your priorities and where do expensive rods lie in that equation?

Most of you will already be owners of decent carp rods; in fact, I would be so bold as to say that around seventy to eighty per cent of you will own rods which will suffice for most carp fishing situations that you may face. People tend not to fish different waters willy nilly, so a rod purchased for one type of water can be used year in and year out. Most are good choices, many are correct choices and only a few are so badly picked that the incorrect choice is going to cost you fish. However, if you are looking to purchase new rods or feel that you are being let down by your current rods, what considerations should you look towards? Normally, these considerations will relate to distance fished, action and so on, but before we look to these, let us look at one or two general points.

Rod Quality

Don't automatically think that the more expensive a rod is the better it will be and, in particular, the better its quality will be. I personally have had expensive rods break on me within six weeks' usage when other rods at half their price have endured five years of punishment. Whether it is a symptom of this day and age I am not sure, but cost does not always equate to quality.

Although as a customer in a shop you will not be able to assess there and then just how good quality a rod blank is, you will have to hope that it is of the quality offered. Look at the blank itself. Is it cracked or flat-spotted? Scratches and matt marks on a gloss-finish blank signify problems, so avoid rods with these signs at all costs. Rods which have been on show for some time and which are occasionally dropped by customers will be marked with scratches and lots of grubby fingerprints.

Don't just look at the rod on show, but look also at the rod in the rod bag which you are going to buy. Most rods have female and male sections to them. As a rule of thumb, the thicker the blank at the point where they join the more use and abuse it can take. Look carefully at this area. Run your finger around the female section. Is it smooth or does your fingernail reveal some hairline cracks? A crack will result in a broken spigot sooner or later. Each side of the spigot should be whipped with good quality thread to provide extra backbone to the blank's inherent strength. Personally, I also like to see the male part of the spigot filled with cork or similar substance which will provide a certain degree of rigidity. However, this male part should neither be too long or too rigid or it may inhibit the natural action of the rod.

Having examined the blank itself, take a good look at the rod rings as well. Personally, I prefer single-legged rod rings as they seem to flow nicely with the rod when it is subjected to extreme pressure. Long-range ringing is discussed in Chapter 7, but as a rule I don't like to have more than eight rings (including the tip) and less than six rings (including the tip) on a 12ft rod. Again, the best test for these fixtures is to run the inside of your little fingernail around the inside of the ring. You will feel hairline cracks on your nail; again, avoid these rods like the plague. A hairline crack will fray all lines, and a frayed or cut line is a line which is going to cost you a fish sooner or later! As a final point, rod rings obviously shouldn't be able to move around so check that the whipping is up to standard and not the bodged job you see on many cheaper rods.

At one time the handles on all rods used to be made of cork of one form or another. However, foam, Duplon and moulded hard rubber now seem to be the in-vogue materials with cork being considered *passé* by many people. Handles of new rods are usually a form of synthetic foam, and I cannot criticize this in any way. All I would say is that you must make sure it is fixed rigidly and doesn't move up or down the blank. A handle extending approximately 4–6in around each side of the winch fitting is about right, although today full-length foam handles are favoured by some anglers and rod builders. Butt grips tend to be made of hard rubber which is an ideal material. The actual reel fitting should be one which holds your reel firmly and securely, but which is not uncomfortable and does not cause you problems when playing fish or when distance casting. It seems that most fittings are Fuji FPS fittings (or similar), so those should not be a problem. Providing you take your reel off now and again, and keep dirt and grit out of the winch fitting, butt grips should be fairly problem-free.

You may, of course, feel that checking a rod for quality to this extent is totally over the top, but remember that when you purchase a rod you may have to live with it for many years. Is it really worth risking your hard-earned cash on rods which you haven't even checked for quality? Such a check on each rod you consider will take a few minutes at most. Also, don't be put off by pushy tackle dealers – it's your money so take your time and do the job properly, even if the shop is full and the dealer is assuring you that he checked the rods personally. Discretion is the better part of valour – and more reliable in the long run.

Blank or Made-Up Rod

Unless you are an accomplished rod builder I would urge you to purchase a made-up rod or have a blank made up by an expert rod builder. Whilst it may look easy in print to make up a rod and even easier when a professional is doing the job in front of you, it really isn't. If it all goes wrong it can prove to be a very expensive mistake and one you needn't make. Certainly, purchase a blank from a reputable firm if you want to, but do have it made up by an acknowledged rod builder. From my own knowledge I can recommend the rod builders listed in the Useful Addresses section (*see* pp 186–188) if you wish to follow such a course.

Personally, I prefer to obtain rods ready made up and I would urge readers to the same. However, if you feel you need a rod tailored to your own personal requirements then tread carefully.

Having looked at the quality of rods and blanks versus made-up rods, let us now look at the criteria you must consider when choosing a rod for your fishing. You must choose a rod which is suited to your own fishing, not one recommended for Harefield, Savay, Cassien or Darenth. Whilst it is nice to have a rod which has been endorsed by one of the carp world's so-called superstars, this may be a rod designed with a specific purpose in mind – say, a rod which will place a stringer over 150yd or heave a giant carp from the depths of Cassien. Ask yourself if you really need that, then look at your water, its size and requirements and work towards a rod on those terms.

Rod Considerations

In respect of any water you fish and any situation in which you find yourself, a rod has to meet certain guide-lines. These are listed below:

1. The rod must be of the correct strength and design to allow you to put a bait to the carp in your water where they are prepared to feed. Whilst it is nice to own and use soft rods which are ideal for margin fishing, these are of no use if you usually need to cast a 2–3oz bomb 70yd out to the main feeding area. Sure, carp may venture nearer in now and again but your rods must be able to place your end tackle in the carps' main feeding area.
2. The rod must be able to hook and land the carp from the water once it gives an indication or run at which you can strike. Again, not all waters are open gravel pits devoid of weed and snags, as many of us well know. Some waters are covered in weed from head to foot and have lots of snags, so that carp generally need to be bullied or led firmly away from such areas. Your rod must therefore be strong enough to utilize the breaking strain of the main line and the strength of the hook; it is no good putting a bait in the correct

spot and getting pick-up after pick-up if you cannot apply such pressure on the fish as to make landing it a realistic possibility. This point mainly relates to soft general-action rods which, although they are a joy for playing fish, don't have sufficient meat or backbone in them to allow you to exert significant pressure on a fighting fish.

3. The rod must be of an action and design to suit the individual and not just his pocket or 'pose factor'. It is a fact of life that the rod business has its own personal factions. There are Armalite fans, Horizon fans, Pursuit fans and so on, each believing that their rod is the perfect one and refusing to swap it no matter what new kind of rod comes on to the market. All anglers are of different builds and abilities, so consequently rod choice will vary from person to person; some will prefer fast taper rods while others prefer through-action rods. You must make sure that if your rod satisfies criteria 1 and 2 above it is also a rod that you yourself can live with. For example, if you are 5ft 5in and weigh 9 stone then a 13ft rod of 3lb test curve will feel unwieldy in your hands, even though it can cast to most spots. To conclude, make sure you pick a rod that satisfies your personal preference as well as fitting the other criteria, and do not pick one just because it is 'in vogue' at the time.

Rod Action

In theory there are three main actions to be found in rods. These are fast taper, medium taper and slow taper. As this book is a book on practical carp fishing rather than theoretical carp fishing, I will keep this section short.

Fast taper rods These have a stiffer tip section and in my eyes make the best long-casting rods. The fast taper design coupled with a stiff butt section leaves all the action concentrated in the top third of the rod. Once you are used to such a stiff rod you shouldn't have any problems with hook pulls or line breaks; until you are used to them be careful.

Medium taper rods These have a lighter action and tend to bend a lot further down the blank than fast taper rods once pressure is exerted. The majority of rods on the market are medium taper as these types of rod cover most general carp fishing situations. This is a good choice for a general-purpose rod.

Slow taper rods A better term to describe the slow taper rod is a through-action rod which can bend from the tip almost to the reel seat. Indeed, my little stalking rod which is slow taper has been known to bend so far in hook and hold situations that the winch fitting has creaked under the strain. These types of rod allow you to really bend into a fish, but they do have limitations when trying to throw a large lead a long way. The 'sloppy' action of the rod tends to absorb the power of your cast, and unless you are a very good caster you will struggle to push a reasonable lead more than 70–80yd.

In an ideal world where everybody had unlimited funds, I would recommend you to have various sets of rods to cover all the situations you would find yourself in. You would have some soft rods to stalk with, some brutes to push three-bait stringers into a headwind, a slim lightweight fast taper rod to floater fish with and so on. However, let us be realistic and say that the set of rods you do purchase will have to be a compromise. From my own fishing experience and by watching others, I would have to say that the set of rods you purchase will have to do everything from floater fishing to snag fishing. For that reason I choose fast taper rods of around 2½–2¾lb test curve which allow me to cast over 100yd, but which I can still use carefully in the margins and for stalking. It is no good purchasing lovely, soft taper through-action rods if you find that the carp at 80yd or more are out of range. You can always use a fast taper rod close in, but you will be pushed to fish at a distance with a rod designed for margin fishing.

As I said earlier, rods are picked on a personal view and what may suit me may not suit you, Rob Maylin or Andy Little in exactly the same situation – it's a thing called personal choice. For that reason it is difficult for me to suggest that you choose a particular rod and expect you to be happy with my choice. All I can do is let you know which rods I have been very happy with, and those rods my friends have used and been happy with as well.

Original Horizon Rod This 12ft 2½lb test curve rod is a lovely fast taper rod which has served me for five years and continues to do so. It will put a bait out over 120yd yet can be used in most situations with a little thought. This rod is available from Rod Hutchinson stockists throughout the country.

Daiwa Amorphous This 12ft 2¾lb test curve rod has a softer taper than the Horizon, but due to its Amorphous blank it can cast a little further and is somewhat more forgiving under the tip. However, it will cost you a Horizon and a half so be prepared to dig deep. This rod is available from all Daiwa stockists.

Armalite This 12ft 3lb test curve rod is one many of my friends favour as it has quite a marked through-action which really allows you to wind them up and put a lead a long way. The blanks are almost indestructible and are ideal for the more clumsy amongst us. This is available from the majority of carp tackle stockists.

The three rods above are ideal starting points to look at when choosing a rod in the 1990s. I know there are other good rods – for example, Rod Hutchinson's IMX range, Maylin's Extreme Pursuits and North Wester's Dyneema's – but as I have not used them I would advise you to use your common sense and think, look and try before you buy.

REELS

Whilst I think it's fair to say that rods are the prime item of tackle in any carp angler's kit, it seems that reels don't have far to go to catch up with that status. Reels are certainly nearly up to rods in terms of price, but are they in terms of quality?

Like rods, fishing reels have their own bands of devotees – some top anglers swear by Shimanos, while others swear by Daiwa, Ryobi, DAM and

so on. When anglers of the calibre of Rod Hutchinson, Kevin Maddocks, Andy Little, Kevin Nash and John Wilson all choose different reels often to do the same job, it is clear that once again you will have a wide range of options, with no one reel being the complete carp angler's choice when compared with others.

Much of what I said about fishing rods for the carp angler also applies to the correct choice of reel. Do not follow fashion and change or update your reel merely because a well-known angler says you should do so; rather, do it if you feel the reel is a genuine aid to your carping in relation to the outlay. I would guess that many of you fish waters under 10 acres or so, so you will not need

Fish like this one test tackle to the full.

huge casting reels or reels developed to tame hard-fighting catfish or Cassien carp. If you feel you do need to equip yourself with a new reel or wish to update your current reel, what considerations should you look to?

1. The reel must be one which will allow you to cast your hookbait to a place where carp are willing to feed. As when choosing a rod, you must look at the waters you fish or are likely to fish and decide what kind of reel will suit you best. As I said earlier, most of you will be fishing waters under 10–15 acres so huge casting reels like Daiwa's SS3000s and Shimano's 8000s may not be needed. What you are looking for is an affordable reel which will allow you to cast around 100yd or so.

In my opinion, the ideal position in angling is to be able to fish without a shock leader (*see* Chapter 5), so improving control on fish and decreasing the likelihood of damaging fish. To be able to use 3oz leads direct on your main line, you will need to be able to use 12–15lb straight through to absorb the shock of the cast. Obviously, this strength of line has a thicker diameter than 8–10lb line. As the line diameter increases, your distance will also be somewhat reduced. For that reason reels with larger than normal spools have a great advantage over normal-sized spool reels as you can put thicker line on them and still be able to propel a baited end tackle over 100yd. Of course, when I refer to larger spools I mean that they are larger from the lip of the spool to the back of the spool rather than in terms of depth (the latter doesn't really affect casting distance). I think that one of the best reels in this situation has to be the Shimano 4500 reel which has been entitled 'the carp angler's reel'. These reels offer large spools to facilitate distance casting with straight through 12–15lb line and, importantly, they are reasonably priced as well. Shimano does offer a ball-bearing version of this reel which is nice if you can afford it (or feel you need it), but to be fair is not entirely necessary.

2. The reel must be balanced to the correct rod if its true potential if to realized. You will probably have heard of the term 'balanced tackle', which usually concerns the match angler but does have its part to play in carp fishing. There is absolutely no point in purchasing three good long-casting reels if you are going to match them with sloppy or poor rods which will not be able to propel a bait any distance. Similarly, a silly line choice or wrong lead choice can prove just as detrimental. It is far better to save your money up and purchase rod and reel combinations than to purchase them piecemeal; indeed, by playing your cards right you will probably get a better deal from your local tackle dealer if you do so.

So, having decided the considerations which will affect reel choice, you should also look at the features which accompany each reel as these too will influence your decision.

3. Baitrunner system. Ever since Shimano brought out the baitrunner system (or, should I say, made it famous) it seems that every angler and his wife has wanted to whack one on their reels. The production and popularity of Shimano's 1989 carp reel range (4000, 4500 and so on) really brought the baitrunner home to the general public, and since then it has been baitrunner this, free spool that, and bite and run the other! Think back to what I said earlier – is a baitrunner really necessary on every new reel, or is it a case of companies following the latest in-vogue thing? I'll leave you to make your mind up on that one!

Playing fish and utilizing the baitrunner system is covered in Chapter 10, but what I will say here is that if you truly feel you need a baitrunner-type system then look carefully at the one that is built into your prospective purchase. Is it easy to use? Will you get it confused with your clutch settings? Are you likely to knock it on or off while playing a fish? Can you tell at a glance whether it's on or off? Have a play with the reel in the shop to see if its characteristics suit you and not the man who's getting paid to endorse the product. I know that some of my friends prefer the free spool system (DAM), some like the bite and run system (Daiwa) and some like the good old Shimano version. When I say that these are the choices of

Andy Little, Kevin Nash and Kevin Maddocks it's easy to see that there is a degree of scope for you to choose your favourite!

Clutches

It doesn't seem so long ago that the carp world was divided into two camps with regard to reels. One side chose ABU reels due to their incredible workmanship and clutch, whilst the others preferred Mitchells for their durability and no-nonsense reliability. However, it seems that every reel boasts of brilliant clutches so you do have a wide choice if you, like me, prefer to play a fighting fish off the clutch. Whilst I know some anglers do prefer to backwind (in other words, play fish by giving or taking line by use of the handle), I have always preferred to fish off the clutch. Using this method, I can increase or decrease pressure on a fish with a simple movement of the clutch knob (hopefully sited at the rear of the reel). Again, I will cover playing fish in Chapter 10, so I will leave the topic at that so you can make up your own mind as to what suits you best.

If you do prefer to fish off the clutch you will need to check your prospective purchase to see if its qualities follow your playing technique. A clutch knob situated on the spool itself will be comparatively hard to use as at times a fish will be pulling line from the clutch while you are trying to undo that front stardisck. The old Mitchells did suffer from this problem, so consequently most Mitchell devotees were backwinders. I've actually seen an angler cut his finger on line being pulled from the front of the spool – he ended up with a lacerated joint which was not a pretty sight. This may also cost you a fish when you least expect it and for that reason I avoid front clutches like the plague. Even my big Daiwa SS3000s are kept only for long casting and not snag or general fishing unless I have no other choice.

Having located the clutch on your reel and checked to see if it is easy to locate in a hurry, the next point is to see if it actually works. Everybody, and I mean everybody, seems to claim their clutch system is silky smooth and a veritable dream come true. In reality, very few can live up

to these claims. In my opinion, the best ever clutches on a reel belonged to ABU's Cardinal 44X/55X/66X series, followed closely by ABU Cardinal 55s and 57s. I haven't seen any other clutches come close to these, so without disclosing which are the worst from what I consider an adequate selection I will leave it to you to use your common sense to find out which are which before you buy the reel.

It is also a fact that the quality of clutches varies between different examples of the same reel. In an ideal world this shouldn't happen, but in reality it does. Insist that the owner of the shop spools up your prospective reel's spool and that you test the clutch for smoothness before you buy the reel. Considering the prices of some makes the dealer should not quibble, and if he does then go elsewhere.

A good clutch does not need to be yanked to get it going, and testing it is simplicity itself. Fill the spool up with line, thread it through all the rod rings and ask a friend or the shop owner to hold the reel. Then, as you hold the line, pull carefully whilst the clutch is tightened gently or unscrewed. A good clutch will pay off line smoothly with no sudden surges or halts. As with leading around with a plumbing rod, your hands will tell you if everything is right or not. If it isn't, then don't buy that reel or design of reel unless you want to lose fish at the rod tip. Find a reel with a good clutch and stick with it. Do this check on each reel body you intend to purchase; I bet you will be more than surprised at the variation in efficiency – I know I was.

Additional Features

Finally, have a good look at any other features the reel boasts of. Can you tighten up your reel handle without stripping the thread completely? Does that folding handle fold away easily and, more importantly, is it likely to fold away accidentally in mid-flight? Is the anti-reverse conveniently located and are you likely to knock it on or off during a fight? Does the bale arm turn over each time it is engaged or is a helping hand needed to do the job? Will it stay over when you are casting out? If it does flick over mid-cast you will end up with an almighty crack-off, you may break a rod or, even worse, you could easily cause somebody serious injury with an untethered lead. To check this feature all you need to do is open the bale arm and shake the reel from side to side – if it flicks over occasionally you will have problems.

As Jim Gibbinson says in his book *Big Water Carp*, he has yet to find the perfect carp reel, so it is vital to check just what you are buying. Finding out on the bank that the reel is not up to that which you desire may be too late. Big carp don't fall to just anybody's rods very often, and when you do get your chance it is silly to mess it up simply because you were too lazy in a tackle dealer's shop when you bought your reel.

BUZZERS

As I sit and write this in mid-1992, it is obvious that the buzzer market has seen a tremendous influx of products in the last twelve months. Updated Optonics, brand new Foxes and a revamped Delkim are just some of the models that are now competing for a share of this very lucrative market. Believe you me, the money that has been ploughed into these products in terms of design and advertising has been phenomenal, so it is apparent that the manufacturers are aware that the demand is still here for whoever gets it dead right.

Whilst there will be some anglers who claim buzzers are not necessary, I would have to disagree as I think they make fishing effective and relaxing. I can accept that the rustle of silver paper and the sight of a jangling dough bobbin do take me back to fond memories, but they also bring back memories of huge bag-ridden eyes, missed chances and exhausted anglers. I am therefore truly grateful for progress in this area.

I will not cover the development of the buzzer in this book as it has been covered in many other carp books. What I will say is that today's buzzers are not totally different from the early buzzers and in my mind have been merely improved upon rather than radically developed (apart from the sensitivity adjustment, which is new). No doubt as I write this somebody will come up with an all-dancing model, but until they do I will stick to my point.

If you find your buzzers acceptable then don't change them just to be one of the bankside poseurs. A buzzer is only a good buzzer in my book if it satisfies two main criteria throughout all sorts of weather conditions. These are:

1. It must be totally waterproof. I have found very few buzzers to be completely waterproof as supplied direct from the manufacturer. Over the years I must have split, dried out and rejoined my buzzers hundreds of times. My main criterion in selecting a buzzer is to pick an indicator which is totally waterproof. Due to the lifting of restrictions on close season fishing and our ability to catch carp all year round, more and more carp anglers are fishing for carp twelve months of the year. In doing so they encounter all sorts of seasonal weather variations – scorching sun, driving rain, the lot. In order to fish all year round it is vital that your indicator does not let you down. If your indicator is susceptible to penetration by rain then sooner rather than later it will let you down. You just cannot afford to have buzzers playing up in the rain so that you have to rely on visual indication or clicking clutches. Big carp takes are all too infrequent and things being as they are, the takes you get will probably happen when your indicator is on the blink. That could cost you the fish of a lifetime – it may have happened to some anglers, but don't let it happen to you!

If your current choice of buzzer is letting you down now and again, I would seriously think about changing it as soon as possible to a model that is more reliable. A working indicator can be the difference between an indication at which you can strike and sleepy oblivion, so do think carefully about whether you should really go for those new carbons or reliable buzzers. I know buzzers can be improved by mounting speaker covers on them (Kevin Nash or Fox's versions), while coating the inside with a silicon gel is also a very good idea. If you go into any army surplus store or hardware shop you will see various gels for sale which can be used to coat your circuit boards. One of these will often do the trick and, providing you do give your buzzers a good airing at home, you may be able to get away with what are really substandard indicators.

2. It must be sensitive and have effective indicators. Whilst reliability is the main criterion by a mile, it is also very important that a buzzer is sensitive enough to indicate a take from a wary fish, that the volume is sufficient to notify the angler, and that he is able to identify the correct rod and not find that it has blown out of the rests in high winds.

Most indicators nowadays are sensitive enough, be this via a sensitivity control or eight-paddle wheel enclosed in the body of the indicator itself. Personally, I don't know why indicators have varying degrees of sensitivity as I would always want my indicators as sensitive as possible. Many takes can occur whilst you are asleep at night so buzzers must either be loud enough to wake you from your stupor, or work off extension boxes which can be placed close to your head.

LEDs which continue to flash and therefore show which rod had the pick-up, are a good idea as sometimes in winter a carp may be hooked via a single bleep but may not dash off; instead it will merely sit with the hook in its mouth, confused or lethargic.

Isotopes on either side of your rod groove are of limited value as I've yet to even look at them when I get a run; usually I would look at the relevant spinning clutch or glowing isotope. A deeply cut section on which to rest your rod is vital in order to prevent the rods being blown from their rests in high winds or lifted from their resting place by fast-taking carp. How many people have woken up to find the rod tip in the water, the buzzer cocked to one side and a heavily weeded fish? A good design can cure all this, so don't let it happen to you, please.

In the end, I'm sure you will be able to make up your own mind on buzzer choice. However, I will look briefly at some of today's buzzers and give an unbiased view on how they rate for the 1990s' carp fishing needs in my eyes.

Standard Optonics, Magnetronics and Compact Optonics

Ten years ago these were your only real choice, but time has marched on and to be fair these are now not the only choice in the buzzer world. When bought they need thorough waterproofing with a silicon spray, carp ears to stop your rod blowing out, an extension box into your bivvy, and an opti polo and bolt to lock them to your buzzer bar. They are possibly good first buzzers for limited carp fishing, but if you intend to fish all year round you may need to look elsewhere.

Optonic XL

This top-of-the-range Optonic was introduced to keep up with the times. At full volume and on high tone these are certainly loud enough, but they do consume batteries monthly for a person who fishes regularly. They are certainly a lot more waterproof than standard Optonics but they do still need proofing. As with the standard Optonics you should equip them with a twitcher wheel for sensitivity and you need to purchase opto-bolts to avoid buzzer lean. You also need to watch that the rear knobs (volume and tone) don't fall off. However, they are competitively priced and a good model to move up to.

Bi-Tech Viper

This original version nearly got everything right, but one or two flaws upset what was potentially a very good product. For sensitivity they are unrivalled – in fact, at times they are even a little too sensitive. A good spray of silicon will solve any weather problems and a good volume output, variable tone, nicely cut rod case and bright LEDs all go in its favour. However, the ball joint design is abysmal and I have actually had buzzers pop off in mid-take at some fisheries. This can be cured by sawing off your ball joint and taping the buzzer direct to the buzzer bar. Whilst this does work, it invalidates your guarantee and makes battery changes a real chore. At the price they are excellent value indeed, and anybody who is willing to do some work on them, who tends to stick to smaller waters and who fishes in winter would be well advised to try them.

Fox Buzzers

Released in a blaze of publicity in June 1992 these buzzers (Micron SX, Micron and Mini Micron) may prove to be market leaders if the waterproofing situation has been sorted out in the way it is claimed to have been. They certainly look the part and on this fact alone they will appeal to a lot of carp anglers. Sensitivity is brilliant, volume is ear-bending, tone is variable and it has a strong latching LED as well. A new hard case protects the buzzer in transit, an offset Swinger attachment allows you to use your jack-plug attachment and a superb little extension box even includes an anti-theft device. However, original versions did have problems with waterproofing even with the speaker covers which became available. Having now extensively tested the buzzers, I can confirm the problem has been solved completely.

Daiwa Sensitron

Like the Bi-tech Viper, this buzzer was a brilliant idea which was let down by one or two design faults. Sensitivity control is good and allows you to strike at the merest flicker on the rod tip. Up until June 1992 the waterproofing was a problem and very few people had a good word to say about them, but I have tested the new versions extensively and the majority of problems have been rectified. Volume is a little on the low side but will probably keep Jim Gibbinson happy! A sounder box is now available and although the volume is passable, placing in your bivvy should ensure that you don't miss any indications.

New Delkim

I think that it's fair to say that the old Delkims coupled with Cardinal 55s used to be the most sought after tackle items all over the UK, and when you ended up paying twice as much for a second-hand one than you did for an original one then you knew they had got it right. However, Del has updated the buzzer for the 1990s and, if my original impressions are correct, he seems to have got it right first time out. It's waterproof, it has an incredible sensitivity control and I really can't fault it. It's loud enough, has variable tones,

has a strong LED and a nicely cut rod groove. All I can add is that due to its somewhat unusual design you probably won't see many on the bank to start with, but I bet that come late 1993 it will be *the* indicator to have – unless all the competitors get their acts together.

Bobbins, Swingers and Monkey Climbers

Up until 1989 when Cliff Fox brought out his incredible Swinger, it seemed that it was a case of monkey climbers or nothing. Whilst it is fair to say that these bobbin set-ups had been improved over the years since their introduction in the 1970s, even the most friction-free, state-of-the-art ones had their problems. The main problem was an inherent one in that a take from a carp pulled the line at one direction whilst the movement of the bobbin could only be at right angles to that (*see* Fig. 16). In layman's terms, your line wants to go one of two ways and the bobbin wants to go at right angles to that. As a consequence, a large amount of friction (depending on the quality of the bobbin and needle set-up) is created which is not always an ideal situation. Whilst in the summer you may get screaming takes which register on any set-up, wary fish or lethargic fish in winter may not tolerate that resistance and either drop or get rid of the baited end tackle.

The old favourite of a bobbin on a piece of cord was probably the ideal alternative, but unfortunately was very susceptible to wind movement, getting caught in bankside vegetation and getting jammed in the butt ring (*see* Fig. 17). While anglers such as Harry Haskell and company extolled their virtues, very few took up the good advice and continued to miss positive indications. However, courtesy of Cliff Fox we saw the introduction of the brilliant Swinger indicator which seems to have been the answer to our problems. Whilst it did take off slowly at first, the Swinger has almost replaced the bobbin on the lakes I fish and I'm sure it will continue to grow in popularity as more and more anglers become aware of its advantages.

I am sure you will be aware of what a Swinger-type indicator looks like and also of all the press

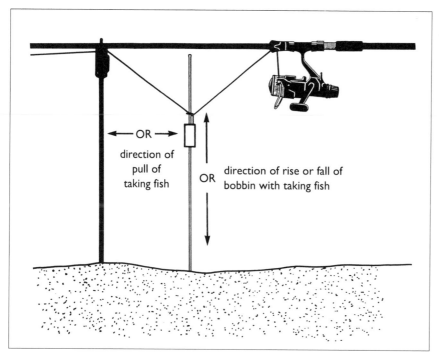

OR

direction of
pull of
taking fish

OR

direction of rise or fall of
bobbin with taking fish

Fig. 16 Monkey climber problems.

coverage they have had should also have made you aware of their advantages over conventional set-ups. As the Swinger is hanging on the line it does not have to move at right angles to the direction of pull as conventional bobbins do, so friction is restricted and takes are registered more easily. Grit and mud thrown up from rain splash cannot impede its progress as there is no bobbin to climb up the needle. By moving the counterweight up towards the rod you increase the sensitivity of the arm as the weight on the bobbin area is decreased (*see* Fig. 18). Indeed, you can find a point of neutral balance by siting this counterweight carefully. Takes on such a balanced set-up will register as huge lifts on the Swinger arm. The greater the registration the more likely your indicator is to sound, and the more likely you are to strike into that fish. Incidentally, the longer the arm, the more sensitive you can make your Swinger.

By moving the weight down towards the bobbin end you will decrease sensitivity as this area is more weighted and it will take more of a pull to move it. However, with drop-backs the nearer the weight is to the bobbin the greater the drop

will be and, as I said earlier, the more chance your indicator will sound and the more chance you will be able to strike into the carp. In Chapter 7 I look at how to set up your Swingers to best advantage, so I won't dwell on that point here.

I was actually tempted to leave out monkey climbers here because I am convinced that a correctly set up Swinger will always be more effective than a needle and bobbin set-up. However, it is apparent that some people do still favour this type of traditional set-up, despite the advantages Swingers have. If you are thinking of the monkey climber type of set-up you may have to purchase a number of different sets of bobbins or a single bobbin which can be made lighter or heavier by adding or removing metal or brass discs. Unlike the Swinger, which has a slidable counterweight on the arm which can be set up for neutral weighting, a weight on a needle and bobbin set-up has to be taken off or added to in order to change its effect.

The reason for this need for variable bobbin weight is that sometimes you will be fishing at range (80yd or more) where the carp are more than likely to give drop-back indications or not

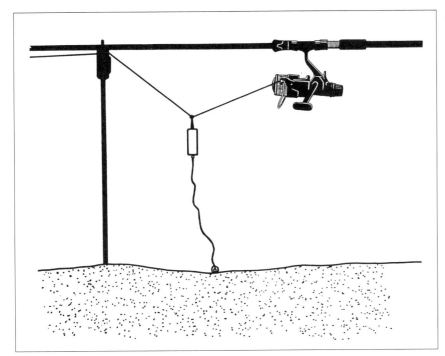

Fig. 17 A bobbin.

bolt straight off. With a light indicator there will be nothing to move the line over the sensor to cause it to sound (due to line stretch and so on), and you may miss that vital pick-up. With a heavy indicator the weight of it will keep the line taught and a slackening of the line will move the line over the sensor, so triggering the sound. I won't go too much into that now as it's all covered in Chapter 7. As well as this heavy 'drop-back' type bobbin, you will need to purchase lighter ones where you are fishing for slow takes (in other words, not a bolt rig type set-up) and you will probably want a set of medium-weight ones for general carp fishing. So, all in all those coupled with isotopes, needle bars and needles can come to a lot of money which would probably be best spent on a single set of Swingers.

BANKSTICKS, ROD RESTS AND ROD PODS

While the rod pod seems to be increasing in popularity there will always be a place in my tackle box for good banksticks and rod rests. You will,

if you pick up any carp magazine, see literally dozens of different manufacturers offering various designs of bankstick and rod rest at variable prices and of variable quality. Most are of similar design so it would be unfair for me to single out any one firm for accolade; all I can do is let you know what has served me best over the years. Many other manufacturers also offer good quality products, but do be aware that just as many others are putting shoddy, overpriced and ill-thought-out products on to the market as well.

If I can I will always use a twin-rest stainless steel buzzer bar at the front and a similar one at the back. These have been well publicized in my magazine articles, but for those of you who are unaware of what exactly a twin-rest bar is, it is a buzzer bar which allows a bankstick to be screwed into each end of it beneath the buzzer itself. In effect, this gives you a rock-solid set-up as the buzzer bar itself cannot twist round a central point no matter how much weight you put on it (*see* Fig. 19).

Normal buzzer bars which have a central bankstick point only have a tendency to rock from side to side when subjected to cross winds or heavy

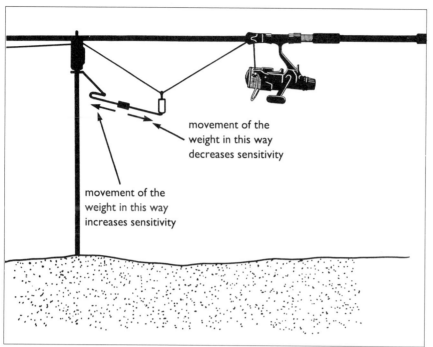

movement of the
weight in this way
decreases sensitivity

movement of the
weight in this way
increases sensitivity

Fig. 18 Swinger
adjustment.

rod and reel combinations. Whilst this may not seem important when you get a single bleep in the night, you do need to be sure it's an indication of a taking fish rather than a poorly constructed set-up creaking in the wind.

I have heard it said that to carry up to four banksticks to utilize this system to the full is too much weight to carry. Well, I have never found that at all. The two dual buzzer bars I use are Leslies versions and all four banksticks are Obelisk 16in short versions which are very well made indeed (*see* Fig. 20). All the components fit inside a folded-down bedchair (without needing to be broken down) and are placed inside in a bedchair bag. It is absolutely simple and I am totally convinced that this is the most effective set-up – even if it may not be in vogue in the 1990s. As I've said before, choose the set-up which suits you best, is the most effective system you can afford and is not just a set-up favoured by those who are paid to endorse it or who will gain financially by its sale.

There are occasions where it is impossible to push banksticks into the bankside. Such situations can occur on reservoir bankings, hard-

baked clay banks, rubble-strewn banks and platforms. Normally this problem would have to be solved by using the tripod adaptor and screwing in three rod rests to form a tripod. However, this could mean that you end up using a total of six rod rests and you still aren't guaranteed a rock-solid set-up. The problem was solved in the early 1980s when Gardner tackle brought the first commercially made rod pod on to the market, which was aimed at the mobile angler who wanted to carry all his rods on his set-up between swims. Gradually these have increased in popularity, and with KJB's Rod Pod and Fox's Super Pod you now have state-of-the-art rod pods.

If you feel a rod pod is necessary for your fishing then I would suggest you think carefully about which one you choose. Unfortunately, not all rod pods are able to accept 12ft or 13ft rods, some only accepting certain buzzer bars and others only accepting certain types of indicator needles. Take a look at all the various designs that are being used on your local lakes and see how they perform in the flesh. High winds will tip over some flimsy versions I have seen and others do not allow you to drop your rod tips below the water level to combat drift and the like, so be alert to these points.

Rod pods do have certain advantages, and a well-chosen rod pod may suit your fishing situation ideally. However, do not imagine for one second that you can order a stainless steel version over the telephone and expect it to perform miracles. It will not, so think and look carefully!

LANDING NETS

Whilst I have been putting the book together I have seen the advent of another expensive landing net, and whilst it seems to be absolutely spot-on in all areas, I wonder if we haven't become a little too overconcerned about the tackle we use at times. I can almost guarantee that sometime in 1993 I will see anglers using this type of expensive net, yet they will still claim that they cannot afford to buy a particular bait, or to join such a syndicate. Priorities, priorities!

A landing net must fulfil two criteria to be classed as effective; any more than that and it becomes merely superfluous to requirements. These criteria are listed below:

1. The net must be a manageable net for carp. Some years ago I was given an excellent net for carp fishing – the Chris Brown (CB Developments) net. However, due to its weight it was a net best wielded by a fellow angler whilst you guided the carp into it. It was a very well made net and superbly strong, but due to its weight it was unfortunately not a net which could be held out at arm's length to net fish which either refused to come any nearer or decided to change direction in the last moments of netting. Late in 1988 I lost a very big carp at the net due to my inability to hold it out, and decided I must change to a more manageable, lighter net. It would be very easy for me to say that the net was to blame for that missed opportunity, but as I have stressed throughout this chapter it was not the tackle that let me down but that choice of tackle.

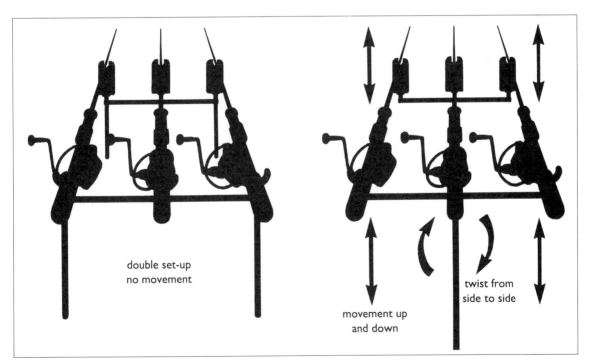

Fig. 19 *Double bar versus single bar.*

If you do fish with a partner all the time and if you do fish next to each other all the time then by all means pick a sturdy net which can be wielded by your partner. However, I bet there will come a time when you are on your own and unable to move your net quickly enough so that a carp will be lost at the net. Don't be caught out like I was – it's a hard lesson to learn, especially when it's a big fish that you lose.

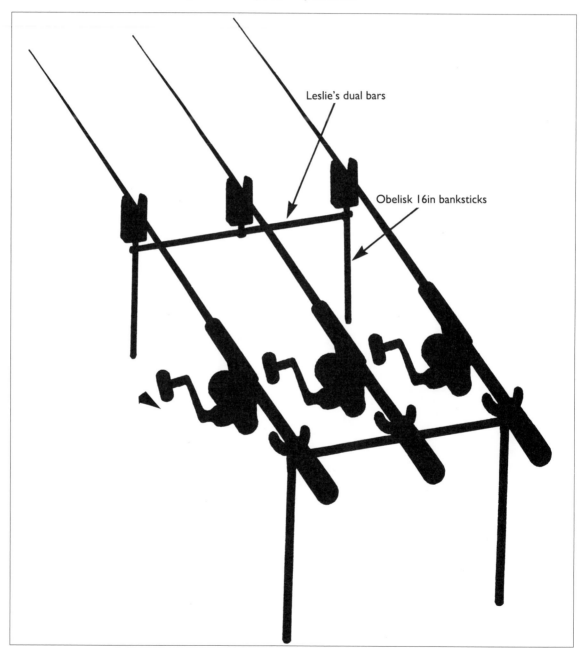

Leslie's dual bars

Obelisk 16in banksticks

Fig. 20 *A stable set-up.*

2. The net must be strong as well as manageable. Clearly, as well as being manageable a net must also be strong enough to net the carp you are fishing for and be able to take the demands that modern-day carping puts on it. I have seen some lovely landing nets on the market which have been designed with weight in mind, but unfortunately I would gauge their longevity in months rather than seasons. A quality piece of tackle should last you at least two or three seasons, and if it doesn't then you really haven't picked the right item for the job.

Landing Net Guide-Lines

1. Length of handle. In these days of 12ft and 13ft rods you have to remember that the longer your rod is, the further out you will have to push your net to reach the fish. Whilst it is very easy to say that you should just draw the carp into the net the closer it gets to you, the more likely you are to pull out of it – particularly if the carp is virtually under the rod tip. How many people week in and week out lose fish because of that fact alone? Take a look at Figs. 21 and 22, and the advantages of a longer handle will be plainly apparent. I like to keep the handle to around 7ft 6in as any more than this makes it unwieldy and susceptible to breakage at or near the connecting point between the spreader block and handle. The whole situation of playing and netting fish is discussed in Chapter 10, so let's move on.

2. Spreader block. To be fair, problems with spreader blocks have almost come to an end with the quality gear you can buy nowadays. There used to be problems due to breakage at the block, softening plastic and nets popping out, but the 1990s have seen an overall improvement. With toughened plastic spreader blocks I do like to locate an

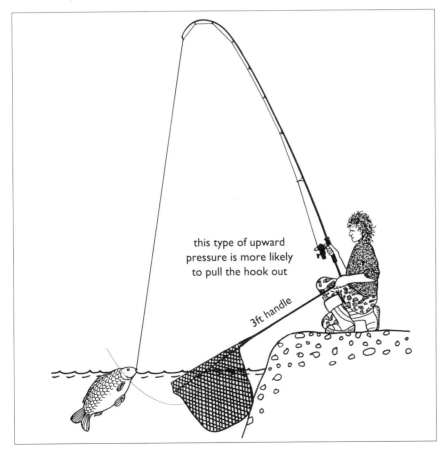

this type of upward pressure is more likely to pull the hook out

3ft handle

Fig. 21 *Short-handle problems.*

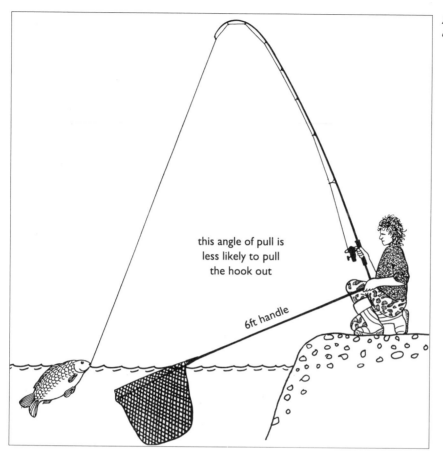

this angle of pull is
less likely to pull
the hook out

6ft handle

Fig. 22 *Long-handle advantages.*

isotope in the V so you can see exactly where the handle joint is, even in pitch blackness. I know Kevin Nash's nets do come with a slot to accommodate an isotope, but with a little thought I am sure most other blocks can be adapted to take one.

3. Net material. As discussed in the section on manageable landing nets you will need to push and lift the net in the water, so your material will need to be of sufficient size to allow easy water flow. It stands to reason that the larger the diameter of the net holes the easier the passage of water but you do have to balance hole diameter with care for your carp. Scales can catch in very large free-flow nets and this can nip them off, cause damage to the carp and encourage the spread of fungal-related diseases. I am quite happy to use my Kevin Nash net as it comes, but if your potential purchase has very large diameter mesh then think very carefully before you buy it.

4. Size of net. There seemed to be a craze among manufacturers a few years ago to make bigger and bigger nets, but thankfully they have now seen sense and keep most models to 42in or 45in. I can see a case for having 50–60in nets for catfish and eels, but remember that as the size of the net increases so will it be more difficult to push through the water.

These are the considerations I would look at before choosing a landing net. However, as a pointer I will cover some specific nets I have used over the years and you can decide whether they will suit your needs or not:

Gardner Net This is a very popular net which is an ideal compromise between the weighty Chris Brown net and the lightweight Solar net. It will suit most readers of this book, and at its price is a most affordable and dependable net.

Chris Brown net I did mention this earlier in the section – providing you do fish with a partner it is ideal. It has a handle of ideal length, strong spreader area, brilliant mesh and is very well made. The trouble with it is that it is so heavy in comparison with today's carbon-fibre specials and is almost impossible to hold at arm's length.

Rod Hutchinson Carbon net If this were still on the market it would almost be the carp angler's perfect landing net. Unfortunately, however, Rod ceased to make it four or five years ago. This was the first net I ever used that could be held out at arm's length when it was wet. It was a brilliant idea, was superbly made and was incredibly light. Its only problem was that due to its weight factor clumsy people like me used to break the handle by standing on it or backing it into overhanging trees. If you do see one for sale then buy it immediately.

Kevin Nash 42in Hooker net When I finally put the Hutchinson net to rest I had to find a replacement – this is the one I bought and up until recently it has been the best I've seen. It is almost as light as the Hutchinson version, but has a slightly longer handle and solid plastic spreader block. Mine is drilled to accept an isotope, but as I said earlier anyone can do this with care. I have had problems with the net cord working free

of its cover, but apart from that these nets are the best available if you don't want to splash out on Locke's Bow-Loc.

Solar Bow-Loc net This is probably the best net on the market, and if it performs as well as it feels then I think it will sell extremely well. The Bow-Loc is made from reinforced carbon fibre, and even though it has a 6ft 3in handle can be held out at arm's length with no problems. Martin Locke is full of good ideas as he has incorporated a clip near the block to clip the bottom of the mesh in (you can therefore sink it easier and not catch it on buzzer tops). The handle itself is detachable from the block area via a spigot joint, so it is unlikely you will take anyone's eye out or spear your bivvy. Providing its reliability matches the design features this is your ideal landing net – but at a price.

GENERAL LINE

Although I discuss particular line choice for different types of fishing later on in this book, I will spend a few paragraphs here looking at line for general carp fishing situations. After all, many of you will just want line for the majority of your carp trips. To be fair, this line will most probably

A Kevin Nash landing-net spreader block – excellent.

suffice for most situations and only in extreme cases will you need to pick a particular brand or vary your breaking strains.

I think that over the years there has been a gradual increase in awareness that a good main line is vital to success in carp fishing and that it is not an item like a rod licence or season permit that can be renewed every twelve months or so. We do all know this, but it has only been in the last couple of years that I have actually seen people making the effort to purchase line regularly, and good line at that.

Hopefully you will appreciate just how important a good main line is when you think that, coupled with a sensible choice of hook, hook-length and swivel, it is your direct connection with the carp. If any one of those items is suspect then you have every chance of losing that fish. As your main line will be the major item amongst them, it is vital that it is the correct type. Obviously, an incorrect choice of main line will be compounded by its length and importance in comparison with the other items.

So, what qualities should a good general main line have?

1. It must be of consistent quality throughout. Clearly, you want a line which is of a usable quality not just for the first 60yd but throughout its whole length. I know you can purchase huge spools of cheap bulk line from sea shops, but I have found that the quality of a line such as this will be 'varied' throughout its length. You only need one weak spot in an otherwise good batch of line to cost you a fish.

2. It must have a good knotting ability. There are some main lines which appear to be very good, yet knot absolutely terribly. All you need to do is tie a knot in the line and test it – you will be surprised at the ones that don't knot well!

3. It must not be of too great a diameter for its rated breaking strain. Remember, the smaller the diameter of the line the better it will cast and the easier the takes will register (there is less water resistance). Clearly, a very strong line with a thick diameter *must* be balanced out against a lesser rated line strength of finer diameter.

4. It must have significant abrasion resistance. Most carp waters have some points of abrasion, be they snags, weedbeds, gravel bars, loose stones or floating weed. Remember that although fine lines do cast well they suffer from abrasion. Lines such as Sylcast and Berkley are renowned for their abrasion-resistant qualities.

5. It must be reasonably priced so you can afford to replace it regularly. It would be nice if everybody could afford to renew extremely good quality line every month or so, but unless you are particularly rich you will have to balance expensive quality against affordable lesser quality lines. I have noticed that recently some brilliant main lines have been imported, but most are in effect luxury items. You are far better off purchasing an affordable good quality line like Berkley, Brent or Sylcast and renewing it regularly than purchasing a 200m spool of an expensive brand which is too costly to renew as necessary.

6. It must possess a certain degree of suppleness and stretch. With today's popular choice of hooklengths having little or no stretch and some distance rods having little or no give in them, it is important that your line does possess some give so that it can absorb the lunges that fish make. Pre-stretched lines with little or no give may be alright for short-distance floater fishing, but for most carp fishing situations, your line must have some give. Unless your reactions are incredibly good, there can be times when a fish will catch you out, so the correct choice of line can be vital to stop breakages.

Hopefully, the above information will give you some help when choosing a suitable main line; I will actually recommend certain brands and ratings when I discuss particular situations but always bear those six considerations in mind when choosing your main line.

Before I go on to look at items which I term 'sundries', I will look quickly at the maintenance of the 'big five' I have just discussed: rods, reels, buzzers, indicators and line. Just because they cost a lot of money does not mean they will last for ever if abused, as I've found out to my cost.

TACKLE MAINTENANCE

Rods

Very little needs to be done to keep your rods in working order, providing you take care when transporting them. A wipe down with a wet cloth now and again gets rid of dust and grime, and also helps your casting (this is discussed again later). If you are using fish oils then you will need to give your Duplon a soap over every month or so as the oil does build up – even if you are not soaking your boilies in it.

Reels

As reels are full of moving parts, they do need looking after if you intend to keep them more than a couple of months. Spools should be taken off once a month and the area behind them cleaned and roller bale arms should be cleaned meticulously to ensure that they do roll. Rear clutches tend to accumulate grit between the discs so wipe that area where possible, giving your reels a general wipe over with a damp cloth to stop grit creeping into open areas – no matter how small the area, the grit can creep in.

Buzzers

These are the main items you must maintain if you want them to keep working all year round. No matter what manufacturers claim, always use alkaline batteries and always change them every three months. After heavy rain split your buzzers in two and dry them out thoroughly with a hairdryer or in the hot cupboard. A small dab of line grease around joints keeps moisture out, and a wipe down with a damp cloth keeps grit down to manageable proportions. All this may sound excessive to some of you, but if one item is guaranteed to go wrong it will be your buzzer!

Swingers, Bobbins, and So On

Swingers actually need very little looking after, and if you bought them in a presentation pack then there will be no danger of them breaking or bending when in transit. However, if you didn't buy a case then don't worry as any good store which sells plastic boxes will be able to fix you up

with a rigid carrying container. Bobbins, needles and monkey climbers should be kept clean and grit-free. These types of indicators rely on the free movement between the needle and climber, so grit, mud and dust are your enemy. Wipe the needles down with a soft cloth, clean the internal bore of your monkey with a cotton bud and generally use your common sense! Buzz bars, banksticks and pods usually pose no problems, and as long as you put them away properly with the screws tightened they should provide you with years of service.

Line

Line does not so much require maintenance as regular checking for abrasions and weak points. You should do this at least once a session when you wind in – wind the line between your fingers and feel for nicks, wind knots and so on in the line. If you have any doubts about the line then respool immediately – you can always guarantee that if you have a problem you are bound to be found out.

SUNDRY TACKLE ITEMS

Although I have covered all the main items that will make an appreciable difference to you catching – or not catching – carp, there are hundreds of other available items that will have an effect on your enjoyment of fishing, even if they don't effectively alter your catch rate. Items such as hooks, hooklengths and leads are covered later in the book in the specialist chapters, so the sundry items I look at here consist of umbrellas, bivvies, rucksacks, holdalls, cooking equipment and the like. I will keep to the items that I know are good and will describe why I have chosen these particular makes.

Umbrellas

I know that many of you will not be session anglers or winter carp anglers, so the correct choice of umbrella is just as important to you as the choice of bivvy is to the session angler. As I state when I look at winter carp fishing (*see*

Chapter 9), you will only fish well when you want to fish, and you will stop wanting to fish when you are cold and wet. More and more anglers are now starting to avoid weekends when fisheries are crowded, and instead prefer mid-week overnight sessions after work, packing up just as the feeding spells end. For me, such sessions start as early as March or April and run through until late September, so I have to make sure I am well protected from the elements without having to lug around a bivvy with its accompanying pegs and poles.

I am personally a big fan of the Steadefast 50in Wavelock umbrella as I have found that, providing you do site your bedchair far enough back and your umbrella at not too acute an angle, you can keep totally shielded from the elements. Obviously, this only works if the rain is coming straight down or from behind; when it comes straight into your face it's time to reset your umbrella. As they come, the Steadefast umbrellas are almost perfect; I simply replace the pole with a screw-in Gardner one which, coupled with a T-bar, will go through almost anything. I

have also covered each rib point of my umbrella with a triangular section of old groundsheet or Wavelock and glued it tight (*see* Fig. 23). This stops the ribs popping out and prevents the thread from perishing at the point where it holds the umbrella rib to the Wavelock skin.

Another useful tip is to make sure that you sew the rib to the spare material that hangs down with Silkworm at least twice along each rib. This keeps the ribs in firm contact with the skin, decreases the chance of your umbrella blowing inside out and keeps the skin from flapping around. However, do make sure that it is the spare skin you tack the ribs to and not the outer Wavelock, or you will end up with water dripping on you at the first downpour.

Most umbrellas you can purchase now from Steadefast have been adapted so that you can screw the pole in near the umbrella boss, so giving you more room and less pole in your way. Before you leave the shop, do make sure you have bought this kind of brolly.

One step beyond the plain umbrella is one with built-in storm sides which keep the rain from

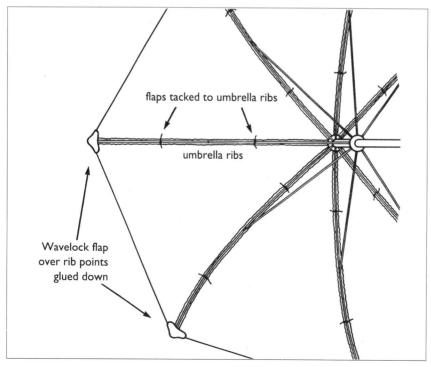

flaps tacked to umbrella ribs

umbrella ribs

Wavelock flap over rib points glued down

Fig. 23 *Umbrella modifications.*

driving into you from the side. These are an excellent idea for somebody who will put in quite a bit of fishing over a season, but who doesn't intend to fish for two or three days at a time, or fish in winter. The beauty of such storm sides is that you shouldn't need to detach them from the umbrella and, compared with the actual weight of the umbrella, they are very light. You can purchase some storm sides which push on or pull off after each session, but as this is time-consuming and places undue wear and tear on the umbrella ribs, I prefer to have mine permanently fixed to the umbrella. I simply purchased a second umbrella, and fixed the storm sides to four panels only with adhesive tape and glue. This is sufficient to protect you and your tackle from most weather conditions, it doesn't obscure your view of the lake and it only requires two extra pegs to pin it down.

Bivvies

The next step up from storm sides is the over-wrap bivvy which turns your umbrella into a weatherproof shelter. This is the theory, but unfortunately some of the more half-hearted attempts I've seen on the market are not suitable for all seasons as they should be, and are even a liability in the winter and in adverse weather conditions. If you are going to purchase a bivvy it should keep you warm and dry no matter what the weather is like. If it is reliable at all it should last you at least two to three seasons without the need for re-proofing every couple of months.

Looking at all these considerations, the model I've been most impressed with is the Kevin Nash canvas overwrap which is now called a Ziggwrap. Because it is made of canvas it is a little heavier than the nylon ones I have seen, but it is totally waterproof, it doesn't flap in the wind and it keeps you warm in winter. Please don't complain that it is too heavy to carry when it gets wet – try weighing out your rods, reels, leads and other tackle and I am sure you will have a big fright as to how little a canvas bivvy weighs in comparison. A canvas bivvy only weighs 7lb – less than the weight of bait you sometimes carry in summer!

Rucksacks and Carryalls

Ever since Kevin Nash brought out his superb K N Rucker, we've seen a growth industry in ruck-bag production and design as the competitors saw just how carp anglers took to them. At the time it was the only choice, and quite rightly so. I'm still a big fan of Kevin's gear and recently obtained one of his new Pursuit 120 ruckbags. In my eyes these are the complete ruckbag for the 1990s' carp angler. Not only are they huge in terms of capacity, but they are highly manageable as well. All the straps are padded generously and a waist strap with plenty of extra padding means that your hips also support the load, so decreasing fatigue on your shoulders – a brilliant idea. I chose the largest one possible, because unless I'm session angling I really want to be able to put all my gear in one bag and do the swim in one go – swinging camera bags and trailing bait buckets are not my idea of fun!

For weekend anglers or those who want to carry lots of food and the like, the Happy Hooker holdall will not be large enough and you will need to purchase a separate carryall. My favourite is Kevin Nash's Monster carryall which will hold all my gear, even when I'm planning a three- or four-day session in winter. Equally well made as the Hooker Pursuit Rucker – you can cram both of them full and still not end up breaking your back or any of the straps.

Rod Holdalls

If I had the luxury of being able to go fishing whenever I wanted and for as long as I wanted, I'd be tempted always to take my rods and reels apart and tie on a new end tackle each time. However, as I work full time I am always on a tight schedule. This means that I don't split my reels from my rods after each session and, like many anglers, my rods and reels stay tackled up together all season. To transport rods kept in this modern way, manufacturers have developed a new style of holdall. You merely have to pull your rods apart, place both parts together, fold your reel handle down and place them in the holdall. This is an absolutely brilliant idea as you can save literally fifteen minutes at each end through not having to re-thread line and re-tie rigs – time you can have a bait in the water fishing effectively. The two holdalls to do the job best are listed below:

High Protection Holdall By Rod Hutchinson, this most resembles a traditional rod holdall with its one-sided zip and the fact that all your rods fit inside it with outside pockets for umbrellas, banksticks and so on. However, the similarity with the old version ends there. Rod took a realistic view at how much rods cost and decided that as a rod bag carries expensive tackle it should provide the best protection possible. Each of the rod chambers is heavily padded and so are the reel chambers. Overflaps with push buttons keep the rods nailed down and everything is as protected as it could ever be. The only minus point is that the holdalls don't balance well when put over your shoulder and tend to topple over. However, if you carry them you won't encounter such problems, and because everything is in one central pocket you can strap them down nicely to roof-racks and carry them through undergrowth without jamming your landing-net poles and umbrella tops in bramble bushes!

Savay Rod Hod With Kevin Nash's version, each rod is contained in its own separate zip-up case, thereby giving each one complete protection. The central area holds your umbrella, landing-net handle and multitude of banksticks, whilst the outer area holds your rods in their sleeves. The big plus of Kevin's design is that, coupled with a Happy Hooker Pursuit ruckbag, your Savay Rod Hod clips to the shoulder top and waistband, leaving your hands free so that you can carry the carryall. Your rod hod will be pointed up at forty-five degrees directly in front of you rather than trailing sideways in the bushes, and your body takes the strain rather than your arms alone – a brilliant design. Its minus points are that you have to unzip three separate cases to get three rods out, and that it cannot be put on a roof-rack as the rod cases flap around and the holdall fills with air. If you do, place it butt-end into the wind to avoid 'air-fill'.

Rig wallets – a useful item for all anglers.

These two ideal rod holdalls may set you back a bit to start with, but they are well worth the investment in the long run. An ideal version would be Rod's holdall with Kevin's way of carrying it – perhaps by the time this book comes out there will be a crossbreed of the two available.

Bedchairs and Bedchair Bags
Top-quality bedchairs seem to be keeping up with top-quality rods in terms of price. If you

have problems sleeping on the bank, however, your main choice will be one of Cliff Fox's bed-chairs. Padded, all adjusting and nicely made, these really do fit the bill. However, if you are on a tighter budget and feel that your money would be better directed to quality bait or good syndic-ates, you would be silly to spend all that money on a bedchair. A normal sunlounger will do the trick if you only fish one night a week or so, and if you do fish more than that at night then I advise you to look towards Lafuma's three- or five-legged versions which are around a third of the price of the Fox's chairs. In my opinion these are far more comfortable than even Cliff's top ex-ample, but they do not have adjustable legs and are a lot more weighty.

Bedchair bags are another brilliant idea, keep-ing your bedchair out of the rain when you lug it between swims. Shaped like an overlarge satchel, a bedchair bag will take a full-sized Fox's bed-chair; inside my bedchair I put both sets of dou-ble buzz bars complete with alarms, back rod-rest heads and banksticks. The bag then zips up to keep the rain out, and the side-pockets will take groundsheets and rod mats. Once your bedchair is out of the bag, it is ideal for storing spare rod cases and your sleeping bag. There are plenty of bedchair bags on the market, but personally I have used ET's version for over four years and it hasn't let me down yet. However, if you can't find one exactly the same, then ones by Nash and Hutchinson are just as good.

Guest Chairs

If you are a session angler it is a good idea to have what is commonly known as a 'guest chair' with you. These small chairs are ideal to keep in your bedchair bag as, providing you pick the right one, they should be nice and light. There are some lovely state-of-the-art chairs around, but if you don't want to spend a lot of money then look around in tackle shops for non-brand name chairs. I know that guest chairs may sound some-what of a luxury, but a comfortable seat other than a bucket or unhooking mat is more likely to have you sitting and watching the water for longer periods than if you were uncomfortable.

Cooking and Eating Equipment

If you decide to stick to overnight sessions or short day sessions, then hot drinks can be brought to the water in large Thermos flasks. For those short sessions it's silly to clutter yourself up with a stove, kettle, milk and so on, so just pur-chase a large Thermos and make sure you don't break it. For longer sessions, or if you feel you must have hot food as well, you will need some form of stove and cooking equipment to prepare your food and drink. Your three main choices are as follows:

Standard gas stove These small gas-canister stoves are ideal for sessions lasting under thirty-six hours as they are very light, very compact and in my opinion more efficient than their larger brethren. You can pick these up from most army surplus stores relatively cheaply, and a gas canis-ter will last you a good month or so.

Coleman multi-fuel stove Some years ago it seemed that everyone used to carry round huge double burners and gas bottles. Due to publicity and availability, Coleman stoves have become just as popular and are a far better choice in my opinion. Your best bet is to pick the multi-fuel model which runs on unleaded petrol and seems less susceptible to clogging of its jets than its 'stated fuel' brethren. Simply open the stove, fill it with unleaded petrol, give it a few pumps and away you go. These work in all weathers, are windproof, make a full boiling cup of tea or cof-fee in half the time that normal gas stoves do and take up little or no room in your carryall. Deficit points are that you do have to be careful with them and that you have to carry a canister of fuel with you. They cost about twice the price of a standard stove and will last you a couple of years.

Double burner or gas-bottle stoves If you tend to take everything including the kitchen sink these may be ideal for you. However, if you fancy hauling a huge gas bottle and burner round with you are either a session angler or are prepared to make a couple of trips. In winter you may have a real problem generating heat due to low gas pres-sure, but I do agree that these are a good idea for the man who really likes his food.

As a footnote to eating equipment, the best cup I've seen and used is the thermal cup which is available from Twilight Tackle (*see* Useful Addresses on pages 186–188). I am sure you can get them elsewhere but I looked for a long time and couldn't find one which was as good. Due to the cup's removable lid, you can be sure a cup of hot tea stays that way, another plus being that if you do leave the lid on overnight you won't find a slug in your cup in the morning. Places like army surplus stores have some nice cutlery available, so if you can't steal some from home then buy your knives and forks from this type of shop.

Clothing and Footwear

I look specifically at winter wear in Chapter 9, but will take a brief look at some clothing and footwear recommendations below.

Over the years I have seen some horrendous sights on the bank – bright T-shirts, Bermuda shorts and the latest designer running shoes. Whilst it's only my opinion, I do feel that clothing should be practical and make you blend in with the background. Obviously, if you are fishing at long range dull clothing is not necessary, but those who climb trees, peer into the water and wave their arms about when clad in bright clothing on small waters only have themselves to blame when fish are spooked. Bright colours against a dull background do put fish on edge and movement in such clothing further accentuates the problem. Personally, I wear army-type fatigues and/or normal jogging gear in dull colours. Choose whatever is comfortable on you and *not* what the latest 'in-angler' is wearing.

With weather in the UK being somewhat changeable, I always carry a set of waterproofs – the time I don't have them will be the time it absolutely buckets it down. There are plenty of different types available but I'm happy with Kevin Nash's Titan oversuit. Due to its 'breathable' Gortex material it is waterproof and you don't sweat in it. Again, it's your choice but do look before you buy. If something has stood the test of time with an angler then it will be a good bet, so ask about for advice!

Normally, I fish in wellingtons all the time, but I accept that there is a case for wearing training shoes if you do fish hard-banked gravel pits or nice grassy waters. A pair of waders is absolutely essential as you never know when you may need to wade those extra 10yd out into the water to further your casting.

Insurance

Have you ever thought how much your tackle is worth nowadays? And have you ever thought how much it is worth to somebody else? Unfortunately, in today's climate it is a sad fact that people will steal your tackle if given the opportunity. Some of these thieves will be non-anglers and yes, some will be anglers as well. Angling attracts a cross-section of people and unfortunately there are dishonest people involved in it too. It doesn't seem so long ago that you used to be able to leave your tackle on the bank, go home for a bath, come back and it would still be there. Now you can't even leave the stuff in your car! Something I can't stress enough is that you must insure your tackle; money won't make it better but it does help. Most carp anglers' tackle is worth a tidy sum and as a consequence is a big draw to the more dishonest in our society.

Tackle insurance is also useful for those occasions when you smash one of your rod tips in the car door, stand on your landing-net handle or leave the buzzers in the car-park. Better safe than sorry!

I shall not recommend any particular insurance company as you will need to choose the one that suits you best. Some cover theft from home only, some cover breakage as well, and some cover all risks. Do look carefully at the policy and pick the best you can afford. They are all within every anglers' budget and will be money well spent.

5 MODERN CARP RIGS

Probably one of the most talked about aspects of carp fishing is that of carp rigs and all that goes with them. How the carp feed or how strongly they are feeding on a particular bait seem irrelevant, and many anglers seem to cast out their favourite rig, thinking that if it's good they will catch and if it isn't they won't. This actually is not true at all because your rig should be varied to suit the carp and not your own personal preferences. The more time I spend on the bank the more I am convinced that few people actually think about what they are doing and prefer to copy rather than think. There is no need for any angler to fall into this trap because group thinking can only result in a decrease in action to that particular style or method. This is because the greater the number of carp caught on one particular rig, the more likely they are to treat it with caution in future. There is no golden rig available, so don't think that it has to be a fixed lead or otherwise; with a little thought and an adaptation or two, what was failing to register a pick-up or hook a carp can at times produce carp takes within minutes of being cast out.

There has been a lot of material written about carp rigs, so I won't go over old ground again. Instead I will look at one or two basic principles that you must get straight to start with, discuss how certain factors can affect your choice of rig and then detail some proven presentations on which I and my friends have enjoyed success, and hopefully will continue to do so for some time to come.

WHAT IS A RIG?

In order that I can be sure that we are working on similar lines, it is important at this stage that you are clear as to what constitutes a carp rig. I have always viewed and continue to view the rig as the lead and tubing part, whilst the hook, hair and hooklength are termed the presentation. Both rig and presentation when used together are known as the end tackle or baited rig:

| **Rig** | lead, swivel, anti-tangle tubing, beads, stop knots, lead core tubing (and so on) | End Tackle |
| **Presentation** | hook, hair, hooklength, stringer, pop up, bottom bait, balanced bait (and so on) | |

WHAT IS THE PURPOSE OF YOUR END TACKLE?

1. To reach the baited area. Your lead will need to be heavy enough to reach your baited area and any tubing or otherwise incorporated must not impede this factor.

2. To fool the carp. Your presentation must be sufficiently subtle or clever enough to fool the carp into taking it into its mouth.

3. To hook the carp. As well as being a presentation which can enter the carp's mouth, it must hook the carp and not be rejected or fail to find a hookhold.

4. To land the carp. Your main line, hooklength, hooks and knots must be chosen correctly to enable you to land the carp you hook.

5. To be safe. Nothing should be used in your end tackle which could cause any damage or injury whatsoever to the carp in the event that you hook it.

The right choice of hook led to this carp's downfall.

FACTORS AFFECTING YOUR CHOICE OF PRESENTATION

1. Naivety or otherwise of carp. Carp which have seen little in the way of carp fishing pressure are less likely to be wary of certain presentations. Carp which have been caught time and time again may approach certain presentations with a degree of caution.

2. Pressure on the water. Even if the carp are somewhat naive, if the water is subjected to carp angler pressure the carp may feel some degree of unease when feeding – this may not be a result of your particular presentation. However, on a pressurized water which has a close season the carp may become temporarily less wary.

3. Common usage. If a number of anglers are fishing one particular form of presentation and a number of carp have been caught on it, those carp may become wary of it and can find a way to avoid being hooked on that particular presentation.

4. Bait application. If the bait is one which the carp really want they may be prepared to take a 'risk' to get that bait. A bait which has been pre-baited and is attractive to carp may cause them to be less cautious. A bait which has caught carp time and time again may be taken less readily or with a degree of caution.

5. Time of season. As the seasons change so do a carp's body temperature and its feeding habits. The colder it is, the more likely the carp is to pick at its food and not take in baits with great gusto. In the warmer months, or in ideal feeding conditions, the carp may take baits more readily (subject to the above four points).

TYPES OF RIGS

First I will discuss the lead and tubing set-ups you can use to present your hooklengths in the baited area. Generally, these can be looked at in one of two ways: either with tubing or without tubing. There will be no complete answer for all waters, so I suggest you look at those illustrated and adapt them according to the demands of your water.

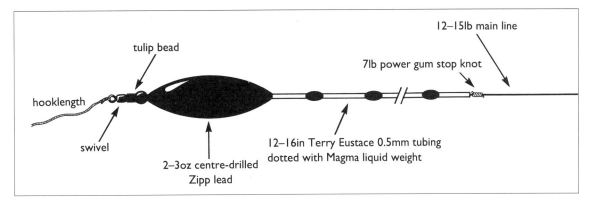

Fig. 24 *Tubed in-line rig.*

Tubing Rigs

The purpose of anti-tangle tubing is fairly self-explanatory and, providing you do use the right brand, it should give you peace of mind in that you know your presentation is not tangled around the bomb and swivel. A presentation which is tangled is an ineffective presentation because it may not be taken in as easily as it was designed to be, it may not hook the carp as effectively and it is more likely to open up or part when subjected to pressure. An angler who doesn't know if his presentation is tangled or not is an angler who is ill at ease and who is unlikely to fish confidently.

I have included two diagrams of the two tubed rigs that I use for around ninety per cent of my carp fishing and if these appear basic to some, then so be it. I see no need at all to detail complicated rigs with booms and different sorts of tubing connectors. The two rigs illustrated have caught a lot of carp and I am sure they will continue to do so. Usually, I use the 'in-line' rig (*see* Fig. 24) unless I wish to fish tight to weedbeds or at greater range when I use the 'bomb on the end of line' rig (*see* Fig. 25). The latter tends to cast a little better, but because the carp pulls one way and you the other (*see* Fig. 26) it is susceptible to line breakages and snagging. As you can see, with a helicopter-type rig you are not pulling directly at the carp, whereas with an 'in-line' rig you are. This can make a sizeable difference when fishing to snags.

Tubing or Tubeless?

Many anglers prefer not to use anti-tangle tubing because they believe it scares or puts off the carp. Although I didn't use to believe this, I have fished one or two shallow gravel pits where rigs with

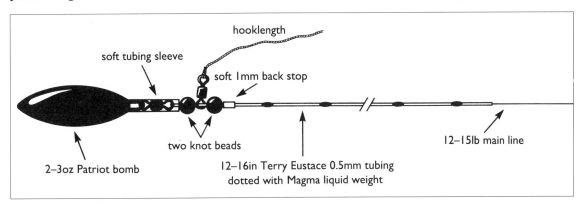

Fig. 25 *Tubed helicopter rig.*

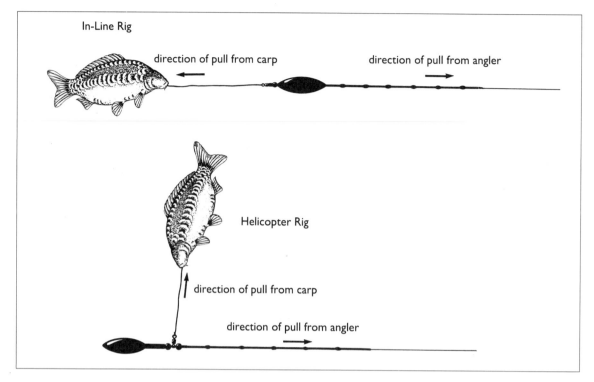

Fig. 26 *In-line advantages and helicopter problems.*

tubing have been outfished ten to one by no tubing rigs, so I do accept that there are occasions where it is detrimental to use tubing. However, on most waters I fish I do use tubing to give me peace of mind and to provide an initial 12–16in of abrasion-resistant material. Where the bottom of your lake is silty, weedy or covered in leaves, it is unlikely that carp will be put off by the sight of this tubing alone and, providing you use it in conjunction with the Magma putty as I have detailed, it will sit tight on the lake bed and not appear obtrusive to the carp.

Tubeless Rigs

If I intend to fish with a shock leader (*see* Chapter 7) or am fishing in circumstances where I believe tubing may spook the carp, I will use a set-up which avoids the use of tubing. Such set-ups are commonly known as helicopter rigs because the hooklength spins round and away from the main line like a helicopter blade (*see* Fig. 27). However, I am not totally convinced that

this rig is fully tangle-proof as I have found that tangles can occur when using pop-up baits or fairly long hairs. To avoid this I add a two-bait or three-bait stringer tight to the hook, as this ensures that if your hook and hair do touch the main line, it does not wrap round but instead bounces off. Fig. 27 illustrates this, and as you can see it is essential that your stringer binds hook and haired hooklength tightly together to create this 'bounce off' effect.

Main Line

Obviously, you must use a main line (with or without a shock leader) which is not so strong as to stop you reaching the target area but is strong enough to enable you to land the carp. Up to a distance of about 70–80yd you will probably not need to use a shock leader, providing you do have a good quality rod and reel. Using, for example, a 2½oz bomb and 12lb main line will allow you to reach most spots, and it is only once you start to cast beyond this sort of distance that you will

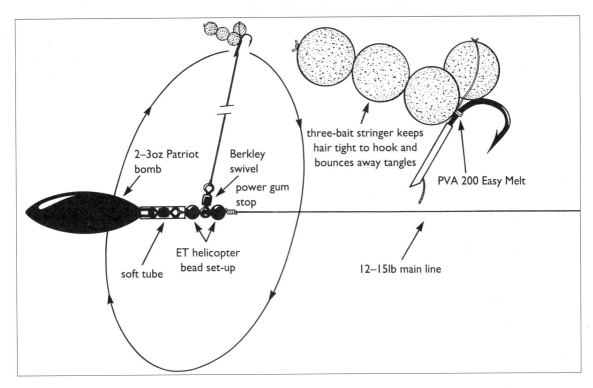

Fig. 27 *Helicopter rig in detail.*

need to use a shock leader (*see* Chapter 7). If you do use a shock leader then please do not use narrow-bore tubing, and do check that your leader knot is secure and that your main line is strong enough to land the carp in your choice of swim. A fine main line will show up takes better, whilst a thick one is less responsive to small pulls.

Because your choice of carp rig will only be an effective one if you manage to land the carp, it is essential that you don't take silly risks to catch carp. Check your main line regularly, especially when you've had a fish or are using it in areas of weed, snags or gravel.

Bomb Size and Fixing

Many rigs in use today are fixed-lead-type rigs and rely on the carp to hook itself against the weight of the bomb. I will look at hooks a little later, but the golden rule is to use as heavy a bomb as possible to hook the carp. Normally, this will be at least a 2oz bomb, but if your rod can cast a 3oz one accurately then use one of these. It

is important that the hook be pulled in against the weight of the bomb, even if only slightly. If the lead is so light that it does not nick the hook in, it may skid out and you will have missed your chance. Obviously, a lead will only be effective at pulling a hook in if its whole weight is felt by the carp. If your lead is able to waggle about, you may as well only have a half-sized lead out there, so do try to use an 'in-line' lead if possible. Its weight is concentrated in one area, and because it is centred it is not likely to move about and is more likely to pull the hook into the carp.

PRESENTATION

Having decided what form of rig you are going to use and why, it is now time to turn to presenting your hookbait in the best possible way to fool, hook and land the carp. This will entail a look at the three major components of all presentations: the hooklength, the hook and the hair. Because I am going to detail thirteen very effective forms of presentation at the end of this chapter, I will not go into each of these three variables too much, but instead will raise one or two points for each which will hopefully direct you to the correct choice.

Hooklength

The purpose of a hooklength is to enable the tethered bait to behave in an acceptable manner so that the carp will pick it up, and also be of a quality and strength to allow the carp to be landed. I could spend thousands of words discussing the merits of super-supple braids in comparison with stiffer manufactured lines, but I feel that you must experiment to determine what is best on your water. All waters are different and it would be impossible for me to describe which hooklength you should choose. However, all I can do is emphasize that my choice of hooklength would be based on a combination of the following factors:

1. Is it supple enough not to alarm the carp to this tethering of the hookbait?
2. Is it strong enough to land the carp?
3. Does it have a certain degree of stretch in it to absorb the initial bolt?
4. Does it retain its strength in water even after lengthy periods of immersion?
5. Is it too supple, therefore making it easily rejectable?
6. Do I feel confident with it?

If your choice of current hooklength satisfies all the above qualities then stick with it until you are convinced that another type or brand would give you a more consistent catch rate. I am happy with Kryston's range – you choose what suits you and your fishing best. One thing I will add, however, is that regarding length of hooklengths, I always use the shortest possible hooklength I feel I can get away with. Generally this is 8–12in, but when everybody else is following a similar pattern the carp may wise up and will start to work out which

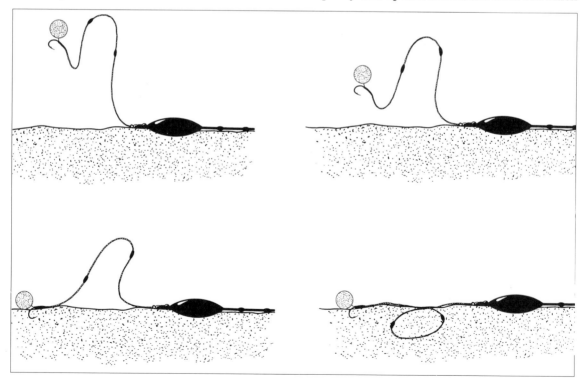

Fig. 28 *The benefits of Magma.*

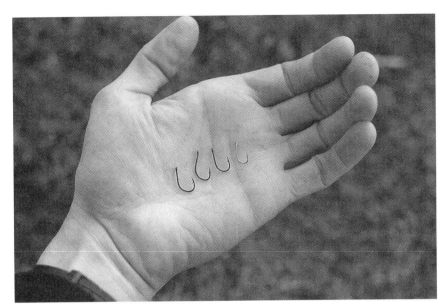

Which one to choose, I wonder?

baits to pick up and which to avoid. You may then have either to increase or decrease your hooklength to catch the carp off guard. However, by choosing a starting point of 12in and varying it as you feel fit you won't go far wrong on many waters you encounter.

You will see that most of the presentations I have detailed have hooklinks dotted with a product called Magma. This is one of Kryston's products and its purpose is to hold the hooklink down on the lake bed out of harm's way. An untreated hooklength, be it monofilament, braid or whatever, will always loop up above the bomb unless you pull the lead back to straighten out the hooklength. I certainly don't advise you to pull back to do this as you may drag the hook into weed and ruin your presentation, or you will lose the effectiveness of movement in it. The Magma liquid weight causes the hooklink to fall as illustrated in Fig. 28, but it doesn't lose any of its inherent suppleness. I know that it looks a little complicated, but it certainly is worth doing as a 'looped' hooklength can get caught up accidentally by a carp's pelvic fins and does look somewhat unnatural – especially on clear gravel pits. The use of this Magma putty is not just restricted to hooklengths as I also use it on my anti-tangle tubing and boom tubes – as you will see in the diagrams.

Hooks

As with hooklengths, I'm not going to force my particular favourites down your throat or tell you that you have to buy half a dozen sizes of half a dozen brands in half a dozen designs. What I will detail, however, are the considerations to be aware of when choosing a hook.

Small hooks are light, and are therefore less likely to be detected by the carp and more likely to be taken into the mouth. However, a small hook with a short hair could be rejected far easier if carp are sucking and blowing at the baits as they do in some waters. A small hook will be comparatively sharper than a larger one, but will be more likely to open up or snap when put under pressure.

A large hook is usually a strong hook but is more likely to be detected by a wary carp. However, a large hook is more likely to catch in the carp's mouth when the carp tries to eject the bait. Large hooks do need sharpening, but they are more likely to stand up to the pressure of an angler pulling at one end and a carp trying to escape at the other.

Sharp hooks are essential for all forms of carp fishing because the initial hooking will take place when a hooklength tightens up against the bomb and the hook catches the carp's mouth tissue. A blunt hook may bounce out and not connect, whilst a sharp hook is more likely to penetrate the tissue and pull in even deeper once the carp bolts off.

Carp hooks are very cheap in comparison with rods, reels and the like, but remember that they perform just as essential a task, if not more so. If this is true then why don't you use a fresh hook after each carp you catch and after each session you finish? The reason why is simply stupidity and laziness. Your hook may well still feel sharp, but water can cause fatigue in the hook and you could lose the fish of a lifetime all for the sake of a few pence. I change hooks each time I change my bait or catch a fish, and I don't lose fish because of hook failures. Can you say the same?

In the section on favourite presentations at the end of this chapter I have detailed my own hook choice in each case, but if you feel a different choice of hook would be advisable then please make it. What matters is that it doesn't let you down and you are confident!

Hair

Although I am willing to stand corrected, I believe that the original purpose of the hair rig in carp fishing was to stop the carp feeling the hooklength and hook when picking up a bait. However, as time has progressed many have forgotten this and a hair is just thought of as a way of mounting a bait on the hook. Keeping the hook and hookbait apart increases the chance that the hook will be dragged into or ejected into the carp's mouth tissue, thereby finding an effective hookhold.

For most of my carp fishing presentations I like to use a hair first to mount the bait, and second so that when it goes into the carp's mouth it causes the hookbait and hook to separate, so increasing the chances of self-hooking. Very supple hairlengths like dental flosses and multistrands allow the hook and hookbait to separate in the mouth, thus aiding self-hooking. If I feel the carp are feeling for the hook and hooklength, I use a long, fine line hair to alleviate the problem and combine it with a small sharp hook to nick home easily. However, on most waters you can start

with a dental floss hair (unwaxed) and increase or decrease its length if action is not forthcoming. The diagrams of each presentation at the end of this chapter illustrate the usual length of hair, but you should feel free to increase it or decrease it as you want to. Nothing is lost by doing this on one rod, and in fact often much is to be gained.

BOTTOM BAIT – BALANCED BAIT OR POP-UP?

Before I continue, I shall clarify some of the terms used with reference to balanced and pop-up baits.

Bottom bait A bait which is identical to the free offerings and which is fished on the bottom.
Balanced bottom bait A bait which, when attached to a hook, hair and hooklength, will just sink to rest on the bottom.
Balanced pop-up When a counter-weight is added to the hooklength in the correct place this just holds the pop-up down.
Critically balanced pop-up The attached counter-weight is just enough to defeat the buoyancy of the pop-up and it sinks slowly so that the counter-weight just rests on the lake bottom.
Overbalanced pop-up The counter-weight is such that it sinks straight down and holds the pop-up firmly on the lake's bottom.

Go to any carp fishery nowadays and I'm sure somebody will say to you something along the lines that only bottom baits catch, pop-ups have blown, balanced baits are old hat and so on. Fortunately, in nine out of ten cases this isn't true, and instead it's a case that the method of fishing that type of bait has been overused and it is time to vary your presentation a little. Personally, on a new water I tend to fish one pop-up 1–3in up, one pop-up about ½in up and a bottom bait. Then I will vary these presentations by use of longer or shorter hooklengths, smaller or larger hooks, shorter or longer hairs and so on before I decide that something is or isn't working. Even then you should keep your options open, and if

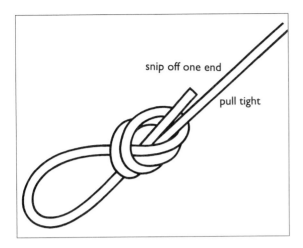

Fig. 29 Hair rig knot.

have found them to work best and how each can be adapted or changed slightly to increase your catch rate at certain times. There are hundreds more presentations detailed in the press each year, but I can honestly say that all of the thirteen listed are presentations I have used successfully and that they are starting points for nearly all of the other variations that may appear in magazines. Most follow a very similar theme, so to help those who have trouble tying up a presentation properly I have detailed how to put together a basic version. I am sure that once you have mastered this version all the others will seem like child's play. If not, please tell me!

somebody is making one particular form of presentation work, try to find out why and how you can do equally as well, if not better.

I shall now move on to the final section of this practical look at carp rigs and presentations by looking at some of the effective set-ups I have used in my carp fishing. Each presentation is illustrated and detailed in full, and I have also included a few lines on the situations in which I

BASIC PRESENTATION PREPARATION

1. Tie up a hair using unwaxed dental floss (the knot is illustrated in Fig. 29), place a dumb-bell boily stop in position and pull it back firmly so that the boily stop sits square in the boily skin (*see* Fig. 30). Leave about 5–6in of dental floss for the hair and trim off with a sharp knife.
2. If you wish to make a pop-up rig I would use a dental floss loop which, when pulled tight, holds the bait tight inside the loop (*see* Fig. 31).

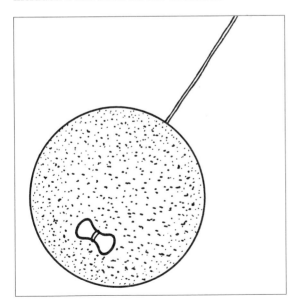

Fig. 30 Sited boily.

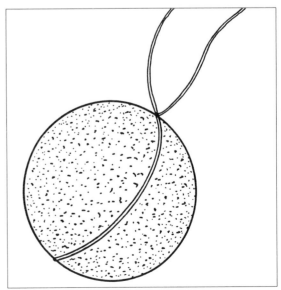

Fig. 31 Dental floss loop.

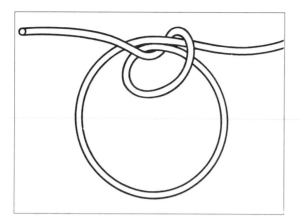

Fig. 32 *Loop knot.*

I have illustrated the knot (*see* Fig. 32), and I can assure you that if you tie it properly the bait will not come off. You don't need to do it this way, but personally I like the way it sits when tied.

3. Having tied your hook to the hooklength, thread your dental floss hair through the eye at least once, and twice if possible (*see* Fig. 33). Most modern eyes are large enough and you should be able to thread your dental floss through without too much trouble.

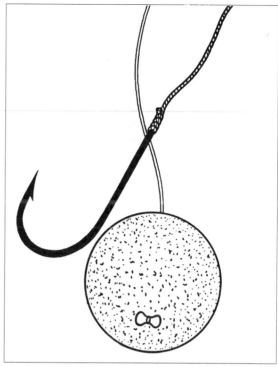

Fig. 33 *Site the hair.*

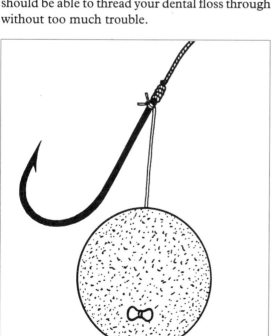

Fig. 34 *Knot it in place.*

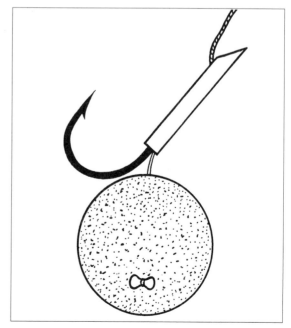

Fig. 35 *Add shrink tubing.*

4. Having threaded your dental floss through and having made sure it is hanging in the correct place, tie it with two granny knots to the eye, making sure this knot is nice and tight (*see* Fig. 34). You can superglue the knot as well, but there really is no need for this.

5. Either thread the shrink tube down the hooklength braid as per normal, or use a line aligner set-up as illustrated and use a needle to pierce the tubing, sliding the shrink tube down it until it covers the area as shown in Fig. 35.

6. I use Terry Eustace's shrink tube in either 1mm (hook size 6–12) or 2mm (hook size 1/0–4) because you only need to administer steam to it in order to shrink it. Simply hold the hook and sleeve over a steaming kettle (making sure not to burn your fingers), and in two or three seconds it will contract to form a nice sleeve over the hair and floss (*see* Fig. 36).

Fig. 36 *Add heat.*

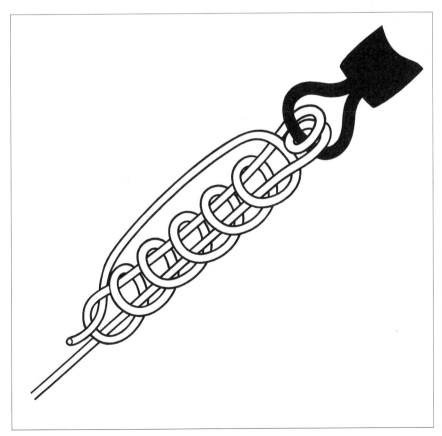

Fig. 37 *The braid knot. Because many anglers have their own preferred way of knotting braids, I will not dwell on which to use or not to use. The one I favour is illustrated, but I suggest you stick with the one with which you are happy. If you are unsure about which knot to use, all 9-Kryston's braids come complete with a leaflet on recommended knots for their products.*

PRESENTATION AIDS

The following are materials I recommend for your presentations.

Hooklength material Kryston Merlin 10lb, 12lb and 15lb; Kryston Silkworm 12lb, 15lb and 25 lb; Kryston Multistrand 15lb.
Shrink tube Terry Eustace 1mm and 2mm.
Anti-tangle tube Terry Eustace ½mm.
Dental floss Johnson's unwaxed version.
Hooks Partridge Z.2 or Boily Hook Z.15; Middlesex Angling Centre Bent Hook; Drennan Super Specialist, Boily Hook and Lure Hook; Gamakatzu Black Carp Hook; Kamasan Aberdeen Sea Hook.

Plus: ET Helicopter beads; Nash bolt leads; Leslies Patriot bombs; Berkley swivels; Nash link clips; Drennan run rings (small and large); DAM float stops; Kryston Heavy Metal putty; Kingfisher baiting needle; Gardner rig glue; Eustace 1mm rig beads; Nash rubber shocker beads; Nash Dumbbell boily stops; Kryston Magma putty; Kryston Bogey putty.

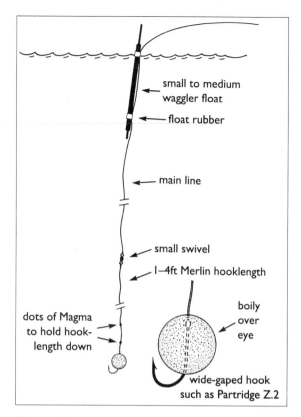

Fig. 38 *Float set-up.*

small to medium waggler float
float rubber
main line
small swivel
1–4ft Merlin hooklength
dots of Magma to hold hooklength down
boily over eye
wide-gaped hook such as Partridge Z.2

FLOAT TACKLE (FIG. 38)

This is a very underestimated set-up which has accounted for a lot of carp, especially in weedy or snaggy waters where it is possible to stalk fish in the gaps in the weed. I know it does look a little crude, but it works well and a bait in a carp's face is far more likely to be taken than one lost in the bottom weed. The float is held on by two float rubbers which does mean that if the fish gets weeded the float will pop off. You will then be in direct contact with the fish and will be able to get a straight pull on the carp. Usually I use a simple hooking set-up of a side-hooked boily pushed up on to the eye to ensure the point is free and can be driven home. Use a wide-gaped hook such as a Partridge Z.2 or Drennan Boily Hook, and keep it as sharp as possible. You can actually present a bait hard on the bottom with this float, but generally I have found that a mid-water bait works best.

MEDUSA RIG (FIG. 39)

This is named after the Greek gorgon who had snakes for hair – can you see the resemblance? All you do is superglue up to twenty-four maggots to the polyball and then use the polyball as you would a pop-up boily. Alternatively, you could use Kryston's Bogey putty to which the maggots will adhere. I usually choose quite a long hair to ensure maximum separation between the hook and bait once it's in the carp's mouth. A small hook is essential so that the rig doesn't look too obvious to the carp, and usually I use quite a short hooklink because this will be fished over a large bed of freebies. To stop your maggots (freebies) burrowing into the mud, scald them with hot water first – this doesn't deter the carp at all.

Providing there are few nuisance fish around or if you can actually see your quarry, this is a

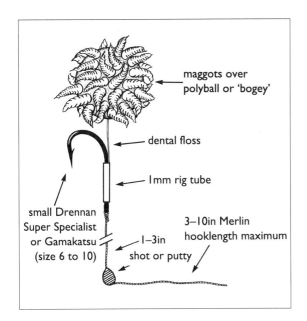

Fig. 39 *Medusa rig.*

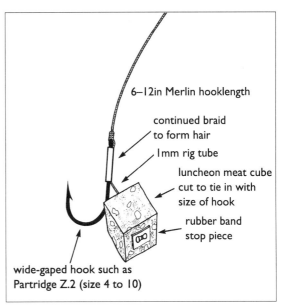

Fig. 40 *Luncheon meat presentation.*

brilliant presentation which works particularly well in winter. If you often use crumbed boilies then this makes a good alternative to a popped-up boily over the crumb. Carp seem to take it with abandon because it is not a method that is commonly used.

PRESENTING LUNCHEON MEAT (FIG. 40)

Not all waters allow boilies, and if you are restricted to luncheon meat you should still be in with a good chance of regular success. The trick is not to use too large a piece of meat and to keep it well away from the hook point. Meat which is side-hooked and which slides down to obscure the point will make hooking carp all that more difficult. Fish your meat on a hair rig (a continuation of the braid) and, providing you use a large section of rubber band held in place by a boily stop, the meat will not come off. Usually I keep my hook-lengths quite short and use a wide-gaped hook such as Partridge Z.2 to make sure the hook nicks home. As it is a self-hooking set-up, do use as large a bomb as possible and keep your hooks sharp.

TRADITIONAL BOTTOM BAIT (FIG. 41)

Earlier I illustrated how to tie a presentation such as this (*see* Figs 30–6) as it is a set-up which many people continue to use. Nowadays, I do use the line aligner in most presentations and thread the braid through the shrink tube with a small needle. With a bottom bait I like to use a simple dental floss hair and make sure that when the boiled bait is attached it hangs as illustrated in the diagram. You can increase or decrease the hair length as necessary, but the illustrated version is a good starting point and will catch on many waters. Always make sure your hook is not too big for your boily and vice versa, and that the hook is the lightest and sharpest you can get away with.

CRITICALLY BALANCED POP-UP (FIG. 42)

This is the typical set-up many anglers use for presenting a pop-up over weed in order to avoid the hook catching in the weed and the bait becoming hidden. If you are seeking to make the bait just sink it is vital you tie it on to cut down

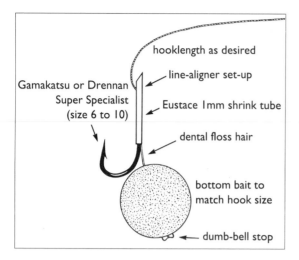

Fig. 41 *Basic bottom bait.*

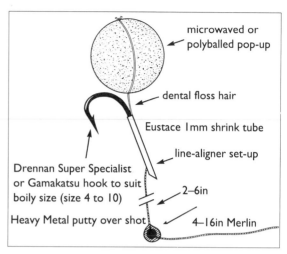

Fig. 42 *Critically balanced pop-up.*

on water intake, and if possible use a microwaved boily or a very tight skinned polyball pop-up. Again, it's the line aligner set-up and the hook is the lightest, sharpest and widest gaped hook I feel I can use. You can try popping it up at all sorts of heights, but 2–6in seems to work best and I usually keep my hooklength beyond the shot to 4–12in. I know a lot of people don't like to use shot on the line, but I have had no problems with a shot on Merlin hooklengths with some of Kryston's Heavy Metal moulded over it. Whether or not you need to critically balance is up to you, but don't think it will automatically catch you more fish. If everybody is doing it, the carp may become wary of a bait that flutters all over the place and you may need to look at an overshotted pop-up. Critically balanced pop-ups do rest well on weed and the like, but they are much used and can be a problem on some waters.

OVERSHOTTED POP-UP (FIG. 43)

In complete contrast to a critically balanced pop-up, the overshotted version nails that pop-up right down. This seems to work extremely well on waters which have seen much use of critically balanced baits. The carp may have become wary of baits which flutter up and down as they

approach them, and as this type of hookbait is nailed down it cannot do this. I usually overshoot by at least a BB to AAA shot which I find are heavy enough to hold the bait down but not so heavy as to stop it entering the carp's mouth. Once in the mouth the heavy shot is more likely to nick the hook home into the bottom lip, so I use an inturned point hook such as a Drennan Boily Hook to find a good secure hookhold. Because you are not reliant on the hookbait floating up and down you don't need to use long hooklengths – I would keep the hooklength to an

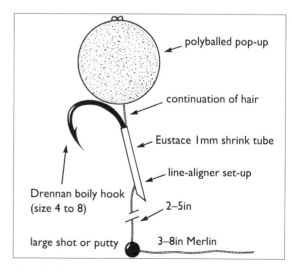

Fig. 43 *Overshotting.*

8in maximum so the carp will feel the pull of the lead sooner rather than later.

BENT HOOK (FIG. 44)

So many articles have appeared about the bent hook that to add to them in this book would be superfluous. If you wish to use them (and are allowed to) they can be very effective and have caught lots of carp. The principle is that the bend in the hook will cause it to flick over each time and nick into the carp's bottom lip. Providing your fish are feeding in a way to utilize this, it does work well, but if fish you catch or see getting caught have the hook in the sides of their mouths then they are feeding in a different way and this hooking arrangement is not necessary. Although it can be used with bottom baits, I use it mainly with pop-ups because I feel it gives a better hookhold and is more likely to sit in that bottom lip once taken in. If you don't want to make your own bent hooks, Middlesex Angling Centre do a version which I can thoroughly recommend. To increase the likelihood of the hook flicking over and finding tissue, superglue your hook knot in line with the eye, and make sure the boily isn't too large for the hook and vice versa.

BIG HOOK SET-UP (FIG. 45)

Because you are using a big hook which will make a larger hole than a size 6 or 8 hook, this is a controversial set-up to some. However, in its defence it is unlikely to tear out and rip a carp's mouth once it finds tissue, and think of how many carp have ruined mouths purely and simply because of small, sharp hooks. I have found the Kamasan Aberdeen sea hook to work best, and I bend it smoothly so that the point is not quite in line with the eye. It must not be bent with an acute bend as a bent hook is or it won't work as well. The two float stops are pushed over the hook point, and once I'm happy with their position I superglue them to stop movement once casting starts. Because it is such a large hook you do have to use a very buoyant microwaved boily to hold it up, and this should always be looped on to keep out water.

As you can see from the diagram, the dental floss is attached to a small Drennan ring (there is no need to crush it) and the small hinge increases the chance of self-hooking. Because of the size of the hook and width of the wire, it is absolutely essential to keep the hook sharp so that it will penetrate once it is in the carp's mouth. A large, sharp hook like this can be very

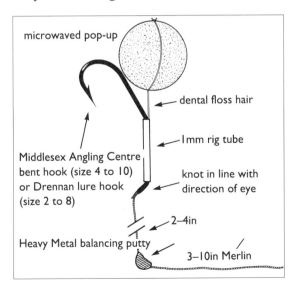

Fig. 44 *Bent hook set-up.*

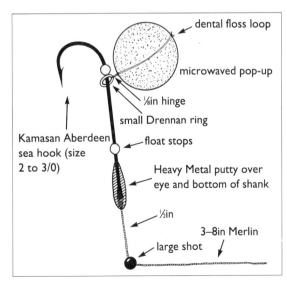

Fig. 45 *Big hook set-up.*

difficult for a carp to get rid of once it has taken it in, so it can be very effective. I prefer to critically balance it and fish it on as short a hooklength as possible so it can pull home against the lead. This set-up works well in both weedy waters and gravel pits.

OFF THE LEAD (FIG. 46)

This is a bit like the float tackle but in reverse – this time the hooklength comes from the lake's bed rather than from under a float. I know it looks very crude, but it does work well when used in the right circumstances. I use it when fishing in weed to present a bait right in the carp's face, and once the carp takes it in it is quite likely to pull the hook home immediately because it is directly off the lead. The bait I use is usually a microwaved and heavily flavoured pop-up which is fairly tight to an inturned hook such as a Drennan Boily hook or Partridge Z.15 hook. You can vary the pop-up distance from 3in–3ft depending on where you want it to sit and why! I have used both Merlin and Multistrand hooklengths, but I do feel happier with Merlin even if Multistrand looks less obvious.

ANTI-REJECT (FIG. 47)

Not all carp feed by picking up a bait and backing off to feel for the hook; some carp suck and blow at baits to test them. Do remember that if your carp are sucking and blowing, a bait tight to a small hook is less likely to find mouth tissue and hook the fish. Bent hooks and short hairs are all right for some carp, but not for all carp by a long stretch. If you use this type of hooking arrangement, once the carp takes it all in and seeks to reject it the hookbait will go first, but the loop will cause the hook to separate from the bait and will hopefully nick into the carp's lower mouth tissue.

This set-up really does work and although it may look complicated to tie, it isn't. It is also very effective, and has caught and will continue to catch a lot of carp. Always use a small, sharp hook and a long hooklink so the carp have plenty of free play. Also, if possible, use a critically balanced microwaved pop-up as this only adds to efficiency. Once you have tied it, see how it sits in the water as it is vital for efficiency that your loop is neither too long nor too short and that the hook is held up away from the weed or silt.

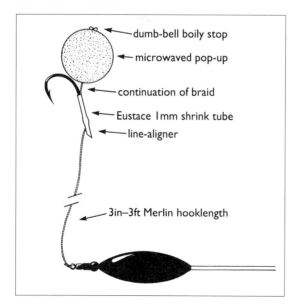

Fig. 46 *Off the lead.*

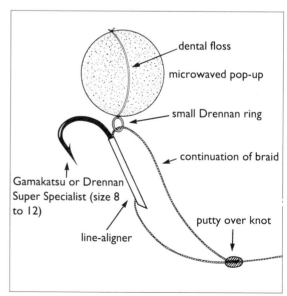

Fig. 47 *Anti-reject rig.*

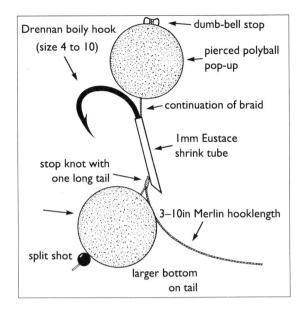

Fig. 48 Pop-up and bottom bait combination.

NAILED DOWN POP-UP (FIG. 48)

This is an effective presentation on many waters and is one I don't see being used much – this can be useful if your water hasn't seen it. The large

bottom bait holds the pop-up down, and because you are using two boilies you have twice the source of attraction and visual incentive of a pop-up. Once taken in it is very difficult for the carp to get rid of it because of the dual boily set-up and large hook. I hope the illustration makes it quite clear how to tie it; all I will add is that you can actually increase the hair length for your bottom bait as you feel fit by moving the shot a little. However, do remember that for maximum efficiency both boilies and hook need to go in the carp's mouth. For the hook I would choose a Drennan Boily hook or Partridge Z.2 or Z.15 which have wide gapes. This set-up is more of an anti-reject set-up than confidence set-up, so keep your hooklink as short as possible.

DOUBLE BOTTOM BAIT (FIG. 49)

Again, this is not a set-up that is widely used, but it does catch a lot of carp when used correctly. Two baits mean double the attraction source, and as they are comparatively heavy bottom baits they are quite difficult to reject once taken in. Use a line aligner set-up to increase self-hooking,

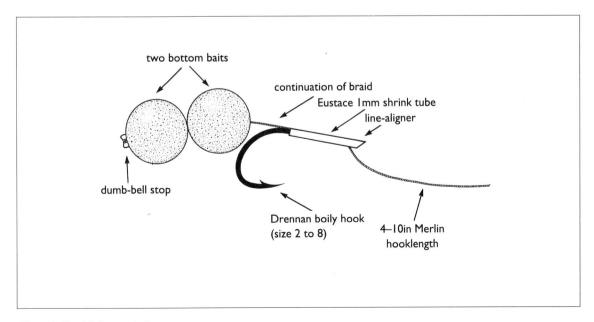

Fig. 49 Double bottom bait.

and if you are using large baits then use a large hook to aid this hooking. For the hook I like the Drennan Boily hook coupled with a fairly short hooklink of 4–10in.

DOUBLE BALANCED BAIT (FIG. 50)

On weedy or silty waters I prefer to present a double bait in a more visible manner and incorporate a microwaved or polyballed bait to lift the hook up. Make sure this is your top bait, and hold the bottom bait tight to it by use of a DAM float stop slipped on to the hair beforehand. I like this presentation to sit on top of weed, so it is critically balanced and usually on a 6–12in hooklength. Wide-gaped hooks are essential to ensure a hold, and incorporate a line aligner for maximum efficiency – look towards a Drennan Boily hook or Partridge Z.2 or Z.15 hook.

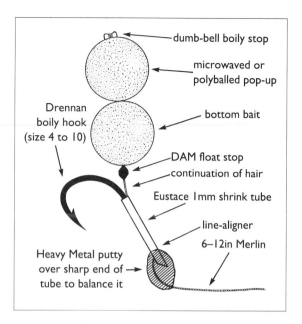

Fig. 50 Double balanced bait.

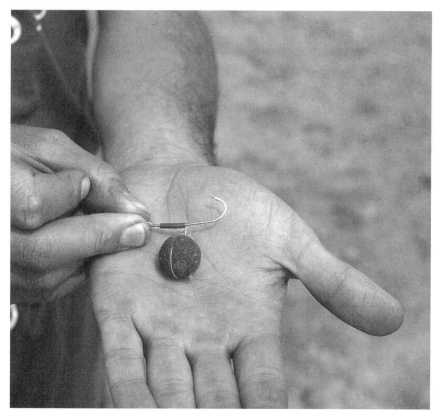

The wrong choice of hook in thick weed cost me a big fish.

6 MODERN CARP BAITS

The prospect of trying to encapsulate a description of modern carp baits in just one chapter is quite intimidating. As we have moved into the 1990s, the whole bait scene has become more and more complicated, and if one thing is guaranteed to have most people running round like headless chickens, it's carp baits. Each time I pick up the monthlies or quarterlies it appears obvious that so many people are completely lost, each new bait piece only adding to this confusion. I cannot promise that all will be clear once you have read this chapter, but I can promise you a section dedicated to making your life easier and helping you to catch carp consistently. I give you clear, concise information which I can almost guarantee will catch you carp, and which won't cost you an arm and a leg in the process.

WHAT DO YOU WANT FROM A BAIT?

In order that things get off on the right foot, I will describe here what I want from a bait – compare it with your own expectations. If it does compare to any sort of degree, then keep reading as I'm sure I can get you clued up and catching carp by the end of the chapter. If your expectations aren't in accordance with my thoughts then you may need to look to more detailed bait articles.

Basically, I expect the following from a bait.

1. It must catch carp.
2. It must catch carp fairly quickly and carry on catching carp consistently.
3. It must be affordable.
4. It must not cause the carp harm.
5. I must be able to have some idea why it does work.

I agree that all these points are very basic, but then I am a practical carp angler who deems an effective bait as one which satisfies points 1 to 5.

The main body of this chapter will look at boiled baits, as these, coupled with particles and Chum Mixers, are what ninety-nine per cent of carp anglers use nowadays. To start with, however, I will take a look at natural baits and convenience baits.

NATURAL BAITS

Maggots

This is not a bait I use a lot because of the nuisance fish problem on my waters – if I put a bunch of maggots out under a float, a perch, bream or eel will be tugging on the other end within minutes. However, I do use them when stalking carp in weedbeds in the summer months, and for this type of fishing they are even more effective than a boily under your float. All you do is find your carp, drop in your float and maggots (*see* Fig. 51), and more often than not a carp will grab them before a nuisance fish does. A trickle of maggots in the holes will arouse most carps' interest and, providing you can find your carp in the first place, this method can be deadly (*see* Fig. 52).

You could use maggots directly on the hook, but my favourite method is to thread between

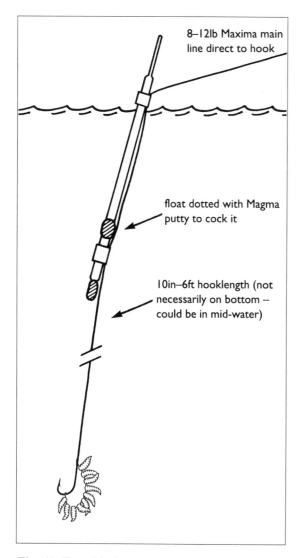

8–12lb Maxima main line direct to hook

float dotted with Magma putty to cock it

10in–6ft hooklength (not necessarily on bottom – could be in mid-water)

Fig. 51 *Float-fished maggots.*

twelve and sixteen on a piece of 2lb nylon. I then tie one end of the nylon to the bend of the hook and the other to its eye (*see* Fig. 53). Your maggots are then free of the point of the hook and, providing it's a sharp hook, you can almost self-hook carp which are cruising between holes in the weed.

Worms

Worms are almost as effective as maggots as a stalking bait, but are, I think, more effective in summer than in winter. In red-hot conditions a worm fished under a float close to weeds can encourage or excite a carp enough to make it pick up that bait when all others have failed. I don't hair rig worms but, having nipped the hook through them twice, push a tiny bit of rubber down the bend to meet them (*see* Fig. 54). This stops them masking the hook point and means that the point is free to nip into the carp's mouth tissue.

CONVENIENCE BAITS

Bread Flake

I use bread purely and simply as a stalking bait for my carp fishing because I have found that it can elicit a response from carp when boilies are ignored. Fish it under a float as you do your natural baits and, if possible, on a hair as well to improve your chance of hooking the carp. The easiest way to make that hair is to continue the hooklength through the eye of the hook once you've tied it on, and leave 1in or so dangling. Clip a small shot near the end of this hair and mould your flake around it (*see* Fig. 55). The shot has two purposes: first, it will weight the flake down; and second, it gives you something around which to mould your flake. I have tried to mould the flake around the hook itself, but I feel that the point of the hook has been obscured at times.

Luncheon Meat

This is a brilliant bait which kept on catching carp until boilies were made readily available; it

Fig. 52 *Setting the scene.*

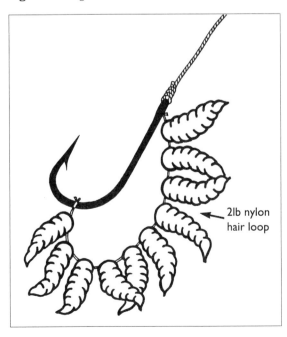

Fig. 53 *Maggot loop.*

2lb nylon
hair loop

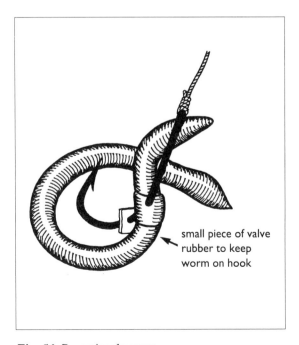

Fig. 54 *Presenting the worm.*

small piece of valve
rubber to keep
worm on hook

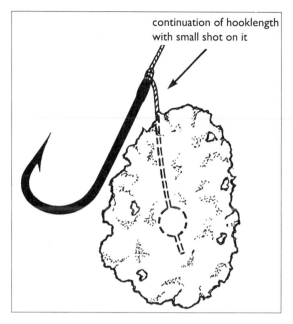

continuation of hooklength
with small shot on it

Fig. 55 *Hair-rigged flake.*

only stopped catching then because few people used it any more. It's not a bait I use a lot, but when a water has a boily ban – which some do – it can be the next best thing to try. You can side hook it as I've illustrated in Fig. 56, but a straightforward 'continuation of the hooklength' set-up is far more likely to self- hook carp (*see* Fig. 57). Don't use huge lumps of luncheon meat as this is unnecessary; small pieces of ⅛–½in at most work just as well, and a carpet of them will cause carp to feed quite excitedly at times. Also, because luncheon meat baits are so oily and fatty, they are naturally buoyant and are well worth using over silty or weedy lake bottoms.

Some readers who have glanced quickly at the sections on natural baits and convenience baits but have dismissed their use as out of date, preferring to use boilies instead. Whilst there's nothing wrong in using boilies almost all of the time, if you are at least aware of the advantages of natural and convenience baits you will be better equipped to tempt carp on those dour days when it seems they just aren't having boiled baits.

BOILED BAITS

What can I say that hasn't already been said about boilies? Probably nothing. It will probably be easier to use this introduction to tell you what I don't intend to cover as this chapter, like the whole book, is a guide to practical carp fishing and not an A–Z of carp baits. The history of boilies and all that goes in them – from milk proteins to blood plasma – has been covered time and time again, so with one or two notable exceptions I will leave the ingredient side of the topic well alone. Instead, I will concentrate on the options available to you, and will discuss one or two of my ideas which have proved to be consistent carp catchers over the years. Whilst some people may disagree with me, I see nothing wrong at all with detailing recipes; you have purchased this book in order to help you catch carp, and catch carp you will. If that means you have to follow bait recipes exactly, then so be it – carp fishing is all about putting carp on the bank, and the included recipes will achieve just those results. First, however, I will discuss your options as far as boilies go.

Ready-Made Boilies

Nobody who fishes for carp can fail to be aware of ready-made boilies; in fact, many of you will start your carp fishing career using them, and many will continue to do so. There is nothing wrong in using ready-made boilies, and I can honestly say that if I had the confidence in ready-mades that I have in my own baits I would use them. Never steer clear of them if you are told that it is not the done thing to use them, or that they don't work well – this is rubbish! Use what you feel confident with – if that happens to be ready-mades, then so be it. All the hard work of field-testing flavour levels and so on has been done for you in advance and, probably more importantly, for many of you they are ready to use. I have used ready-mades quite a lot and have been successful on a number of waters with them. Indeed, I would still continue to use them if I felt they gave me an advantage. A few I can recommend are as follows:

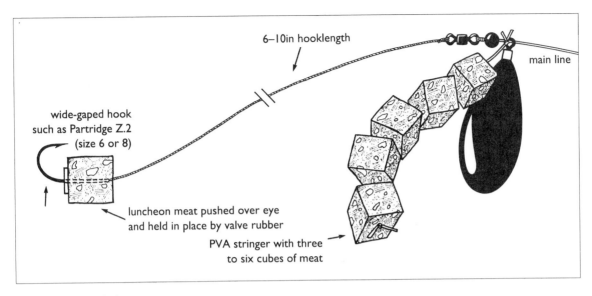

Fig. 56 Side-hooked meat.

Richworth Tropicano, Honey Yucatan and Bird Food boilies.
Crafty Catcher King Prawn and Peanut Pro boilies.

Advantages
1. Ready rolled – no mess in the kitchen or time wasted at home.
2. Perfectly round – your freebies go where you want them.
3. Proven – all the field testing and flavour research has been done for you.

Disadvantages
1. Non-exclusive – you have no edge as anybody can use them.
2. Price – you are paying for the rolling of the baits in the product price.
3. Rigidity – you cannot change size, flavours or colours at will.
4. Confidence – are you merely picking a bait that suits you rather than the carp?

Base Mixes
These seem to be almost as popular as ready-mades nowadays, and many anglers who move off ready-rolled baits purchase base mixes

instead. With these you have a ready-mixed dry powder mix and it is up to you to add colour, smell and attractors, and also to decide on shape, size and hardness. Most of the hard work in designing a mix which will catch and roll has

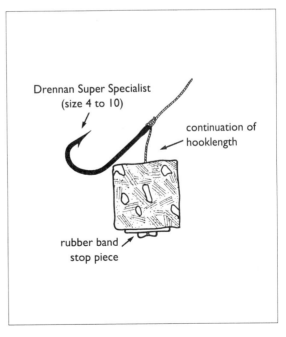

Fig. 57 Spring rig.

been done – all you need to do is make sure you don't mess it up by using excessive flavour levels or boiling it too much. Most of my carp fishing is done using base mixes to which I add the attractors of my choice. Base mixes I can certainly recommend are:

Nutrabaits Enervite, Enervite Gold, Big Fish Mix, Hi-Nu-Val.
Nash Bait Amber Attractor Mix.
Richworth 50/50 Mix.

Advantages
1. Flexibility – you can choose colour, shape, size, smell, hardness and so on.
2. Price – bulk buying of ingredients by the manufacturers keeps prices down.
3. Confidence – you can choose a bait to suit the water, you and the carp.

Disadvantages
1. Rolling – you have to do the somewhat tedious rolling of the boilies yourself.
2. Input – you could put in the wrong attractors and ruin a good base mix.
3. Quality – have you really any idea what has gone into the base mix?

Single Ingredients
I will be brutally frank here and say that most readers of this book needn't even think about putting together a whole bait themselves. Doing so involves deciding on all the dry powders and liquids to use, and ascertaining whether the boily will even roll and boil, never mind catch carp. The more you have to do, the greater the variables and the more likely you are to get something wrong. Don't even think about it; if you are, I suggest you turn to the Further Reading section which details books that cover this area fully. I'm certainly not going to touch the subject because it doesn't belong in a book of this nature. However, I will recommend one or two dry powder ingredients that you can add to normal base mixes.

Robin Red Powder This is a very dark bird food which is rich in spices and oils – carp absolutely love it. When added to a bait it can make that bait a dark red colour and with an increased attraction level. Robin Red is something carp really do get hooked on, and it seems to work well for years.
Egg Albumin A fine, white, milk powder which, when added to a bait, will make it rock

With gear like this you cannot go wrong.

hard on the outside. It is then less likely to be nibbled away by small fish, less likely to break up during catapulting and less likely to let in water, so that your critical balancing will not be ruined at a vital moment.

Green-lipped mussel powder This highly concentrated powdered extract originates from a shellfish. It has a high betaine level which is a brilliant carp attractor in itself, and I use it in most fishmeal bases at up to two level teaspoons per mix.

Having discussed the three main forms of boiled baits, I will now look at the four main types of boilies from which you can choose. I know that there are a lot more, but I can honestly say that most of the carp pictured in this book have been caught on one of the four types discussed, and at least ninety per cent have been caught on the exact recipes I have detailed.

The four main 'types' of boilies you will find are low- to mid-protein attractor baits, birdseed baits, fishmeal baits and finally, mid- to high-protein baits. As today's practical carp angler, you could do worse than stick to those four ranges – when you find an actual need to start changing baits then it's time you wrote your own book!

Basic Low-Protein Attractor Baits
With these baits you are not relying on the quality of the base mix itself but on the attractors you have put into it. The baits usually contain ingredients like semolina, soya powder and maize meal. In theory, such a bait is not supposed to work in the long run, but if you find that it is still working and working well, then don't change it. However, if you do notice a discernable decrease in action then use your common sense. There are lots of mixes of this nature on the market, and I have listed a few below:

Nutrabaits Nutramix 50/50 Mix.
Richworth 50/50 Mix.
Rod Hutchinson Boily Mix.

These mixes work well on most waters and don't cost the earth. Below is a recipe for a bait of this nature which should work as well for you as it has done for me.

Standard Free Offerings Recipe
As far as basic low-protein baits go, this is one of the best I have used and, although it has been designed as an instant bait, it certainly seems to keep on working.

13oz Richworth 50/50 Mix
3oz Robin Red
5 Size 2 eggs
10ml toasted sesame seed oil
20ml Nutramino
3ml Rod Hutchinson Mango-Pineapple Flavour
1ml Rod Hutchinson Intense Sweetener
8 drops Nutrabaits Nutmeg Essential Oil

Boil for two minutes. Freeze and use as necessary.

Microwaved Pop-Ups
These are made from the same base mix as used for the standard recipe.

6oz Richworth 50/50 Mix
2oz Robin Red
2 Size 2 eggs
10ml toasted sesame seed oil
20ml Nutramino
3ml Rod Hutchinson Mango-Pineapple Flavour
1ml Rod Hutchinson Intense Sweetener
8 drops Nutrabaits Nutmeg Essential Oil

Boil for two minutes. Leave to cool for two hours. Place up to ten in a microwave (level 9) and cook for two minutes. Take them out and allow them to cool for five minutes. Place them in batches of ten in the microwave (level 9) again, and cook them for 1½–2 minutes. Take them out and allow them to cool for five minutes. Place them in a freezer bag with 5ml toasted sesame seed oil and 1ml mango/pineapple flavour. Inflate the bag, seal it and shake it vigorously for one minute. Empty these baits on to a hard surface and leave for sixteen hours to harden. Freeze and use as necessary.

Polyballed Pop-Ups
Again, these can be made from the same base mix.

5oz Richworth 50/50 Mix
2oz Robin Red
2oz egg albumin
2 Size 2 eggs
10ml toasted sesame seed oil
10ml Nutramino
2ml Rod Hutchinson Mango-Pineapple Flavour
½ml Rod Hutchinson Intense Sweetener
4 drops Nutrabaits Nutmeg Essential Oil
Wrap-around Cotswold Baits Polyballs (¼in, ½in and ¾in)

Boil for two minutes. Leave to harden for twenty-four hours, then freeze and use as required.

Birdseed Baits (Red and Yellow)
The birdseed boily is a very popular type of base mix because of its price and effectiveness, only slightly overshadowed by fishmeal baits. The boilies are highly attractive to carp, very digestible, relatively cheap to buy and can make excellent long term baits when used sensibly. In short, they are many people's first choice, and rightly so. Most bird-food baits contain quantities of Robin Red, Sluis, Nectarblend, Ce De, PTX and so on. If red bird-food ingredients are used your bait will have a dark red colouration and a spicy taste. If you use mainly yellow bird foods, the bait will be pale in colouration and mellower in taste. Most bait suppliers have at least one or two bird-food baits on their list, and I can recommend that you look at the following:

Nutrabaits Enervite, Enervite Gold.
Nash Baits Amber Attractor Mix.
Rod Hutchinson Red and Yellow Seed Mixes.

If a water is not completely overrun with fishmeal I always look towards a bird-food bait, and in winter, if you do choose a fairly prolific venue, you could do worse than use a yellow birdseed bait as well. Below are a couple of recipes which I thoroughly recommend you try.

You will see that I have included two yellow birdseed recipes as I feel both are equally effective, dependent on the kind of venue you are fishing. Nutrabaits Enervite Gold version is the one I use on hard-bottomed gravel pits such as Willow Park where their density doesn't push them into the silt. I would also be prepared to use a lot as the carp seem to take to it very well indeed – even in winter.

Yellow Bird-Food Base Mix No 1

Standard Free Offerings Recipe
16oz Nutrabaits Enervite Gold Base Mix
5 Size 2 eggs
10ml Nutrabaits Multimino
3ml SBS Cornish Ice Cream EA Flavour
1½ml SBS Strawberry Jam EA Flavour
1½ level teaspoons Cotswold Baits Milk 'B' Enhancer
Colour: red, yellow or orange

Boil for two minutes.

Microwaved Pop-Ups
This is made from the same mix as the standard recipe above.

8oz Nutrabaits Enervite Gold Base Mix
2 Size 2 eggs
10ml Nutrabaits Multimino
3ml SBS Cornish Ice Cream EA Flavour
1½ml SBS Strawberry Jam EA Flavour
1½ level teaspoons Cotswold Baits Milk 'B' Enhancer
Colour: red, yellow or orange

Boil for two minutes and leave to cool for two hours. Place up to ten in a microwave (level 9) and cook for two minutes. Take them out and allow them to cool for five minutes. Place them again in tens in the microwave (level 9) and cook for 1½–2 minutes. Take them out and allow to cool for two minutes. Place them in freezer bag with 1½ml Cornish Ice Cream EA Flavour plus 1½ml Strawberry Jam EA Flavour. Inflate the bag, seal and shake vigorously for one minute.

Empty these baits on to a hard surface and allow them to harden for twenty-four hours. Freeze and use as required.

Polyballed Pop-Ups
Again, these are made from the same base mix.

6oz Nutrabaits Enervite Gold Base Mix
2oz egg albumin
2 Size 2 eggs
10ml Nutrabaits Multimino
2ml SBS Cornish Ice Cream EA Flavour
1ml SBS Strawberry Jam EA Flavour
1 level teaspoons Cotswold Baits Milk 'B' Enhancer
Colour: red, yellow or orange
Wrap-around Cotswold Baits Polyballs (⅓in, ½in and ¾in)

Boil for two minutes and leave to harden for twenty-four hours. Freeze and use as required.

Yellow Bird-Food Recipe No 2

Standard Free Offerings Recipe
This is the version I use when I am fishing weedy or silty waters and when I want my free offerings to rest on top of, rather than in, the silt. Kevin Nash's mix, which I believe is now called the Amber Attractor Mix, is very light and is ideally suited to these silty waters. All you need to do is decide which kind of water you are fishing and pick your base mix accordingly.

16oz Nashbait Yellow Seed Base Mix
5 Size 2 eggs
10ml sesame seed oil
4 drops Nutrabaits Bergamot Essential Oil
3ml SBS Cornish Ice Cream EA Flavour
1½ml SBS Strawberry Jam EA Flavour
1½ level teaspoons Cotswold Baits Milk 'B' Enhancer

Boil for two minutes.

Microwaved Pop-Ups
These are made from the same mix as used above.

6oz Nashbait Yellow Seed Base Mix
2oz Catchum Protein Mix
2 Size 2 eggs
10ml sesame seed oil
4 drops Nutrabaits Bergamot Essential Oil
3ml SBS Cornish Ice Cream EA Flavour
1½ml SBS Strawberry Jam EA Flavour
1 level teaspoon Cotswold Baits Milk 'B' Enhancer

Boil for two minutes, then leave to cool for two hours. Place up to ten in a microwave (level 9) and cook for two minutes. Take out and allow to cool for five minutes. Place again in tens in the microwave (level 9) and cook for 1½–2 minutes. Take out and allow to cool for two minutes. Place in a freezer bag with 1ml Cornish Ice Cream EA Flavour plus 1ml Strawberry Jam EA Flavour. Inflate the bag, seal and shake vigorously for one minute. Empty these baits on to a hard surface and leave for twenty-four hours to harden. Freeze and use as required.

Polyballed Pop-Ups
These are also made from the same base mix.

6oz Nashbait Yellow Seed Base Mix
2oz egg albumin
2 Size 2 eggs
10ml sesame seed oil
2ml SBS Cornish Ice Cream EA Flavour
1ml SBS Strawberry Jam EA Flavour
2 drops Nutrabaits Bergamot Essential Oil
1 level teaspoons Cotswold Baits Milk 'B' Enhancer
Wrap-around Cotswold Baits Polyballs (¼in, ½in and ¾in)

Boil for two minutes, then leave to harden for twenty-four hours. Freeze and use as required.

Red Bird-Food Base Mix

Standard Free Offerings Recipe
This red seed recipe is probably one of the most effective I have used, and on at least half a dozen waters this exact recipe has completely preoccupied the fish, with other anglers hardly getting any takes. However, I have known one or two

waters where it hasn't worked at all, no matter how the attractor levels have been increased and decreased. Therefore, my advice with this recipe is if the fish do seem to respond to it, really pile it in because you should be able to catch a lot of fish in a relatively short time. However, if you are not getting takes and if this is not due to bad angling, then stop using this bait and move on to a yellow seed equivalent.

16oz Nutrabaits Enervite Base Mix
4 Size 2 eggs
30ml Nutramino
8 drops Nutrabaits Bergamot Essential Oil

Boil for ninety seconds.

Microwaved Pop-Ups
This uses the same base mix as the recipe above.

6oz Nutrabaits Enervite Base Mix
2oz Nutrabaits Hi-Nu-Val Base Mix
2 Size 2 eggs
30ml Nutramino
8 drops Nutrabaits Bergamot Essential Oil

Boil for two minutes, then leave to cool for two hours. Place up to ten in a microwave (level 9) and cook for two minutes. Take out and allow to cool for five minutes. Place again in tens in the microwave (level 9) and cook for 1½–2 minutes. Take out and allow to cool for two to three minutes. Place in a freezer bag with 5ml Nutramino and two drops Bergamot Essential Oil. Inflate the bag, seal and shake vigorously for one minute. Empty these baits on to a hard surface and allow to harden over twenty-four hours. Freeze and use as required.

Polyballed Pop-Ups
Again, these are made from the same base mix.

6oz Nutrabaits Enervite Base Mix
2oz egg albumin
2 Size 2 eggs
20ml Nutramino
5 drops Nutrabaits Bergamot Essential Oil

Nutrabaits know I like my bait in bulk.

Wrap-around Cotswold Baits Polyballs (¼in, ½in and ¾in)

Boil for two minutes, then leave to harden for twenty-four hours. Freeze and use as required.

Fishmeal Boilies
I think that it is fair to say that fishmeal boilies have really taken off in the last few years, and not many of you now can be unaware how effective they are. Similar to bird-food baits in that they are relatively cheap to buy, very digestible and highly attractive to carp, fishmeal baits usually consist of ingredients such as white-fish meal, capelin meal, sardine meal and so on, coupled with some form of binding agent. Most people use them in conjunction with a bulk fish oil and flavour, and providing you do stick to reasonable

levels you should do well. I wouldn't hesitate to use them on most waters between May and September, but as I discuss in Chapter 9, I don't use them between October and March. Most companies do have excellent fishmeal base mixes, and I can recommend the following:

Nutrabaits Big Fish Mix, Fishfood Mix.
Premier Supreme Fish Mix.
Rod Hutchinson Seafood Blend.

With many waters having fishmeal boilies piled in by the thousands, I always use as good a quality base mix as I can, just to give me an edge over other fishmeal users. You may not be able to out-bait or outstay others, but if your mix is as good as, if not better than theirs I am convinced that you can have that vital edge. Nutrabaits Big Fish seems to catch at all the waters on which it is used, and doesn't need to be pre-baited or put in by the thousands as some fishmeal boilies do. I have included two recipes which I have taken a lot of fish on, so you can choose the one which suits you best – both are equally as good!

Standard Free Offerings Recipe No 1
20oz Nutrabaits Big Fish Mix
6 Size 2 eggs
10ml capelin oil
10ml herring oil
10ml fish-feed oil
30ml Nutramino
4ml Nutrabaits Tutti-Frutti Nutrafruit
1 level teaspoon Nutrabaits Green-Lipped Mussel Extract

Boil for ninety seconds.

Microwaved Pop-Ups
This is made from the same base mix as used in the above recipe.

7oz Nutrabaits Big Fish Mix
3oz Nutrabaits Hi-Nu-Val Base Mix
3 Size 2 eggs
10ml capelin oil
10ml herring oil

10ml fish-feed oil
20ml Nutramino
4ml Nutrabaits Tutti-Frutti Nutrafruit
1 level teaspoon Nutrabaits Green-Lipped Mussel Extract

Boil for ninety seconds, then allow to cool for three hours. Place up to ten in a microwave (level 9) and cook for two minutes. Take out and allow to cool for five minutes. Place in tens in the microwave (level 9) and cook for 1½–2 minutes. Take out and allow to cool for two minutes. Place in a freezer bag with 1ml Tutti-Frutti, 5ml Nutramino and 10ml capelin oil. Inflate the bag, seal and shake vigorously for two minutes. Empty these baits on to a hard surface, and allow them to cool and harden over twenty-four hours. Freeze and use as required.

Polyballed Pop-Ups from the same mix
Again, this recipe uses the same base mix as above.

8oz Nutrabaits Big Fish Mix
2oz egg albumin
3 Size 2 eggs
7ml capelin oil
7ml fish-feed oil
7ml herring oil
2ml Nutrabaits Tutti-Frutti Nutrafruit
¾ teaspoon Nutrabaits Green-Lipped Mussel Extract
Wrap around Cotswold Baits Polyballs (¼in, ½in and ¾in)

Boil for two minutes, then leave to harden for twenty-four hours. Freeze and use as required.

Standard Free Offerings Recipe No 2
20oz Nutrabaits Big Fish Mix
6 Size 2 eggs
30ml salmon oil
30ml Nutramino
4ml Nutrabaits Cranberry Nutrafruit
1 level teaspoon Nutrabaits Green-Lipped Mussel Extract

Boil for ninety seconds.

Microwaved Pop-Ups
This uses the same base mix as the standard recipe above.

7oz Nutrabaits Big Fish Mix
3oz Nutrabaits Hi-Nu-Val Base Mix
3 Size 2 eggs
20ml salmon oil
20ml Nutramino
4ml Nutrabaits Cranberry Nutrafruit
1 level teaspoon Nutrabaits Green-Lipped Mussel Extract

Boil for two minutes, then allow to cool for three hours. Place up to ten in a microwave (level 9) and cook for two minutes. Take out and allow to cool for five minutes. Place in tens again in the microwave (level 9) and cook for 1½–2 minutes. Take out and allow to cool for two minutes. Place in a freezer bag with 1ml of Cranberry, 6ml of Nutramino and 10ml of salmon oil. Inflate the bag, seal and shake vigorously for two minutes. Empty these baits on to a hard surface and allow to cool and harden for twenty-four hours. Freeze and use as required.

Polyballed Pop-Ups
Again, these use the same base mix.

8oz Nutrabaits Big Fish Mix
2oz egg albumin
3 Size 2 eggs
20ml salmon oil
2ml Nutrabaits Cranberry Nutrafruit
¾ teaspoon Nutrabaits Green-Lipped Mussel Extract
Wrap around Cotswold Baits Polyballs (¼in, ½in and ¾in)

Boil for two minutes, then leave to harden for twenty-four hours. Freeze and use as required.

Protein Baits

From the late 1970s to early 1980s, protein baits were a very popular boily to use, but with the advent of the ready-mades and subsequent popularity of bird food and fishmeal boilies, they seem to have decreased in popularity. However, they can be excellent baits and should not be ignored. Protein baits have the advantage of being very nutritious to the carp; a good base mix will also last for years and the resulting protein boilies will usually improve and not deteriorate! They consist of ingredients such as casein, caseinate, lactalbumin and egg albumin which means they can work out very expensive. However, when compared to what we now spend on tackle they are actually very reasonable. I have used them a great deal and can recommend the following:

Nutrabaits Hi-Nu-Val.
Rod Hutchinson Protein Mix.

Although there is no doubt that protein baits are not used as much as they used to be, that is not because they are not good carp baits but rather because fishmeal and birdseed boilies are so much cheaper and more fashionable. However, this base mix is one I would use in winter on waters with low stock levels, where there is no 'going bait' and where only odd fish will be caught. I should add here that it is essential that you change baits every twenty-four hours because they work better when fresh, although I cannot tell you why this is true. There is also no need to microwave your pop-ups because of the light nature of the base mix ingredients – even ¼in polyballed ones will stay up for as long as is needed.

Standard Free Offerings Recipe
20oz Nutrabaits Hi-Nu-Val Base Mix
6 Size 2 eggs
10ml Nutrabaits Complete Food Oil
2ml SBS Cornish Ice Cream EA Flavour
1ml SBS Strawberry Jam EA Flavour
6 drops Nutrabaits Bergamot Essential Oil
1 level teaspoon Cotswold Baits Milk 'B' Enhancer

Boil for seventy-five seconds. Freeze for at least twenty-four hours and use within twenty-four hours of defrosting. If the bait is any more than twenty-four hours old once out of the freezer, do not even put it in the water.

Polyballed Pop-Ups
This recipe uses the same base mix as the one above.

8oz Nutrabaits Hi-Nu-Val Base Mix
2oz egg albumin
3 Size 2 eggs
10ml Nutrabaits Complete Food Oil
1½ml SBS Cornish Ice Cream EA Flavour
¾ml SBS Strawberry Jam EA Flavour
3 drops Nutrabaits Bergamot Essential Oil
¼ teaspoon Cotswold Baits Milk 'B' Enhancer

Boil for ninety seconds. Allow to cool for six hours and then freeze. Use as required, but keep for only twenty-four hours after defrosting.

Basic Boily-Making

When I first started carp fishing the idea of making my own baits horrified me. It all sounded too complicated and my initial efforts only went to substantiate that. Mixes dried out on me, I used too much flavour and eggs of the wrong size, I boiled them for too long and so on. However, a million bait mixes later and I have now got it off to a fine art.

The only way to make your own bait efficiently is to have a plan and to make sure that you do not deviate from the plan whilst you are making your bait. All the recipes I have included in this chapter are recipes anyone can copy and, providing you follow the plan I've included below, you can make your own bait quickly and efficiently. Start by making one or maybe two mixes during an evening, and don't be in any rush to finish them. Once you have mastered this art it will seem an absolute doddle, and I guarantee that you will then be able to churn out bait like there's no tomorrow. If you have had nasty experiences while trying to make up mixes you may be a little sceptical, but do persevere and you shouldn't have any problems.

1. First, and probably most importantly, make sure you are properly sited to ensure trouble-free rolling. You must be in a place where you can devote yourself to the task in hand and not have to keep stopping to allow people to make cups of coffee and the like. I usually make mine in the garage as it's nice and cool, there's lots of space and I don't get disturbed. However, if you are lucky enough to have your own kitchen then that is probably the best place.

Make sure you have more than enough base mix, eggs, flavour, oils and so on to do as many mixes as you can in the evening (*see* Fig. 58). It is no good at all making one mix up and then finding you haven't enough flavour left despite an over-abundance of everything else. A quick visual scan will tell you how much you have; if you are running low on a particular ingredient then make sure you order some more as soon as possible.
2. I always use free-range eggs in Size 2 from a local farm because I know the quality is good and that they are almost always the same size. Don't be tempted to use second-rate, out-of-date eggs because they can ruin an otherwise good mix. Always keep to the same sized eggs because once you start mixing various sizes the 'effective' flavour level in your mix will have changed. A lot of my mixes are six-egg mixes, so the first job is to crack six of these eggs in a large bowl and whisk them round with a fork not a blender (*see* Fig. 59). I don't use a blender because I feel it

Fig. 58 *Preparation.*

Fig. 59 Add the eggs.

too little of something. Bulk oils and the like are measured in large measuring cylinders, flavours are measured with pipettes and essential oils are measured in drops from their own droppers. If you accidentally put too much in it may ruin a mix, so throw it away and don't risk it on the carp. Colour is always added at this stage, even if it's in powder form. Both Nutrabaits and Cotswold Baits do excellent powder colours and I use half a teaspoon per six-egg mix.

Once all your attractors have been added, give the mix another whisk with the fork to ensure equal dispersal into the eggs.

4. Now we come to the stage where some people start to get things wrong, namely adding the base mix to the egg mix. Most mixes take 14–22oz of base mix per four to six eggs, but do remember that if you have added fish oils, minamino compounds and the like you have a lot more liquid in there than that from just six eggs. I suggest you keep adding dry mix by hand and mixing thoroughly with a fork or wooden spoon until it becomes very firm. Usually I will put around 10oz in at once and whisk that round, then add the base mix a handful at a time until I get a nice, firm consistency (*see* Fig. 61). Do not pour all the base mix in at once or you won't be able to mix

puts too many air bubbles in a mix which can cause it to float. Whisk until all the egg is beaten and it is a fairly even liquid throughout.

3. The next job is to add your attractors to the eggs (*see* Fig. 60). Always measure out your attractors very carefully as your bait may not be as effective if you have added either too much or

Fig. 60 Add the flavour.

Fig. 61 Whisk.

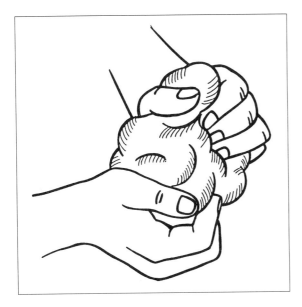

Fig. 62 Knead.

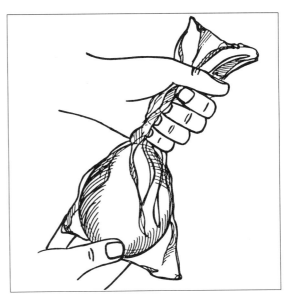

Fig. 63 Bag up the mix.

it evenly with the liquid. Use a good-quality fork that doesn't bend, and then pick up the mix once it is fairly firm and has stopped sticking to the fork. Smearing your hands with olive oil is also a good idea as it stops the mix sticking to them.

5. Having lifted all the mix into your hands, start to knead it (*see* Fig. 62). It will probably be a little bit sticky, so put a bit more dry base mix into your basin and keep rolling the dough in it. Once the mix is correct it will stop feeling sticky, and although moist it won't stick to everything. Practice will teach you best, but a quick way to check if the consistency is correct is to roll a piece in your hand. If you can make a round boily shape without it losing shape then it is fine, but if it goes soft and resembles a peanut rather than a marble, it is still too moist and needs a little more dry mix.

6. Having got the mix as you want it, it is essential that it doesn't dry out, so pop it into a freezer bag (*see* Fig. 63). A six-egg mix makes a lot of dough and you will be surprised how soon it can dry out, especially when you are taking your time getting used to doing the job properly. Popping the mix into the bag keeps it moist and stops it from becoming too dry while you are half-way through making the sausages.

7. Next, pull small lumps of mix off the main mix so that you can roll your sausages. Obviously, the size of the lumps you need to use will depend on the rolling table you use. I like to use 20mm baits, so for my sausages each lump needs to be half the size of a tangerine. However, if you are using 14mm baits, half that size again will do. Once again, practice will make perfect, and after a mix or two you will almost be able to gauge exactly how much to pull off.

Put the lump on your piece of plyboard, Formica or whatever, and give it a couple of rolls with the correct side of your Gardner rolling table. A bit will come out of the side – chop this off by rotating the table at ninety degrees and pushing down. Don't leave the sausages out in the open, but cover them up with a spare freezer bag as this keeps them moist and stops them from drying out (*see* Fig. 64). I roll all my sausages out before I put them through the rollaball, so it is imperative that my mix is still moist; if it was dry my baits would split or would have holes in their middles where they had not bound together.

8. Next, place one sausage on a table and roll the top portion back and forth (*see* Fig. 65). I use a Kingfisher long rolling table which is brilliant because it allows me to move the top table up and

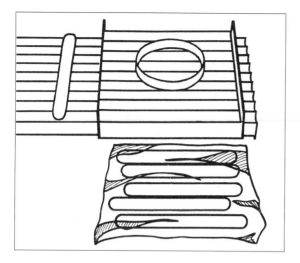

Fig. 64 *Place the sausages on a table.*

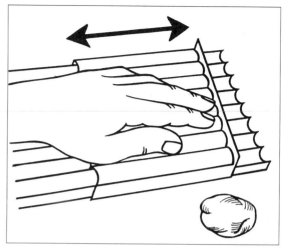

Fig. 65 *Roll the sausages backwards and forwards.*

down by 6–8in so that my baits are nice and round. Personally, I still work on one sausage at a time because I feel I get a rounder ball that way. You need to use a firm, consistent pressure on top of the table (but don't push), and if you have too many sausages on it the outside ones either don't get the same pressure or stick to the middle ones. Do it carefully and get it right!

9. As you can see in Fig. 67, the boilies are perfectly round – exactly what you are trying to achieve. When casting over 70yd, a boily which is not round will veer off course and will perhaps draw carp away from your hookbait rather than to it. However, if you have spent some time doing this stage properly, you should be able to drop them with accuracy next to your marker time and time again.

10. I roll my completed boilies out on to a hardwood base or plastic sack so that they still retain their shape and don't stick as they do to the towel-type material some people use. If your mix is too sticky, the boilies will stick to the board and when you try to put them in the boiling pan they

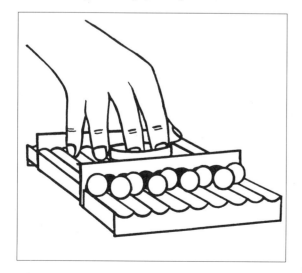

Fig. 66 *Apply firm pressure.*

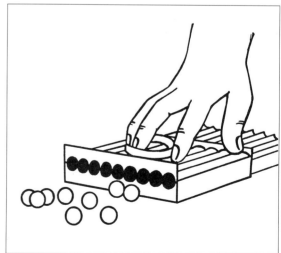

Fig. 67 *The end result.*

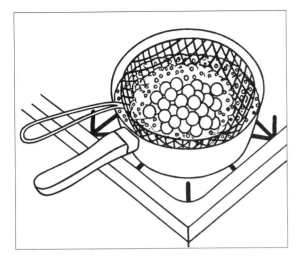

Fig. 68 Boil your baits.

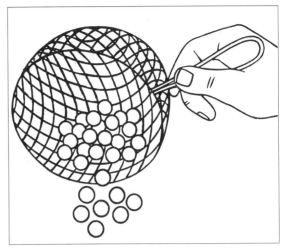

Fig. 69 Shake your baits out of the sieve.

will become misshapen as you pull them from the board. Get it right next time!

11. Having rolled out all your mix into perfectly round little balls, you now need to boil them so that they gain a skin. I usually boil mine in the kitchen and use a fairly large pan of water with an aluminium colander in place of a sieve. Some people advocate the use of chip-pan sieves, but I have found that the mesh-type material marks the boilies and ruins their round shape. A colander is smooth and your boilies stay as they should be.

Boil the water, put your colander in and add no more than half a panful of boilies to the boiling water (*see* Fig. 68). The water should only just go off the boil as you add them, and will start boiling again in seconds. Give the boilies a quick stir with a large wooden spoon to ensure that they don't stick together, and time the relevant period as I have detailed in my recipes or as shown on your boily instruction leaflet.

12. Once they have boiled for the correct time, lift the colander out, move the pan off the ring so it doesn't boil over and take the colander of boilies into the garage. Tip the boilies out on to a towel and go back to boil another lot (*see* Fig. 69). It's as easy as that! I usually leave all mixes except milk protein mixes overnight to dry, bag them up in 1–3lb mixes in good-quality freezer bags and then put them in my chest freezer.

Twenty Points to Aid Your Bait-Making

1. Make your baits in a cool place so they don't dry out.
2. Don't put yourself in a position where you have to rush as you may make a mess of it.
3. Always write down your recipes so you don't forget a good one.
4. Stick to the base mix and don't add an ounce of this or an ounce of that.
5. Keep dry mixes cool and out of direct sunlight.
6. Keep flavours and oils in a fridge if possible.
7. Never exceed recommended dosage levels.
8. Find a good source of eggs and stick with it.
9. Find a good recipe and stick with it.
10. When mixing, use a fork that won't bend and a bowl that won't crack.
11. Keep your hands clean and make sure you haven't handled soaps, petrol or other strong-smelling substances beforehand.
12. Make your own bait yourself; friends tend not to be as careful if it's not their bait.
13. Make sure you replace your table and rollaball each year to avoid misshapen boilies.
14. Don't try to put too many sausages in your rollaball; one at a time isn't that much slower and produces better baits.
15. When you have rollaballed them, put the baits on dustbin liners so they don't stick or go out of shape.

16. Don't put too many boilies in to boil at once or the water temperature will drop and you will end up with soft baits.

17. Don't exceed 120 seconds when boiling or you will boil out the flavour in many mixes.

18. Remember that colour attracts anglers rather than fish.

19. Always freeze your bait for at least twenty-four hours – it tends to be more effective.

20. Use good-quality freezer bags or you will end up with boilies all over the place!

Making Pop-Up Boilies

I detailed in Chapter 5 just how effective pop-up boilies can be. However, having seen one or two apologies for pop-up boilies, I would like to explain the two best methods I have found for producing them. One method is for microwaved boilies while the other is for polystyrened pop-ups.

Microwaved Pop-Up Boilies

Whilst I cannot say for certain exactly which method (microwave or polypop) is most effective, I tend to use microwaved pop-ups when I want small pop-ups or intend to leave the baits out in the water for any period of time. Small microwaved pop-ups work particularly well because even a 12mm or 14mm microwaved pop-up will hold up a size 4 hook, whilst a 14mm polystyrened pop-up would hardly hold up a size 8. Microwaved pop-ups are far more buoyant for their size, so you can use smaller pop-up baits per hook. Also, because a microwaved pop-up is usually rock-hard it seems to keep out water for longer and is therefore ideal if you wish to leave baits out a long time or wish to have baits critically balanced for a long time.

Typical microwave production is detailed below:

1. A microwave will evaporate some of the flavour, so I use twice as much flavour in the baits I intend to microwave. So a typical four-egg mix which needs 6ml of strawberry for bottom baits will contain either 6ml in two eggs or 12ml in four eggs when produced in a microwave.

2. As your microwave will make your boilies swell to nearly twice the size, roll your double-flavour mix into 12mm size for eventual 16mm pop-ups, or 14mm size for eventual 18mm pop-ups.

3. Once you have made your mix, have rolled it to the correct smaller size and have boiled it for the correct period, leave it to dry for one to three hours.

4. Place the baits in batches of no more than ten in the microwave (level 9) and cook them for two minutes. Take them out of microwave and leave them to cool for five minutes.

5. Then pop them back into the microwave in batches of ten again and cook them for two minutes at level 9. Take them out of the microwave and leave them to cool for two to three minutes.

6. Put them in a freezer bag containing a small amount of your chosen flavour, inflate the bag, seal it, give it a shake for one to two minutes and then pour the boilies out on to a table to dry. Don't put them on a towel or the flavour will be absorbed into the towel and not the boilies.

7. Leave the boilies to dry for twenty-four hours, freeze them and use them as and when required.

This is a general guide to microwaving boilies and should not be accepted as spot-on for each and every base mix. Some need up to three minutes in the microwave whilst others only require 1½ minutes. With each of the recipes included in this chapter I have detailed the times exactly, but if you prefer to use your own recipe you may have to experiment a little.

Polystyrened Pop-Up Boilies

Now that Cotswold Baits have an excellent range of polypops, this too is an excellent way of making pop-ups, and if anything is a little easier than microwaved pop-ups. Polystyrene pop-ups are not as buoyant as their microwaved counterparts, but because the mix isn't microwaved it's almost the same as the freebies you put out. I cannot say if this matters or not, but I can say that if possible I prefer to use polypopped pop-ups rather than microwaved ones. You, of course, should make up your own mind and use that which you have confidence in and which works best for you.

Typical polypopped boily production is detailed below:

1. As you want the skin of the boily to be as impervious to water as possible, you should use egg albumin as a hardener to your mix even with coarse fishmeal or birdseed base mixes. I usually use it on a ¼ egg albumin to ¾ base mix ratio (in other words, 4oz egg albumin to 12oz Big Fish Mix, and so on). Note, however, that flavour levels do not change.

2. Having made the paste, you will find it very sticky due to the egg albumin. This means that rolling the paste round the polypops can be a chore; don't give up.

3. Cotswold have a super range of ¼in, ½in and ¾in polypops which will cover all sizes of pop-ups from 16mm to 26mm. Make sure your polypop is surrounded fairly evenly by the paste.

4. Boil for twenty per cent longer than you would your normal boily mix, just to make the boilies hard and less likely to let in water so that they will stay popped up for longer.

5. When you have boiled these polypopped hookbaits, put them on a towel and give them a good roll about. This will dry off any wet edges which could otherwise let water in.

6. Once they start to dry out, leave them to harden for twenty-four hours so that they are rock-hard before you freeze them.

Again, this is only a general guide to polypopping hookbaits, and you may need to experiment slightly to produce the ideal pop-up for your mix and presentation.

Boily Crumb Baits

Although some anglers have been using boily crumb for years, it doesn't seem to have taken off in as big a way as I expected, especially after some of these anglers' results were made public. Quite honestly, the results on all waters I know where this bait has been used have been devastating, and it has put a lot of so called 'uncatchable' fish on the bank from very difficult waters.

What is Boily Crumb?

Boily crumb is normal base mix that is put through a blender or liquidizer to create a crumb, rather than being left as little round balls or cubes. This is both very easy to do and very effective. You can make your crumb in minutes (providing your boilies have been made), and if you can put it where fish are prepared to feed the results can be spectacular.

How to Make the Crumb

1. Using bait which has already been rolled into cubes or boilies, simply pop a handful into the top of the blender, shut the top, turn on the power and it will crumb your baits for you. Very easy indeed! The beauty is that you can even crumb ready-made shop boilies and, whether you use fishmeal, birdseed or protein boilies, it is very effective indeed.

2. To make crumb from base mix, make up your mix in the normal way for boilies with eggs, attractors and sweeteners. Once you have made the large ball of paste, roll it into sausages but don't put it into the rollaball, instead leaving it in its sausage state. Providing your pan is big enough you can boil the sausages in the pan whole (stick to the usual time period of 60–120 seconds), thus saving you a lot of messing about with the rollaball. Let the sausages dry for at least three to four hours and then pop them in the blender. This is a lot easier than making round boilies!

3. Once you have crumbed the mixture, you don't need to use it straight away – simply pop it in a bag in the freezer and use it when necessary. After freezing, do leave it to defrost for an hour or two or it will all float because the moisture will have turned to ice. When you make the crumb it should be moist enough so that you can squeeze it into a throwable form, but when it hits the water it should explode or dissipate, creating clouds of crumb, food and liquid which will fall through the water and carpet the lake bottom. It should not be in pure liquid form or so stodgy that it sits on the lake bed in big lumps. Practice will tell you when you've got it right.

What Base Mixes Can Be Used?

Quite literally, you can use the crumb method with any base mix or boily from the low-protein varieties to spiced fishmeal. I have used it in winter, liquidizing Hi-Nu-Val boilies, and in summer have crumbed Big Fish Mix. As an attractor it's an absolutely brilliant concept.

Plain Crumb or Boily Mush?

Whilst boily crumb on its own is very effective, I have found it to be even more so when I have added a limited amount of liquid to it. Use up to 30ml of whatever liquid you want per lb of crumb. Pour the liquid into a freezer bag, add the crumb, inflate the bag, seal the top and give it a good shake for two to three minutes – you will find that the crumb absorbs the liquid. This adds to the attraction so that even in winter it is possible to have carp competing for food rather than picking at it. Below are a few ideas for quantities of liquid to add to each 1lb of boily crumb.

Nutrabaits Big Fish Mix plus 15ml salmon oil and 15ml Nutramino.
Nutrabaits Enervite Mix plus 20ml Nutramino and 10ml molasses.
Nutrabaits Hi-Nu-Val plus 20ml Carnation Milk and 5ml sweetener.
Nutrabaits Enervite Gold plus 10ml Carnation Milk and 20ml molasses.

Fishing the Crumb

Obviously, boily crumb is only effective if you can place it where the carp are feeding. As you will have to throw it out by hand, you are restricted to a maximum of under 10yd, meaning that it is a brilliant small-water or margin method (*see* Fig. 70). Providing your carp come into the margins, a carpet of crumb should do the trick. In summer I wouldn't hesitate to have 1–1½lb of crumb around each hookbait, and even in winter I have successfully used up to ½lb of crumb per hookbait. Usually I fish very small, critically balanced pop-ups in the crumb (*see* Fig. 71) as the carp hoover it up in a way that is similar to particle fishing. I keep hooklengths very short and, if possible, I try to avoid the use of any free-baits at all. Hopefully the diagram will illustrate the method of presentation sufficiently, but don't hesitate to use large baits or bottom baits if you feel that this is an advantage on your water.

Why Does Crumb Work So Well?

As you know, boilies can be very attractive to

Typical boily crumb areas – holes in the weed, margins, lily pads and the like.

Fig. 70 *An ideal crumb swim.*

carp; to a certain extent you can increase this attraction by putting more boilies in. However, whilst more boilies may equate to increased attraction, they can also fill the carp up long before your hookbait is picked up. A pound of boilies can contain as many as 100 to 200 decent-sized baits, and if you have just three hookbaits out with 200 freebies your chance of a pick-up will only be one in seventy or so. With boily crumb, however, you only have one boily out there (your hookbait), and all the attraction of 1–2lb of boilies but nothing with which to fill the carp up (*see* Fig. 72). As the liquidizing process has broken the skin of the boilies, the crumb has more of an instant attraction and starts working as soon as it hits the water. You can't go wrong, can you?

All I would like to say is that you must remember with crumb that you are not actually feeding the carp as you would do with normal baits, so if you wish to keep the action going, it is beneficial to pile in freebies (rolled baits) when you are not fishing. You also have the added advantage that this is a new method which very few people use.

PRE-BAITING

Is it Worth the Effort?

The flow chart above is a good basic guide to putting together a baiting campaign and, hopefully, you will reap the dividends that such a campaign can produce. Before I follow it through logically, however, you may want to ask why you should choose a baiting campaign when many other anglers don't. My opinion is that a properly put together baiting campaign should usually increase your catch rates on waters you will encounter. Providing you have the confidence and drive to carry one out, you will succeed and it needn't cost you an arm and a leg.

Correct Bait

Clearly, if you are going to put together a course of baiting you must be absolutely sure that the bait you will be using is one which, if properly applied, will catch carp on a regular basis.

Prebaiting flow-chart.

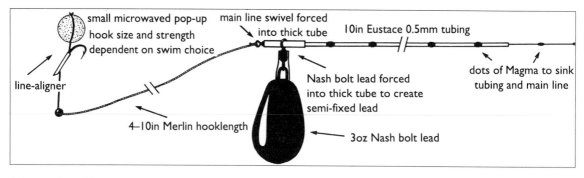

Fig. 71 *Crumb bait presentation.*

Although most baits will catch carp, I would hesitate to recommend that anyone uses a new untried or experimental mix, as occasionally a water won't respond to a certain smell, attractor, oil. I don't know why – it could be down to levels or just bad angling, but unfortunately it does happen now and again.

Obviously, each water has 'best baits' and you are probably aware of your own water's best choice. If you've had a few fish on a bait, that would be a good choice; perhaps somebody else has had some success on a particular recipe and hasn't reaped full dividends with it. Don't be swayed by anglers who claim that a bait will blow after so many weeks – in my experience an applied bait of at least some food value will go on catching for months, if not years.

Will it Work?
I have covered most of the answer to this above, but your best bet is to use the bait you used last

year, providing it caught you fish and that you didn't have every single fish on it several times. If you did catch all the fish on it last year, then there's little point in fishing the same water year in year out. Instead move around a bit – there's a lovely carp scene out there and life does exist beyond your local lake.

Can I Afford It?
Carp anglers don't tend to be millionaires and even if we do sometimes get our priorities wrong, most of us have to watch the pennies. A baiting campaign should take you through a good deal of the season without you changing your bait one iota. If you start having to add semolina, halve flavour levels just to get by or reduce baiting levels, then you've probably wasted all your previous effort. You have to choose a bait, stick with it and fish it until your nose bleeds, so don't buy a few bags of some Hi-Protein Mix or top-notch fishmeal mix if you can't afford to keep pumping

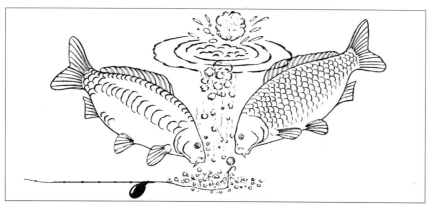

Fig. 72 *Feeding hard on boily crumb.*

quantities of it in from May until September. You will be far better off if you choose an affordable base mix, apply it properly and then reap the rewards.

If you are catching carp consistently and getting them in the press, then bait firms will give you bait at reduced rates – providing you are genuine about it. I know that Nutrabaits, Premier, Zenon and Cotswold always look after their team, and I presume that this applies to most other companies as well. Very few anglers receive bait free, and even if I received free bait from now on I would be hard pressed to generate back the money I have already spent on bait. If it matters enough to you, you will be able to afford it – cut down on life's luxuries or join forces with two other anglers to spread the cost.

Storage
By necessity a baiting campaign involves making comparatively large amounts of bait and then introducing this bait to a water as you feel fit. Ideally, you should make at least three months' bait in advance and then, when you have an odd free night, make some more mixes to top up your stock. Usually I make up around seventy-five 3lb mixes (weighed and rolled boilies) which will see me through from March to May. On free nights, I roll half a dozen mixes so that I can keep topping up the freezer supply. After all, the last thing I want to do is to have to miss a night or two's fishing to make bait when the carp are really having it.

Large amounts of bait will, however, need large amounts of storage room before and after they are made. Dry mix is best stored in large dustbins with permanent lids. These keep it dry, airtight and away from mice and other animals which find their way into garages once the aroma of boilies builds up. I keep flavours in large labelled bulk bottles and enhancers in airtight boxes. You must keep all the ingredients out of direct sunlight and out of harm's way. I also tend to take flavour labels off bottles and just write '1ml' or '2ml' on each one, depending on the quantity I will be including. After all, you don't want anyone copying your recipes and fishing off your hard work.

A common or garden 3ft square freezer will not be large enough and you will need to purchase a chest freezer. You should be able to keep around 200–300lb of bait in such a freezer, and this should do you for quite some time. Boilies are kept in good-quality freezer bags, and I store them in terms of weight rather than numbers. Each of my bags weighs 3lb, so I know that each Tuesday and Saturday I will need to take out five bags and catapult the lot out. This is lot easier than counting out 300 or so boilies!

Unless I am making a protein mix, I tend to make the bait (six to twelve six-egg mixes) in the evening, leave it to dry overnight and then put it in freezer bags the next day. I have not found that this drying-out period affects birdseed or fishmeal baits, and it allows them to harden so that they do not lose their shape when put together in bags. Week by week you will see your bait starting to pile up, and it's a lovely feeling to know that you have 200lb of rolled bait in your freezer which is ready for the carp to eat – it's a bit like having 200lb of confidence in the bag already.

Baiting Up
Apart from choosing the right bait, this is the most important factor in a baiting campaign. How much, where and when?

To start with, I only fish a new water once I have baited it for at least two weeks. If you have experience of a local water then you will know where to bait up. Introducing the bait at points where the carp were caught the previous year is as good a place as any. They won't always be in the same place each year, but my experience is that you will be right more times than wrong follow this plan.

If you don't know where to put your bait then watch others. Don't bait up where other people are baiting up, but, if they are catching fish without baiting up, then who am I to say you shouldn't introduce bait in these swims? If you are to wean the carp on to your bait they need to be able to find and eat it. If your bait is where they are willing to feed you are half-way there already, be those spots snags, weedbeds, island margins or gravel bars – the list is endless.

Make sure your bait will be eaten by carp and not by birds. If coots and tufties are a problem, bait up at dusk or dawn, or whenever these animals are away from the water. Don't just pile the bait in blindly and watch tufty after tufty gulp the lot down as it is a waste of good bait. Use your common sense and discretion. Make sure your bait goes out accurately and goes where you want it. If you don't then your bait will go all over the place and won't be displayed in such a way as to tempt carp or numbers of carp down to feed. Keep your bait in an area no more than half the size of a room (12ft x 10ft) and plaster that area with bait. Don't bait up further than you can cast to accurately. Imagine where you are going to place your rods, and bait to that spot accordingly. Are you going to have all your rods in one spot, or are you going to choose three areas? The more rods you are going to place to one area, the larger the size of that area for pre-baiting. Think before your bait goes to waste, and take your marker rod down if you are unsure.

The more regularly you can bait up, the better. I like my bait to go out into the water on at least three separate occasions each week (including my fishing weekend). Typically, I bait up on Tuesday and Thursday nights and fish from Friday to Sunday. Once I know the fish are having the bait, I do not hesitate to fish after work on Monday and Wednesday to take advantage of my own hard graft. If you can only get down once during mid-week, then bait up on a Wednesday and also on Sunday when you leave. Regularity equals success.

If two or more of you are fishing together, take it in turns to bait up so that you save on cost. However, for at least the first occasion make sure you visit the water together so that you know exactly the spot you should be baiting and at what amount. You will have to be able to trust your baiting partner completely – if you don't then do it yourself. A trio is ideal in my eyes, but finding two other consistent and reliable anglers is easier said than done. Some waters will respond immediately to your tactics, others won't; are your colleagues the type that will stick with you?

As to the amount of bait to use, that itself is the $64,000 question. The amount will actually vary from water to water. What you have to aim to do is to give a large percentage of the carp a taste of your bait over a regular period of time. It's no good putting in 2lb of bait every other day on a water which contains a large amount of carp – say, over 150. They just won't find it in numbers. You can drop in a little once you have them on it, but to start with you want the majority of carp to be able to sample your bait in quantity. This is only a general guide, but for anybody who hasn't a clue on levels, the following figures are useful on all but the very pressurized waters.

50 fish in lake At least 4lb each Tuesday, Thursday and Sunday.
100 fish in lake At least 6lb each Tuesday, Thursday and Sunday.
200 fish in lake At least 10lb each Tuesday, Thursday and Sunday.

That is a lot of bait, but you should use this much if you are to obtain the best possible results from your hard work. Don't be afraid to really pile it in when you're not fishing; if you have a stack already made up at home then you won't be afraid to do it. You have to make a 100 per cent effort with your campaign or there is little point in doing it at all. Once you're fishing, you will have to decide on the amount you want out in front of you when your rods are in the water. Usually, I like thirty to a hundred 18mm baits round each hookbait, but play each water by ear. Once the fish are really having it, you can get away with more bait than usual. Until then, keep it low rather than high.

Luck

No baiting campaign will ever succeed without a certain degree of luck. It will have its ups and downs, but if you work hard, apply the bait properly and don't waiver from giving it your best shot, you will make your own good luck. It's no secret that waters such as Yateley, Longfield, Harrow, Savay, Con Club, Mangrove and Harefield have been turned over by anglers who fish together by applying a bait and reaping the rewards. If these types of water can produce the goods, I'm more than confident that yours will.

Application of Bait Whilst Fishing

How Much Bait?

This truly is a major question in carp fishing, and it is those who get this right more often than they get it wrong who are the successful anglers on the water. Unfortunately, there is no complete answer available, and although I do wish I could tell you what to stick out and know I would be right, I can't because it is dependent on so many variable factors. The factors listed below all determine how much bait you should put out when you start fishing. Because I can't give you the definite answer, you should look at these considerations carefully to see how they may apply to the water you are fishing at that particular time.

Time of Season?

In the early season when carp are starting to move about you can begin to put bait into a water in quantities, but not until you are satisfied that the fish are feeding as well. As the season progresses and water temperatures rise you can increase this level, but do be aware that during spawning the carp may seem to avoid baits. However, after spawning they can be ravenous and it may be an advantage to have a fair bit of bait out in front of you. Once all that is through it is very much a case of playing it by ear; red-hot summer days do not equate to avid feeding by the carp, but the nights may produce action. As water temperatures drop so may a fish's appetite, so cut back on bait or you may ruin your chances.

Numbers and Size of Fish Present?

A fishery absolutely stocked full of fish is a water where you may be able to get away with piling lots of bait in and encouraging the fish to compete for those available baits. Fish which are competing for food, or confident in it, are fish which are more likely to pick up a hookbait and end up on the bank. If your water only has a small number of carp it would be better to find the fish

first, and then present a small amount of bait to interest them rather than overfacing them with pounds of it.

Are they Shoal Fish?

If the fish in your water do shoal up in numbers it may be possible to introduce quite a number of free offerings initially so that you create a bed of bait. This may encourage numbers of the shoal to stay in your swim to feed, and so become more likely to be hooked. A small number of free offerings could well be ignored by a large shoal of carp who are drawn to another carp angler's bed of baits. However, the trick is to know if your fish are shoal fish in the first place. Lots of fish topping in one place and multiple catches indicate shoal fish present in your water. This is a prime consideration.

This carp obviously loved the bait.

What Has Worked Before?

If you are fishing a new water, the best way to get a fish under your belt is to stick to the common baiting levels used on that water and hope your presentation or location will give you an edge. Once you have some fish under your belt then you can start to experiment. Don't pile in thousands of boilies in the hope that you will catch all the fish at once. You may do, but you are just as likely not to.

Type and Size of Bait?

Obviously, if you are using large baits of, say, 22mm or above in size, you won't need to put hundreds out to interest carp; conversely, you may need quite a number of particle-sized baits to create the same level of interest. I'm not totally sure whether I should put out more fishmeal than bird food, but I do know that I would rather have a little out than a lot until I know that water well!

Pre-Baited Bait or Not?

If you have been baiting the water with a bait and the carp are being caught on it regularly, it may be that they are actually searching for that particular bait. If this is the case then you may be able to put more in than you would do if your bait was new to the water. Obviously, if numbers of carp are used to the bait going in and have taken a liking to it, then there's nothing wrong in increasing your baiting level – providing it does not mean a drop in your catch rate.

Number of Anglers Present?

If you are just one of many anglers present on a water and they are all sticking out hundreds of baits, it isn't advisable to follow their lead automatically – unless it is working well for them. Clearly, if that method is producing carp consistently then follow it, but if it isn't then don't waste your bait. Try to create an edge by fine-tuning your presentation or improving your watercraft.

Weather Conditions

Weather conditions will affect a carp's appetite and you should base your baiting levels on how much a carp may want to eat at the time. Clearly, if good summer feeding conditions are followed by a sharp drop in temperature, the carps' appetite may decrease for a while, so cut back on the bait. Similarly, if it's winter time but a good wind has put a lot of feeding carp on the move, you may be able to increase your baiting levels. Use your common sense!

These are just some of the factors that can influence how much bait you should put out when you start a session, but I'm sure there are lots more. If you are looking for a more definite answer to the question of how to apply bait, then I would say that unless you are 100 per cent sure that a lot of bait is necessary, then stick to ten to forty free offerings around each hookbait at most, and only start to change if it's obvious that another type of baiting is working. Do remember that you cannot retrieve what has been put in but you can always add to it if necessary. Think about that before you automatically reach for the throwing stick and start to blitz the water! Baiting levels will always be dependent on how you read the water in front of you at the time. If you use your common sense I'm sure you will get it right. However, if you act like a sheep then . . . well, I needn't continue, need I? Finally, if your swim is full of carp then put a bait to them and not half a dozen mixes (perhaps use stringers if you are in doubt).

So, there you have my look at modern carp baits, telling you what I personally would prefer to use and why. However, at the end of the day bait is only one part of the jigsaw puzzle, and as all the carp pictured in this book were caught on the ideas and recipes discussed here, then something must be right on the bait front . . .

7 LONG-RANGE CARP FISHING

One of the most startling developments in carp fishing has been the refinement of fishing at long range. From its early popularity when you were the man if you could hit anywhere near 100yd, we now see claims that some of the more illustrious carpers such as Zenon Bojko and Rob Maylin are hitting the 160yd mark with accuracy time and time again. I should make it clear, however, that this book is aimed at the general carp angler and that the need to fish at very long distance is restricted to comparatively few waters. Those who can hit over the 140yd mark consistently are very few indeed, and whilst some may query this I doubt whether even one per cent of the total carp fishing fraternity could hit that sort of mark. Mind you, I think only half that number need to fish at such a range in the first place! Fishing at such a distance is hard work, it requires a lot of practice and it can be a very hit-and-miss affair. You will not need to consider refining your tackle and tactics for such distances, but we can still all learn something from such refinement.

This chapter will look at fishing at range for carp – it's up to you to decide what you think range is. My guide-line for fishing at range is over 100yd, but many of you will think of it as any distance over 80yd. Whilst 80yd may not sound a lot, as the information in this chapter will help improve your set-up, casting and approach for distances over 100yd, it will certainly make at least as much improvement, if not more, for distances over the 80yd mark.

WHAT IS LONG-RANGE FISHING?

I was taking a walk around a local lake some days ago and, whilst sitting down talking to one of the anglers, I saw a carp leap out near the island about 60yd away or so. The lad obviously knew what he was doing as he wound in a close-in rod and cast it to the spot without any trouble at all. Thinking back to the early 1980s when I first fished the place, I remembered that in order to hit that same spot from the same swim in the same conditions but with 1980s' tackle I would have almost to run up to the water, give it all I had on 6lb main line, and hope that the luncheon meat and 1¼oz bomb would make it. Believe you me, in those days 60yd was range carping for many of us!

The point behind that little story is that the more you fish and the more experience you gain, the narrower your definition of range fishing. Whilst fishing at 80yd with some degree of efficiency may be a big deal to you this year, I can guarantee that if you do work hard at your carp fishing, in a year or so's time 80yd will just be a nice chuck. It's all a natural progression, and what is one man's range is another's 'steady chuck'.

To fish efficiently at 80–100yd takes a certain degree of thought and practice, to fish at 110–130yd takes a lot of practice, and to fish over 130yd is a very hit-and-miss business for the majority of fisherman in the carp world.

WHY DO YOU NEED TO FISH AT RANGE?

The first thing to point out is that if you don't have to fish at range then don't. Believe me when I say that if I could catch under 30yd at every single venue I fish I would be a happy man. However, whilst I may catch some carp at under 30yd on some venues, I would be short of the main feeding area on many. Undoubtedly there are those people who genuinely like to fish for carp at range whether they are there or not, but doing so is very hard work. The further you go from the bank, the harder it becomes to be accurate with your casting and baiting, presentation becomes a problem and landing fish even more so. So, once again, the maxim is: if you don't need to fish at range then don't.

There are, however, a number occasions on waters when you do need to fish at distance to put yourself in with a chance of catching a reasonable amount of fish. Most readers of this book will have fished lakes over 5 acres or so where a point out towards the middle is as good a place as any. If carp are showing at 30yd, then fish at 30yd. Similarly, if they show at 60yd, then fish at 60yd. If carp show at 90yd you must be prepared and able to fish efficiently and effectively for them at such a distance. Clearly, if fish show at range you should fish at range unless there's a good reason for not doing so.

I would also consider fishing at range if I felt that the water had not been subject to it, *and* if carp were present at range. Note that carefully – fish at range if it has not been done before and you feel that carp are at range. If the margin is full of carp and you are casting over 100yd then you are a fool of the first degree. However, in this day and age many waters are range waters due purely and simply to pressure close in. Hordes of anglers with their bivvies have driven carp further out, so the only solution may be range fishing. One of my local lakes, the Tilery, used to produce a lot of carp at 70–100yd. However, pressure on those carp over the years has pushed them out a little further and it is not uncommon to see them topping at over 150yd out or more.

TACKLE

It would be nice to tell you to go out and buy Extreme Pursuits and Aerlex 8000s, or Amorphous 2¾s and SS3000s in the hope that you would do it, but I know that this is not realistic! Clearly, with the top range of rods, reels and line range fishing becomes easier, but in this practical look at range fishing we all have to keep our feet on the ground, our hands in our pockets and still keep hitting that 100yd-plus mark. As with snag fishing, particle fishing and floater fishing we have to make our existing tackle do the job, until maybe one day – if we really feel it is necessary and if we can afford it – we will go for the top-of-the-market tackle. So for this section on tackle, I will look at *affordable* rods, reels and lines for range carping up to 100yd which will suit ninety-nine per cent of carp anglers, as well as rods, reels and lines for ultimate distance fishing.

Rods

If you already have a rod or rods then you may have to make do with what you have. If it's a 12ft rod with a test curve of 2lb or more, and if you have a decent reel, main line, shock leader and 2–2½oz bombs, you may be able to hit 100yd with a baited tackle. My personal experience has been that the faster taper a rod is (in other words, stiffer), the easier it is to cast at distance, and cast at distance accurately – because of its taper you can get away with punch casting with your arms and upper body only. This is a lot easier than having through-action rods which, if wound up correctly, can cast long distance, but do take some getting used to. Certainly, a good caster could make a through-action rod cast a huge distance, but if you can then try to pick as stiff a taper rod as possible.

If you haven't purchased your rods yet, or are thinking of purchasing new ones, then I will give you a little advice. First, unless you are going to be fishing at huge distances (130yd plus) on a regular basis for a number of years, then don't spend huge sums on rods when you don't need to. That money would be best spent on bait or a good syndicate place. My advice would be to choose a rod in which I personally believe totally – I always recommend this rod to anybody who does not want to spend a large amount of money. It is Rod Hutchinson's 12ft, 2½lb test curve Original Horizon rod – an absolutely brilliant rod that should last you a long time, and which will cast single baits up to 130yd and stringers to 100yd. It is reasonably priced even when made up, is virtually unbreakable and I have used mine for everything from floater fishing to chucking out half-mackerel for pike. Most Hutchinson tackle dealers stock them.

Reels

As with rods you probably already have reels that will be suitable for range fishing with a little care and thought. Looking at most tackle on the bank it seems that Shimanos, Daiwas and DAMs are very popular. Shimano 4500 and 4000, Aerlex 5000 and 4000, Daiwa BR2650 and DAM CD350 are all good carp reels, and if you have one of these then you will have no problems at all. If you haven't then all you need is a reel with a large enough spool to facilitate long casting, which has a good line lay and which is reliable enough to last a season or two.

Look at the spool of your reel, is it at least 1½in wide (*see* Fig. 73)? If so, there is a good bet that it is a suitable choice for most situations. I cover the reason for this a little later in this chapter, but in basic layman's terms once you cast, line comes from your spool. The further you cast, the more line comes from your spool. Obviously, every time that line touches the spool lip there is considerable friction, and this friction reduces distance. The wider a spool is the less times the line

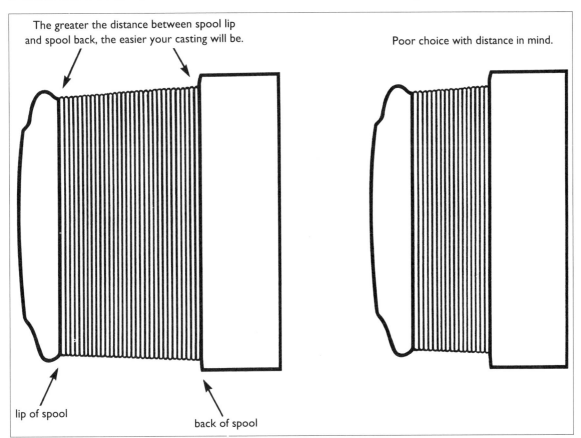

The greater the distance between spool lip and spool back, the easier your casting will be.

Poor choice with distance in mind.

lip of spool

back of spool

Fig. 73 The advantages of a large spool.

touches the spool lip, so the less friction there is and, all things being equal, the further out your baited rig should go. I discuss overloading spools, polishing rods and matching the correct reel to the correct rod to get a true picture later, but if you do understand that general friction principle, then it's a good start. If your reel has a small-sized spool, you may have a problem. If you feel you need to purchase a reel then purchase one of good quality, that is affordable and which has a good-sized spool as well.

Balancing Rod and Reel

Just a small point but a very important one is that if you have a good rod and wish to purchase a reel (or vice versa), it is vital that you make sure that the item you purchase is equally as good for your choice of fishing. This is known as purchasing balanced tackle. For example, a Rob Maylin 12ft 6in Extreme Pursuit *can* cast over 140yd with a good reel attached, but if you put an undersized reel on it and you may not even manage half that distance.

Your rod will only be as good as your reel and vice versa, so if you have to uprate your tackle make sure you don't spend too much on rods so that you have to purchase second-rate reels. Similarly, don't buy top-of-the-range Shimanos and team them up with cheap, second-hand rods which have all the power of a stick of chewing gum. You should wait until you have enough money to purchase rod and reel together. You will be able to see how the reel feels on the rod and you may even be able to haggle a better price for bulk buying!

Line

If you can, it's always best to fish with a main line straight through rather than main line to a shock leader. Once you start putting leader knots in your line you may decrease its strength. Knots can also pick up floating weed in the tip ring and cause it to jam, and you will have to modify your presentation to accommodate 'no-tubing' rigs or 'thick-tubing rigs' to go over the shock leader in the event of a crack off. However, whilst it's nice to be able to use a straight-through main line, this just isn't possible in many cases.

Generally, you will be casting around 2½–3oz of lead, and this needs a line of 15lb test to make sure it can absorb the initial surge of power from rod to lead. A line of 12lb test may be able to take the strain with gentle casts up to 70yd or so, but if you really start pushing it you will crack off and have to set up all over again. Cracking off (when your line parts from the lead in mid-cast) is also very dangerous as a flying lead is a lethal object and can cause grave injury to anyone it hits. I'm sure some of you will be thinking that while you never use a shock leader your 12lb line has always been fine – even with a 3oz lead. I agree that it will take the odd cast, but if you really want to give it all you've got or if you keep thinking the carp are always *just* out of range, then it's time to get your brain into gear and start using a shock leader and main/line combination. Over the years I have met many carp anglers who fish main line straight through all the time and miss out on lots of range opportunities. Sometimes this has been down to just sheer laziness, but in many cases it was because the anglers did not have a clue on how to tie up a shock leader. I cover this later in the chapter, so please do try it. Don't flick past the section as it could cost you fish in the long run.

If I have to fish main line and shock leader combinations I tend to use as high a breaking strain main line as I feel I can get away with, along with a 15lb or 18lb shock leader. My choice of main line to a shock leader has always been Sylcast 6lb, 7lb and 9lb and until I am convinced otherwise I intend to stick with it. In these ratings I have found it to cast very well, have good-quality-abrasion resistance and knot extremely well to high-rating shock leaders. I know some people swear by Brent and Maxima – it's all a case of keeping your options open and choosing what you feel is best.

Shock Leader

As I said earlier, unless you have some of Daiwa's SS3000s or Aerlex's 8000s and rods to match, you will need to use a shock leader of some form or another if you want to cast consistently over 100yd. I have explained the whys and wherefores in the section on balancing rod and reel above, so if you wish to be a consistent carp catcher in *all* conditions, you will have to master tying shock leaders and have confidence in using them. Whilst I agree I would not use them unless I had to, I certainly don't feel uneasy using them and I'm sure that after a few sessions you won't either. Being able to use them and use them well means having another string to your bow, and, as so few people can even be bothered to learn how to tie the knot, never mind have a go at using them, it's an edge as well. Remember what I said about distance fishing – how carp can be pushed further and further out? Well, if you are the only one who can get a bait on them you have probably one of the best edges in carp fishing. Savay, Harefield and Tilery are all hard lakes which have been turned over by those who are able to present their bait at range in comparison to other anglers.

Your three main considerations with shock leaders are: type of shock leader; length of shock leader; and which knot to use.

Type of Shock Leader

A length of 15lb Berkley Big Game is all most anglers need for a shock leader for carp fishing. It knots well, breaks at 18lb plus, has a good abrasion resistance and isn't so thick that it reduces range in the long run. However, if 15lb is not quite enough you could always try Sylcast in 18lb

which, although a little thicker, is like a tow rope – if something does go when you are playing a fish it probably won't be your leader. In Chapter 8 on snag fishing I will describe some gravel pits that are so ridden with gravel bars covered in zebra mussels and hard flint that you can be 'cut off' (have a line break) time and time again. Whilst 15lb Big Game and the like may solve some of your problems, you will need to uprate your shock leader if you wish to fish very bad areas. I have never encountered such problems, but having talked to experienced anglers it seems that Kryston's Quicksilver is the ideal choice. Even the Harefield bars don't seem to fray this line – if that's true then you should be able to rest assured that your water won't be a problem. However, ninety per cent of carp anglers needn't worry about this problem at all.

Length of Shock Leader

As I have said, the purpose of *most* shock leaders is to absorb the initial surge of power generated from the cast, with the maximum point of strain situated at the main line and swivel join. In theory, therefore, a shock leader could be just long enough to allow a sufficient drop of the lead and still be on the reel spool as the release point is reached (*see* Fig. 74). However, if you were to tie a shock leader to just that length, you would probably crack off time and time again as not *all* the force is taken up in that split second as the

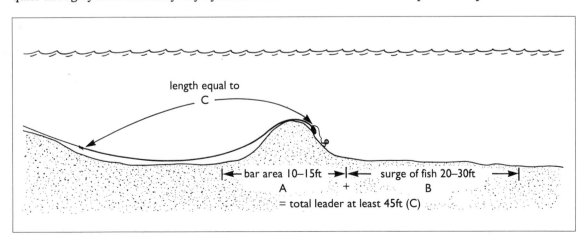

length equal to
C

|← bar area 10–15ft →|← surge of fish 20–30ft →|
A + B
= total leader at least 45ft (C)

Fig. 74 *Leader length.*

lead is released. Instead, you should tie on a leader that is equivalent to length A–B in Fig. 74, and with at least six turns of leader on the spool already. I know some writers advocate anything up to ten turns on your reel, but I suggest that if you are a complete novice at leader fishing you should only require eight turns. As you get used to it and get more proficient at tying, you can decrease the number of turns safely to a minimum of four. However, do what suits you best and not necessarily what I have found works best for me.

Setting the leader up is very easy: all you need to do is thread your main line through all the rings and tie on your leader (as discussed later). Then wind on your leader until you have four to six turns on the spool. Following that, simply cut off the leader with scissors at a point where there is at least 36in of leader between rod tip and cutting point. That allows sufficient leader to which you can tie your bombs or swivel; it is also better in most circumstances to have a little too much leader than not enough.

Obviously, the longer the leader the more your distance will be reduced. However, its length should always be balanced so you are using a long enough length to avoid crack-offs. Time and experience will show you what is best, so don't be put off by all the lengths I have quoted. They are not gospel, and you must use what you are confident with.

Sometimes you may fish a shock leader because of its abrasion qualities rather than simply its casting abilities – perhaps if you are fishing to bars or snags. Clearly, your shock leader in this instance needs to be long enough to cover that snag in question and also the surge of your fish. The diagram shown in Fig. 74 explains this, but as you can see your leader needs to be a combination of 10–15ft to cover the bar area and 20–30ft on top of that to cover the initial surge of the fish – in other words, you need a total leader length of at least 45ft. Personally, I would use a leader of 60ft to cover every eventuality. Never take risks unless you really feel that you are *totally* sure of the guide-lines. My advice is don't risk it, please.

Which Knot to Use?

Almost every carp book seems to include a different type of leader knot. I'm sure that all are equally as good, so all I will do here is include a diagram of the knot I use and which hasn't caused me any problems (*see* Fig. 75). I've no idea or interest in what it is called; all I do know is that it does work and unless I start to have problems I don't intend to change it. It works for me and I hope it will work for you too. If it doesn't then try one which is illustrated in another carp book – for example, page 185 of Jim Gibbinson's *Big Water Carp* or page 52 of Rod Hutchinson's *Carp Now and Then* or page 89 of Tim Paisley's *Carp Fishing*. One thing I would add is that you must never rush your knots, always wet them before pulling tight and pull them together gently. If the main line looks at all 'crinkly' then redo the knot – it will only take thirty seconds to do so and it will be worth it. I usually tie my leaders up at home which does help, and I suggest that you also do this if you can. You won't be rushed and things always seem a lot easier away from the elements.

As I said earlier, later in this chapter I will look at ultimate range fishing, where range to *some* extent is dictated by budget. However, I will now cover the peripheral items which go with your main tackle.

Buzzers

Clearly, the same indicators that you use for your general carp fishing will also suffice for fishing at range, providing they are sensitive enough to register indications. As range increases so does the stretch in your line, and your ability to pull tight to the lead will also be decreased. The further out you are, the greater both the line stretch and slack line, and the more a carp has to move the lead

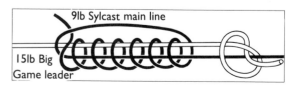

Fig. 75 *A leader knot.*

before your indicator sounds. The more a carp has to move before you have any indication, the more chance it has of getting rid of the baited hook, dragging you into a snag or weed and generally not being caught. So as the carp has all the balls in its court, it's up to you to have the most effective form of indication at your end of the tackle.

No matter what set-up you choose, your buzzer must be as sensitive as possible. If it's a Fox, Delkim or Sensitron then put it on maximum sensitivity; if it is an Optonic then put in on an eight-paddle twitcher wheel.

Rod Rests and Buzzer Bars

As you are fishing at range and may need to strike at single bleeps, you have to make sure your rod rests, buzzer bars and so on don't move at all. Buzzer bars swaying in the wind cause false bleeps, leaving you unsure as to whether it was a carp or not. Personally, unless I am fishing all three baited tackle to one tight area (in other words, no more than 10–15yd apart), I try to fish my buzzers on single banksticks and have my main line from reel to bomb in a direct line. A direct line equals minimal resistance equals more chance of a registration!

Monkey Climbers and Swingers

I tend to fish one of two ways depending on whether it's a windy day or not. Whilst that may sound silly, it isn't, and I will describe the two methods below with the aid of diagrams.

Tight Bowstring Method (Fig. 76)

This is the method of registration I use over eighty per cent of the time – *not* because it's far superior to the other method but because the other way has its limitations, as I will describe later.

First, cast your lead to the desired position and, having mended the line, pull back as tight as possible so you can almost feel the lead. I use a lead of around 3oz so I can really pull tight to it; under 2½oz and you may move the lead – this can mean disaster for your presentation. Having satisfied yourself that the line is as tight as possible in all the circumstances, put the line into the back clip sited directly above the lip of the reel spool. Clip your heavy bobbin on to the line and tweak the line slightly to the lead again. This should drop the heavy bobbin ever so slightly and, providing your indicator is sensitive enough, should also give you a single bleep.

Any takes will register in one of three ways. The first type is a screaming take – line pulls out of the clip, the clutch screams and you hopefully have a self-hooked fish. The second type is when your bobbin starts to drop down the needle. Quickly tighten up to this 'drop back' and strike as hard as you can. These types are a little more difficult to hit. The third take is the one that lifts the bobbin slightly, the line then tightens and sometimes (if you are lucky) you will get a single bleep. Again, strike these takes as hard as possible as they are indicative of a fish which may not bolt off but

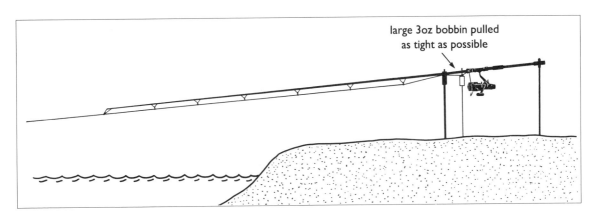

large 3oz bobbin pulled as tight as possible

Fig. 76 The tight bowstring method.

which has just pricked itself. It may well scream off, but you must not miss that chance, so hit it and hope. If you missed it, get your bait out to the same spot as soon as possible.

Slightest-Touch Method

Another way to set up your indicator system is as illustrated in Fig. 77. Unfortunately, due to its very nature whereby any movement of a fairly slack line will move the Swinger and sound the alarm, its use is restricted to small waters which are not greatly affected by wind and undertow, and/or waters in winter which tend to be still rather than windswept. I have used this method at Willow Park, Surrey in almost water-freezing conditions and found it works absolutely brilliantly – so, see if you think you can use it as well.

Again, cast out to the desired spot and pull the line as tight as possible into a back clip as with the first method. When you have done this and the line has settled, put on a Swinger with the counterbalance about half-way down the stem. Unclip the back clip and slacken off your clutch (or baitrunner). With the tension being so great, the Swinger will try to move skywards and your line will want to pull free from the spool in order to relieve the tension. Simply keep pulling line from the spool via the clutch or baitrunner until the Swinger stops going up against the rod each time. By moving the counterbalance weight slightly either way you will find the perfect balance point of that still line. Any line movement at all on the Swinger will cause it to shoot upwards

or drop downwards, so giving a large number of bleeps and your chance to hit that take.

As I said earlier, you can only get away with this set-up in still conditions as wind will upset it. I have tried to use it in weedy waters, but it does not work as well here either, because all the debris, weed and algae tend to lie on the sunken and still line, stopping it from moving on gentle takes. However, this method is another string to your bow, so don't forget it!

END TACKLE

If you can actually get away with fishing straight-through main line and still hit 80–100yd accurately each and every time, then most of the standard end tackles will suffice. For fishing main line only I would use either of the two end tackles illustrated in Fig. 78. Both are very effective for the kind of carp fishing most of us do, and whilst you may read all sorts of articles on round leads, lead-core fly lines and the like by carp anglers who fish pressurized waters, the illustrated rigs will serve you well for a long time on the waters you fish. You will see that these rigs include tubing, the merits of which I discussed in Chapter 5. I would be happy to use these rigs on most waters, providing I felt that the use of tubing was not likely to put off the carp to any noticeable degree.

However, as I pointed out in the section on whether to use shock leaders, if you want to hit 100yd plus in most conditions with general carp

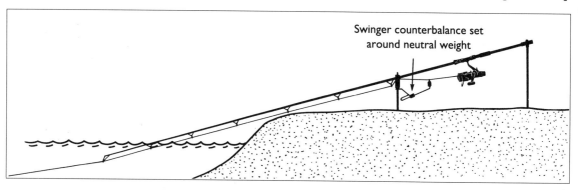

Fig. 77 The slightest-touch method.

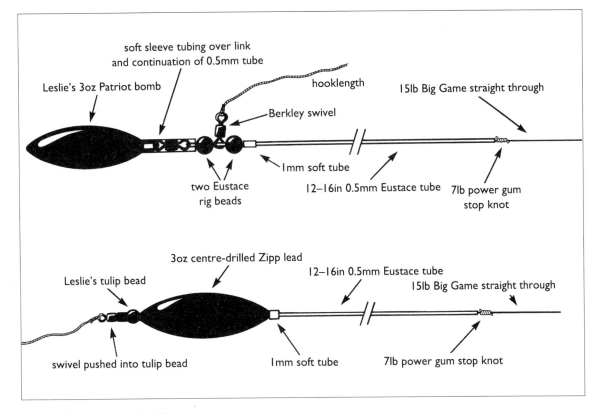

soft sleeve tubing over link
and continuation of 0.5mm tube

Leslie's 3oz Patriot bomb

hooklength

15lb Big Game straight through

Berkley swivel

1mm soft tube

two Eustace
rig beads

12–16in 0.5mm Eustace tube

7lb power gum
stop knot

3oz centre-drilled Zipp lead

12–16in 0.5mm Eustace tube

15lb Big Game straight through

Leslie's tulip bead

swivel pushed into tulip bead

1mm soft tube

7lb power gum stop knot

Fig. 78 *Long-range end tackles.*

tackle, you will have to use a shock leader. Although it is not immediately obvious, if you don't change your end tackle as well you could end up with a potentially dangerous rig purely and simply by having that shock leader knot some 30–60ft back down the line. Below, I explain why this is not obvious at first.

Imagine that you are casting out and crack off due to poor timing, the bait arm flipping over in mid-cast and so on. The law of averages says that, all things being equal, your line will break at its weakest point. With a leader of, say, 15lb and main line of 9lb, that breakage will be on the knot and on the main line side rather than the leader side. Obviously, your rig will be somewhere out in the water, and if a carp picks it up and bolts it will probably find some kind of cover eventually. The swivel will then either pull free of the tulip bead or the swivel will slide down the leader line. What you have then is a 30–60ft piece of line with

a carp at one end and, because the ½ml tubing can't pass over the leader knot, a lead at the other. You can imagine just how dangerous this is when you think that it is likely that a carp will tangle itself up to some degree. At best it will tear itself free, so ripping open its mouth, and at worst the carp will be tethered up and may die. That's a horrifying thought isn't it? Don't think for one second it won't happen to you because you crack off – it may happen, and because of that you would be a fool if you continued to use it. I really can't spell this out enough, so please do think about it. Geoff Boots has covered this in some detail on pages 88 to 91 of *Carpworld 24* (*see* Further Reading for more details), so if you do have the chance give it a read and give our carp and your carp a chance.

Now we know the problem, how can we solve it? There are a number of solutions, and I illustrate the two I use below.

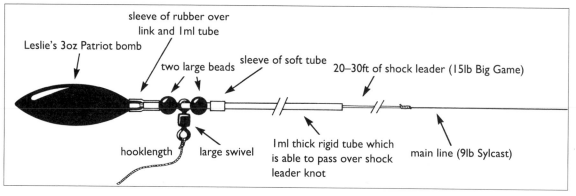

Fig. 79 *The thick-tube method.*

Thick-Tube Method (Fig. 79)

From what I have seen over the years, carp anglers seem to be divided over their love or hate of tubing. I shall not go over the same old ground I covered in Chapter 5, except to say that if you are a tubing fan then this is the method for you when you are range fishing with a shock leader. I hope the diagram is self-explanatory, but the important point to note is that the thick tubing has an internal diameter large enough to pass over the shock leader knot on the shock leader side. You must, and I stress *must*, check that it will pass over that knot and that it passes over the knot with ease. If there's any doubt over this then don't use it, or use larger tubing. Because of the diameter of the tubing, the beads, swivels and so on must also be larger and therefore more visible. On clear waters like shallow gravel pits this may be a problem, so think carefully about whether the set-up is suitable.

No-Tube Method or Tadpole Rig (Fig. 80)

I first saw this at a BCSG meeting where it was being shown by Dave Thorpe. The rigs are now readily available from Leslie's of Luton, and you should have some if you do fish at range with a leader.

Again, I hope the diagram is self-explanatory, but I will cover all the basics of the method so that hopefully you will see its advantages when using a leader. As purchased, the bomb (2½–3½oz) has a long, wire tail-stem built into it, this being long enough to accept the tadpole-shaped rubber, both beads and the swivel. All you do is simply thread your leader through the tadpole inner, both beads and the swivel, and tie it to the small ring of the stem. Then slide all the components down on to the stem, setting it up so it is ready to fish. The wide end of the tadpole (nearest your rod) stops your bead and swivels leaving your stem unless a fish picks up a

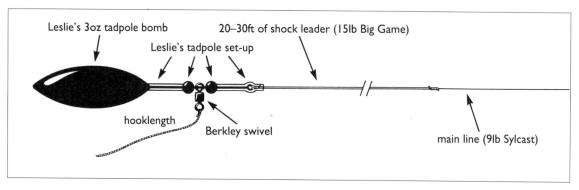

Fig. 80 *The tadpole rig.*

cracked-off lead. Then, with minimal pressure, the beads and swivel on the rubber can slip over the loop on the end of the stem, so freeing the carp from the lead. It is a brilliant set-up, and one I use regularly if I have dropped tubing and feel I have to use a leader.

Although in theory both set-ups are not tether rigs, you do, however, have to think very carefully before using them in weedy waters with a shock leader. Anybody who has ever used a leader in a weedy water will know that the leader knot has a tendency to become covered in algae and weed, and can be difficult enough to wind through your top ring let alone to allow tubing to pass over it or the tadpole arrangement. So you do have a problem in such circumstances which can, in reality, only be solved by using straight-through main line without a leader.

PRESENTATION AT RANGE

In Chapter 5 I covered all the different hooking arrangements I feel are acceptable today, and to be quite honest just because you are fishing at range you should not stop fishing an effective hooking arrangement. Unfortunately, when you are casting a long way you cannot easily watch your baited rig for tangles, so be careful if you think that your rig is likely to tangle. There is no reason why it should do so, providing you change it or adapt it so it can be used at range confidently. Because you are generating such force with your cast, and because that force will be transmitted to all items on your line to a certain extent, you have to be very careful that the fine hairs don't break, the boilies don't fly off, the counter-balance weights don't move and so on. This is the reason why I always tend to use basic hooking patterns if I can – the fewer the components in the rig, the more chance it has of reaching the target zone in one piece.

Just because you are fishing at range, however, there is no excuse to chuck any old rubbish out there. Whilst it would be nice to imagine that carp don't inspect rigs half as much at range, this isn't true; an inefficient rig at 130yd is just as much of a waste of time as it if it were at 30yd. A carp will not even be able to pick up a tangled rig, so don't waste your time risking it. If you are occasionally bringing back tangled rigs at range, then don't sit there and accept it but instead start thinking about what is going wrong. Why is it tangling up? Why is the hook turning back on itself? Would a shorter hair help? Should you use shot rather than a piece of putty? By tying up parts of your rig with PVA you will be able to ensure that they will not whirl about catching all and sundry, but at the same time the PVA should not be so thick as to defeat the main purpose of the hooking set-up. Although you will probably stick to the basic presentations, like all things in carp fishing, if there is a problem don't accept it or give up, but find a solution and catch those fish! A little work goes a long way, and because so few people are prepared to work at it, if you do then you will be successful.

LONG-RANGE CASTING

I think one of the main problems people seem to have with long-range fishing is getting the baited tackle out to the required spot with accuracy. Even with the correct tackle and shock leader, hitting the same spot time and time again seems to be beyond the ability of many carp anglers – the baited tackle will hit that spot occasionally, but ask them to do it again and they will struggle. If you wish to be a consistent carp catcher it is absolutely vital that you are able to put a bait at range to the same spot time and time again. Whilst it is an asset to be able to cast out a long way, it is just as important to be consistent with that casting. In Chapter 2 I did go into some detail on how important it is to put your in the right spot time after time. The consistent carp catchers are those who catch more than one carp in a session, or who catch carp on a regular basis. This isn't down to luck, but is down to the fact that they can put their bait to the right spot exactly, whilst others put theirs somewhere in the general area. At times the latter may be acceptable, but over the course of a season the accurate casters will have a greater catch rate. I am sure you have seen anglers who claim to be great casters on your water, but unless they can hit the same spot consistently and regularly then they might as well not even bother. Odd fish are caught on chuck-it-and-chance-it tactics, but not as many as are caught by accurate casting.

The method I use to cast at all ranges (30–150yd) is illustrated in Figs. 81 and 82, and Figs. 84 and 85. I know there will be many anglers who don't agree with this style of casting and who believe that their way is far better, but this method has worked for me and I will continue to follow it until I am convinced otherwise. If you are having problems with your casting at present or feel you could improve it, try the illustrated method as it is a style many anglers favour for accurate casting. Hopefully the diagrams will be self-explanatory, but I'll describe each to help you in case you have problems.

Preparation (Fig. 81)

I have heard it said that long casting is seventy-five per cent technique and twenty-five per cent tackle; I certainly wouldn't disagree with that figure at all. In order to perfect accurate casting you must have a nice, unhurried casting action along with the correct tackle. However, before you cast you must make sure your preparation is as good as could be expected in all the circumstances.

If possible, don't wear tight clothing or restrictive jackets when casting as this will impair arm and body movement. A jerky cast caused by your jacket tightening up under your arm is an incorrect cast and won't be as accurate as it could be. Obviously, if it's raining you will have to compromise to a certain degree, but if it isn't then don't limit yourself by a poor choice of garment.

Your left hand grips the rod butt (which should be clean and not muddy, oily or slippery). Your right hand holds the reel stem, with the finger nearest your thumb holding the line tight to

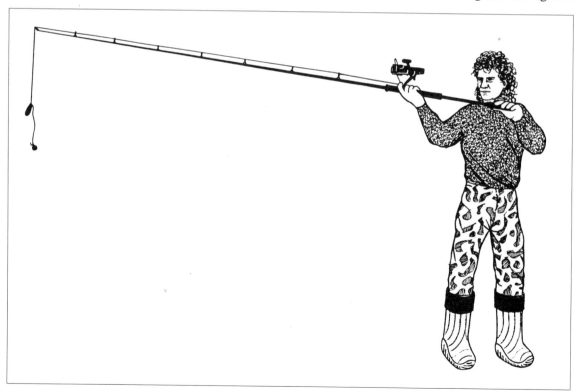

Fig. 81 *Long-range casting – preparation.*

the rod. Do make sure your bale arm is open and not likely to close in mid-cast. Some reels have a tendency to do this if you leave your handle at half-cock, so check in advance the best position in which to leave it whilst casting.

Have a 30–36in drop from rod tip to lead, the lead positioned some 2–4ft above the ground. Make sure the rig is ready to cast and is not tangled. Look down the rod to ensure that your line is going through all the rings and directly through your tip ring. If it is looped round your tip ring, at best you will cut down your distance and at worst all the power will be transmitted to that rod tip area and snap it. Keep the left leg slightly in front of the right leg and spread them about 1–2ft apart.

Aim (Fig. 82)

The rod has now been brought just above your head as you intend to drive it forward in a straight line. Do not cast if your rod is at an angle over

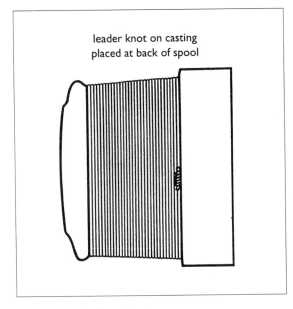

Fig. 83 Leader knot siting.

your shoulder or the baited rig may not go in a direct line. This type of cast is called the overhead cast and will suit most anglers for the majority of their fishing. Your body is facing directly towards the area and you should also be siting up your mark. Hopefully you will be fishing towards a swim marker or shadow on the water so you know exactly how far to cast and therefore how much power to apply.

Remember that your rod will make an arc above you, so make sure that there aren't any overhanging trees or passers-by in that zone. If your rod does touch a branch, leaf or piece of grass, your rig may pick it up, so make sure nothing is going to get in your way.

If you are fishing a shock leader, make sure the leader knot is to the back of the spool as illustrated in Fig. 83. A knot situated near the front of the spool will constantly 'pluck' line as each of the six turns of leader pass over it. At best this will cut your distance down, and at worst it will jam up and you will end up with either a broken rod, a crack-off or a rig which has drilled straight down into the margins in front of you. This trick only takes a second or two, so don't risk breaking that rod or snapping that line just out of laziness!

Fig. 82 Aim.

Fig. 84 *Power.*

Power (Fig. 84)

We now get to the very important stage of your casting: the smooth casting action which many people seem to have problems with. Using your left hand (which is holding the rod butt), start to pull the butt back smoothly whilst your right hand drives forward. This should be a smooth movement and not a hurried jerk which will send the lead nowhere in particular. Your body will naturally move forward above your hips, but do not move your feet or swivel because doing so will cause you to lose accuracy. Keep your head still at all times.

Release (Fig. 85)

My preferred release position is when the rod is at forty-five degrees to the ground – if Roman ballistics are anything to go by, this should be the ideal angle of release. Aim a little higher than you need to so that you can feather down your cast into the desired spot if necessary. You can always slow a cast down, but once it's left your finger you can't speed it up. If you do need to slow it down, don't just stop it dead in mid-flight if it is going too far or you will crack off or drive it into the water 30–40yd out. Simply start all over again and do it right this time. When you do release your lead, try to keep the rod pointing directly in line with the desired spot. Again, if it's not going in the correct direction you cannot do anything about it except cast it again.

At this early stage you should be able to see your rig fly through the air, so do look to see that the boily and so on are still attached. If the boily is going to come off then it's likely to happen at this stage so, if in doubt, wind in and do it again.

When your baited tackle hits the spot and the lead hits the bottom, if it is a calm day you can flick the bale arm over, tighten up to the lead and set up your preferred indication system. When you flick your bale arm over, make sure your line is laid down correctly and isn't looped over. A wind knot at this stage could prove disastrous, so make sure it is bedded in properly on the spool and isn't behind the spool, over the reel handle or anywhere else. If it is a windy day, you will

Fig. 85 *Release.*

have to be very quick with this step; any delay will allow a bow to develop in the line which can be detrimental to effective bite registration and indication. However, just because you do it quicker doesn't mean you should do it incorrectly!

Never overtighten to the lead because if you do so and then move the lead 'by accident', you may drag the hooklink into weed and so ruin your chances of having a pick-up. On waters which have silty or weedy bottoms it is unlikely that this will happen accidentally as your lead will be embedded in the mud or detritus. However, on gravel pits it is possible to overtighten accidentally, and if your hook drags along the bottom it may dull the hook point and decrease your chance of effective penetration in the carp's mouth. Little things like this are always worth considering as they can form the fine line between success and failure.

Perfecting the Distance

Although you might not believe it at the moment, there will come a time when you will be able to judge a cast of around 100yd or so if it is going too far. Believe me, with practice, a good eye and some thought you will be able to master long-range carping. However, until then if you are to be sure you are spot-on each and every time you will have to have a precise mark at which to fish, or a certain way of ascertaining if you are in the correct spot each time. There are quite a number of ways of doing this, but I will describe the three I favour.

1. This first method involves fishing to a marker float. Providing you can get your marker float out to the prescribed spot, an excellent way of making sure you are in the correct spot each time is to leave the marker out there during the length of your stay. Whilst this sounds good it does, however, have a number of drawbacks. Having all that line out to your baited area, you are just asking for a carp to pick it up when you get a take, thereby causing all sorts of difficulties with two lines out to one fish. You could, of course, wind down your marker so it is tight to the lake's bottom but you still have all that line running out and a pike float sitting in your baited area.

If you do want to fish to a marker, you should really put the marker in the correct position, mark on a piece of paper its line of sight *and* mark your line with liquid paper so you know just how far out you are. When you have cast your hookbait to the correct mark, wind your marker back in and put it behind you in the swim, so moving out that possible source of tangles. However, each time you want to replace your baited rod to

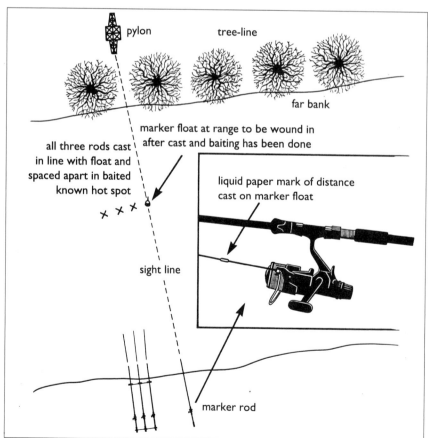

Fig. 86 *The marker rod at distance.*

a marker you will need to recast the marker first and then cast the hookbait at it. This, of course, means that you have twice the level of disturbance in your swim each time and, things being as they are, the wind will probably get up and stop you putting your marker out to the same spot again!

2. The second method is in fact very similar, but instead of using a marker float time and time again, you use it once and then mark all your fishing lines with liquid paper between butt ring and reel (*see* Fig. 86). Make sure you have marked down sight lines for each rod in turn so that you know precisely at what trees, pylon, opposite bivvy and so on, your rod is being cast. Then it's just a case of lining up your mark each time and casting out towards that mark. Once your liquid paper mark starts to show as the line nears the target zone in mid-cast, start to feather it down so that the mark is no more than a rod's length beyond your rod tip. Then tighten up and, with luck, the mark will be in roughly the same position as it was when you originally cast out.

I am sure some of you will think that you won't be able to do this, but I know that you can – providing you cast smoothly and don't feather the cast down too hard. If you do drop a couple of yards short, cast out again. Do not leave it and hope, because your rod may be out there for hours before you need to cast again. It is a lot more sensible to recast it properly first time around!

After each cast always put more liquid paper on the same mark as it does tend to wear off in time. I use white liquid paper for Sylcast lines which are brown, or green liquid paper if I'm using white Berkley Big Game line. Both are available from any good newsagents and I've never found them to damage the line.

3. If you don't feel you can trust yourself to feather the line down each time, then another good method is the band, tape or rubber band method. All you do is put your marker out and put your baited rods out to it. Then, when you've marked the line with liquid paper, pull off a couple of turns of line via the clutch and put a piece of black electrical tape on the spool. Rewind the line again to the liquid paper mark and you're all set up. This is an almost foolproof method in that each time you do recast, the line cannot come off beyond the tape or rubberband, and by the time you have tightened up, your mark should be in the correct place. Don't worry that your cast may be stopped dead in mid-cast by the band, as the reality is that providing you don't cast stupidly it will gradually slow down and as the line is not completely tight in mid-flight, any jerking effect will be absorbed by the slack in the line. You don't have to use electrical tape – rubber bands and the like are just as good.

So, there you have three good ways of marking the distance each time you cast out at range. As I said earlier, you may not believe it but experience will help you, and soon you will be wondering what all those initial self-doubts were about!

GETTING THE FREEBIES OUT

Although the old maxim 'better to have one single bait in the right place than to have a hundred in the wrong place' does apply, there is often a case to be put forward for having your hookbait resting in a group of freebies. Whilst I don't think you need to have your hookbait surrounded by freebies *all* the time, it is nice to be in a position where, if the need arises, you can put them out. As stated earlier, I'm sure that with practice everybody who has decent tackle will be able to cast at least 100yd accurately and up to 120yd in the right conditions. However, once you've mastered that technique, how do you get your freebies out to the same distance as your hookbait? There are quite a number of ways, but I will simply deal with the methods I use – I'm positive they will work for you as well.

Stringer Method
I discussed the stringer in Chapter 5, but this is a method many people like to fish when long-range carping. It is certainly something I like to use, providing it does not affect my ability to hit the

target zone accurately and regularly. Normally, I fish a two- or three-bait stringer tied off the hook which does stop tangles when you are not using tubing. Do remember, however, that a stringer attached to your hook by PVA may affect your presentations, so don't tie one to a 3in pop-up and automatically expect the pop-up to be popped up over the stringer as it should be. The weight of the stringer may drag the pop-up into the weed, so you may not have the presentation out there that you thought you had!

A stringer will magnify the normal smell round your hookbait, but even so it may not interest nomadic carp travelling yards away because they may not come close enough to pick up on the attraction. If you can't be certain your stringer is exactly in the hot spot, it may be advisable to use a scattering of bait – as I shall discuss later.

Necklace Method

By threading the baits tight to the lead and PVA loop, you have a very aerodynamic and weighted load which can usually be cast further than a hookbait alone due to whirling hooklengths and so on. Within ten to twenty minutes you should be able to put a couple of pounds of bait out to the area, using three or four baits per necklace. The minus points are that the sixty to eighty casts that are needed to get all the bait out there do create a lot of disturbance which may or may not be detrimental. It also takes up a lot of PVA!

Catapult Method

A normal catapult such as a Drennan Feederpult will generally be able to put a fairly hard 18–20mm boily around 80yd out with accuracy, providing there is little wind. With a wind in your face you can subtract at least 10yd from that; with a wind at your back, add 10yd. Over the years I have found this brand to be the best around and, providing your boily is hard enough, round enough and big enough, you should be able to put out a nice carpet of bait at that range. I've since tried Fox's new Rollapult and the Wychwood Reddipult, and although these add a little distance, to be fair, baiting up at over 100yd is not usually possible with any catapult.

Throwing Stick Method

It seems that most anglers have a throwing stick now, despite them having been on the market for only a few years. However, whilst eight out of ten carp anglers have one, I doubt if three in ten are even moderately proficient with one. If you don't believe me then stand behind an angler who is using one with perfectly round boilies – he will probably be all over the place with them. Stand at the side of a pond to watch variations in distance and you will be amazed at the inaccuracy of most people. This is due purely and simply to lack of practice, a lazy arm or too much effort.

The only way to be proficient at using a throwing stick is to practise, practise and practise some more. People do not naturally become good stickers, but become so through practice and hard work. Until you are accurate enough, do not put bait out when you are fishing as in my opinion bait that falls all over the place whilst you are fishing is detrimental rather than advantageous. Certainly, practise at the end of a session to pile out your remaining baits or to pre-bait, but while your rods are in their rests and you are fishing, leave it alone! Round boilies, heavy boilies, a clean and polished throwing stick, and practice will all increase your range; misshapes, soft baits, a sticky inner and laziness will all impede your range. One thing I would say about putting bait out is that if conditions are favourable, do get it out straight away rather than messing about with your bivvy or bedchair because if you do leave it for thirty minutes or so, the wind is bound to be up. Don't say I didn't warn you – it has caught us all out before!

How Much?

I covered much of what I want to say on this subject in Chapter 6, but I will make one or two points on quantity of bait whilst range fishing.

If you are the first angler who is able to really exploit fishing at range on your water, I would advise you use single hookbaits as often as you can. A bait where a carp has never seen one before tends to work well on all the waters I've known and, providing that it is a bait which the carp are willing to pick up, it's on a form of presentation in which it can be picked up and it is in a place where it will be picked up, I am ninety per cent sure you will score on a regular basis. Between visits or after fishing I may be tempted to stick a few baits out in such an area, but I wouldn't feel it necessary to do so, or detrimental not to do so.

If the single bait approach *anywhere* at range has been used, you may well have to start searching and working hard to find the most *productive* spots at range. All I will say is that it is vital that you record distance and direction of each rod to see which is productive and which is not. It is no good having a take and then having no real idea where that take came from, except that it was 'somewhere out there'. Again, I would be tempted to fish single hookbaits at the spot, but would possibly amplify their presence by way of a stringer, or flavour capsule or dip.

If your fish are shoal fish *and* the method of a large bed of bait hasn't been used, it can be advantageous to fish a bait (pop-up, stringer and so on) over a large bed of bait. However, putting a bed of bait out at 100–120yd is far harder than trying to put a bed of baits out at 60yd. Your throwing-stick arm will get tired from constant use, the dreaded tufties, ducks and swans will start to wise up and it will take a long time to put

3–6lb of bait out at this distance. However, if it hasn't been done it *can* be productive.

In a nutshell, at range I would have as little bait out there as possible when fishing unless I felt it necessary to educate or pull fish down into that area to feed.

EXTREME-RANGE FISHING

I was tempted to devote a chapter to extreme fishing (130yd plus), but because so few anglers need to fish at such range, because so few will be able to fish at such range, and because so few will be able to afford to fish at such range, it has little practical use to readers of this book. Instead, I will keep the information basic and not give details which will be irrelevant to many anglers.

Once you start looking at 130–160yd casting and effective angling, you are talking about very specialized fisheries, the need for expensive purpose-designed tackle and a considerable amount of hard work and graft. While such extreme-range fishing may be necessary on waters such as Harefield, I honestly don't think that most anglers will need to worry about it. If you do feel your water is a similar fishery and really want to start improving your technique,

Daiwa SS 3000s, the best money can buy.

A large carp taken at extreme range.

tackle and awareness then please look at the suggested additional reading matter in the Further Reading section at the end of the book. I do occasionally fish at extreme distance so I have included details and thoughts on tackle towards which you can look.

Rods

To go for extreme-range fishing in a really big way, look for 12ft fast-taper rods of at least 2½lb test curve and *not* more than 3lb. My personal choice is Daiwa's Amorphous 12ft, 2¾lb Infinity, but I know many do rate Rob Maylin's Extreme Pursuit and Rod Hutchinson's 12ft 3½lb test curve IMX.

Reels

To utilize the full potential of your rod, you do need to purchase a reel capable of long casting. Top of the range is Daiwa's SS3000, with the Shimano 8000 Aerlex and Daiwa's PM400H not far behind.

Balanced Rod and Reel

This is vital in all carp fishing situations but is indispensable for ultimate range carping. You must have a top-range rod and reel which can hit over 130yd consistently in all conditions. Until you have both, you might as well have neither, so be prepared to dig deep into your funds!

Line

No special line is really needed, but I would stick to 7lb Sylcast main line if I was confident that I was not going to get snagged up in weed or cut off on a gravel bar. If conditions dictated, I would move up to a 9lb Sylcast main line and make the shock leader as short as possible.

Shock Leader

Unless you are an exceptionally good caster and can cast 130yd with straight-through 15lb main line, you will need to have a leader of some form. For big punches and 3–4oz leads you *must* upgrade your leader material to a minimum of 18–20lb breaking strain. My choice is Big Game in 20lb and on as short a length as possible to increase range.

Buzzers, Rod Rests and Indicators

There is very little difference here from the tackle you would need to use up to 130yd. However, remember that the further out you go the more magnified will be any problems or defects your tackle has. Lines need to be bowstring-tight, with heavy monkeys set spot-on. You should not tolerate any form of movement in your rod rests.

End Tackle and Presentation

You will have to cut out tubing and make your rig as streamlined as possible to get those few vital yards that can make the difference between success and failure. Streamlined leads, short hooklinks, short hairs and small baits all increase range by a certain percentage. If you really feel unsure about a tangle due to lack of tubing, then PVA *one* free offering tight to the hair, hookbait and hook. This will almost certainly cut out tangles, will not reduce your effective casting range too much and will double the attractor signal of your bait.

Casting

There is absolutely no leeway here at all – you must have a practised and smooth action or all the tackle you have just bought will be wasted. This casting technique does take some time to master, so those who purchase rods and reels without having the ability to use them to the full will have to wait until they do so. No amount of money will give you technique.

Getting the Freebies Out

To be able to put a freebie out over 130yd definitely requires more than a catapult. You may be able to get away with a one-bait stringer or a two-bait necklace, but you certainly will have to look towards a King Cobra throwing stick or the like. As with casting, it takes a long time to master the use of such a throwing stick and you will only put baits out with any degree of accuracy if they are rock-hard, dense, perfectly round and if your throwing stick is the correct one and is well maintained. Your effective distance will, to a large extent, be governed by wind direction as well at this sort of range. A back wind is an advantage, providing you can put enough height on your freebie to allow that wind to carry it. A slight wind in the face is also an advantage because it gives your bait lift for the last 30yd or so. Side winds are a definite disadvantage, and a strong head wind is the kiss of death!

Don't be intimidated by the last section on extreme-range fishing as very few anglers will ever need it to use the information it contains. In fact, I can confidently say that some anglers will *never* need to cast over 130yd. However, it is an advantage to be aware of what is available, and if you do have the money and inclination to purchase these rods and reels then it makes casting up to 130yd a lot easier!

BOATS

No chapter on long-range fishing would be complete without at least a few words on putting your hookbait and freebies out via radio-controlled boats or inflatables.

Radio-Controlled Boats

Love them or hate them, radio-controlled boats are allowed on some carp waters and are readily

Weed, lilies, trees and bushes – carp in abundance?

available, so we shall have to get used to them. As they allow you to place all sorts of no-tube combinations and complex presentations, and drop them with freebies precisely in the correct spot, they do give you a distinct advantage. If boats are allowed and you want to use one, then do so and accept that your results should be comparatively better than those who don't use them. This doesn't mean that you are a better angler, just an angler who is using an edge. Similarly, if somebody else is using them and catching numbers of carp, don't feel downhearted – compare your results only to those of anglers not using a boat.

Inflatables

One step beyond radio-controlled boats is the inflatable dinghy, whereby you actually drop your baited tackle and freebies by hand. You can place your hookbait in clear spots if you can see the bottom, and huge beds of mini-particles and the like can be put out with deadly effect. As before, your results can be better than those of bankside anglers so don't kid yourself about your own ability if you do well.

However, do be very careful if you use an inflatable – the tragic death of Andy Mundy shows how dangerous they can be.

8 SNAG FISHING

Most people who fish for carp will encounter some form of snags and snag fishing in their water. This may be as little as an overhanging willow branch or distant tree-fringed margin. Mind you, it could equally be some sunken trees, a sunken landing stage or worse. Most waters have snags, and if there is one thing that is guaranteed to make an angler inefficient it is a snag of one form or another.

You can picture the scene, can't you? A sunken bush shows its tip some 20yd out, probably a good haunt for carp throughout most of the year. So what does our angler do? He chucks a bait at it and scatters a few freebies around the general location of the visible snag. He gives no thought at all as to how big the snag is, what lies between him and the visible snag, whether his tackle, which is geared mainly to margin fishing, is up to the task, and so on. In other words, he has gone on to auto-pilot and, if by some fluke he does get a take and it snags him up, there will be some rod bending, line cracking and cursing. However, it's not the carp's fault but the angler's! A little thought goes a long way in carp fishing, and nowhere is this more true than when fishing to snags.

In this chapter I will take an in-depth look at snag fishing so that hopefully the risk factor is lessened for you. You don't always need to fish to snags, but let's hope in future that when you do you have a good chance of getting it right and ending up with a carp in your hands rather than a fluttering line in your rod rings!

WHAT ARE SNAGS?

This is an almost never-ending list as anything from thick weed to a sunken barge could be classed as a snag; what is a snag to one man may just be a feature to another. Below I list the main snags you may encounter in waters and discuss how difficult I have found it to extract carp from such features.

Visible sunken trees These are a typical feature in many waters I've encountered and one near which carp tend to spend a great deal of time. A visible snag is a lot easier to fish to, but remember that it will also attract the lazy carper who just chucks out in its general direction with no thought whatsoever. This can result in lost fish, and this in turn *can* mean that carp in such areas may be edgy due to continual hooking and losing.

Invisible sunken trees These are very difficult to fish to and are all too common on some waters. No matter how you attempt to map out such an area, you will never get the true picture unless you swim over it or drift over it on a boat. Obviously, if you locate 'the spot' it can be to your advantage as you will know exactly where to cast and the lazy carper won't even know it's there. However, trying to land your carp will be your main problem.

Sunken branches and boards Show a child an iced-over water and the first thing he or she will do is start skidding tree branches across its surface. This is all good fun until the ice melts and you end up with debris all over the place. The same goes for those stormy autumn days when branches are blown into the water and end up in the most unexpected places. Some, of course, will float, but other larger ones will sink. Generally, these branches will drift along until they meet some form of resistance such as weed or mud – this goes a long way towards explaining why some gravel bars are covered in snags and why some weedbeds contain immovable areas. Like the sunken tree pieces mentioned above, if you can locate a sunken branch it's a good bet for a carp, but it's also a hit-and-miss affair trying to find them and land fish from them.

Weedbeds If one thing is guaranteed to hold carp for months it's areas of thick weed growth. Loved by carp and carp anglers alike, these areas are a magnet to both and one of your best bets on most waters. For unknown reasons some carp anglers steer clear of weed, but by doing so they cut down on their options somewhat. Providing your tackle is sensible, your bait is placed in the appropriate spot and that you are alert, you can land fish from such areas with regularity.

Lily beds These are brilliant in summer as carp love to bask around them. They are also a good choice in winter when food items collect around them, providing feeding areas in low temperatures. I used to have trouble landing carp from lily bed areas until I learnt that the trick was not to pull their heads off if they got in them, but instead to try to lead or con them out. Berkley's Big Game is brilliant in such areas.

Masonry and poles Time and elements such as wind and rain play havoc with fisheries, and on some of the waters I fish it's not uncommon to find broken landing stages, mooring poles and discarded masonry out in the water. Again, carp do frequent such areas but landing carp from them is a very hit-and-miss affair. These snags tend to be almost impossible to extract carp from, and you will find your main line and hooklengths part with frequency.

Gravel bars and zebra mussels If any of you have never fished a gravel pit before you won't believe the problem that such areas can cause. Quite literally, you can have a screaming run, pick the rod up and find your line frayed and fluttering in the rings. Such cut-offs are down to gravel bars, zebra mussels and the like, and are frustrating to say the least!

WHY FISH SNAGS?

The answer to this is a easy one – because you are usually in with a chance of a take. Perhaps it would be easier to ask why carp frequent such areas? I know that many anglers used to believe that carp laid up in such areas in the day to relax or escape from pressure. However, I have caught far too many carp at night and when there has been a lot of pressure on such areas for this theory to be *totally* true.

Whilst I certainly believe that pressure will push carp into snags, I believe there are just as many other carp in there for different reasons. Clearly, if nobody has ever fished to those snags the carp may choose them as holding areas, moving out to feed later in the day or at night. Personally, I just think that carp like to be in such areas, but I'm not sure why. It could be a result of the high natural food stocks you find there. I know that when I have dragged snags out they have been literally alive with food. Mind you, that would probably apply to other areas as well. It could also be a result of the fear aspect – such snags or heavy weed growth offer them protection from anglers' lines. That is, of course, until anglers cotton on to such areas and everybody starts casting at these snags! The carp will then move elsewhere – but they will be back! Whatever the reasons, snags are good places to fish.

Hopefully, I have now convinced you of the advantages of fishing to snags – now all I have to do is get the game plan sorted out. Snag fishing is like all other aspects of carping: you identify the problem and then decide how to approach it. Those who solve the problems quickest catch first; those who solve them more often than not catch consistently. All you need to do is first identify what problems there will be when fishing to your snag, and then identify the answer to each problem.

GAME PLAN FOR SNAG FISHING

The game plan consists of the following steps: find and map out the snags; have the correct tackle to land the carp; have the correct approach to land the carp; and follow the plan through.

I shall now look at each step in a little more detail.

Finding and Mapping Out Snags

No matter how visible or apparent a snag looks, no matter how much you've been told about that snag, and no matter how much you know or think you know about that snag, it really is advisable that you map it out beforehand. Whilst it may not be necessary to actually draw a map, it's vital that you spend time with a spare rod to feel for snags and so on. No doubt some of you will think that this is all too much like hard work – well, it may be. However, if you want to catch carp, and particularly big carp, nothing should be too much work for you. Every time you see prolific big fish anglers in the paper with a huge carp, you know their success is not a result of luck but that it is all down to hard work. You too can do it if you just try hard enough.

When fishing to snags I always have a spare rod set up so that I can lead about to feel the nature of the bottom. By casting around for up to half an hour at a time I know how far the snag extends, if there's anything between me and the snag, where clear patches are, and what the nature of the bottom is. You may think that this scares the carp off, but although this might happen initially I have found that they will soon be back. If your plan is correct you should catch them rather than lose them.

I simply take my old SS6 fibreglass rod loaded with 12lb Sylcast and, using old leads, spend as much time as I can mapping out the area in front

of me. If I intend to fish this spot on a regular basis, I will mark my findings on a piece of paper. Memories are funny things and once darkness falls it can all change in terms of perspective. A quick sketch takes no more than a minute or two and will save you a lot of grief in the long run. Things like tree lines and direction of cast can all be logged down carefully – it is worth it.

Take a look at the two sketches showing two swims full of snags (*see* Figs 87 and 88). These are not imaginary swims from make-believe waters, but are two swims on one of my waters, the Motorway Pond. Both swims are full of snags so I will describe how to approach them to find out the best spot for a bait.

Starting with the swim shown in Fig. 87, assume you have set yourself up in '1 down'. Obviously, there is a group of snags to your left at around 30yd or so, and also to your right at 50yd or so. If you didn't intend to do any work beforehand it would be so easy just to drop a bait on the end of each of those snaggy areas and also one in the edge to catch margin feeders. The trouble is, unless you were lucky you would probably lose any fish you hooked in snags you didn't know were there. However, half an hour's work with a leading rod will have shown you the true size of the snags, one or two sunken snags and a nice bar running between both areas.

A rod cast at point A means that you have to hit and hold or you are lost, as is the case at point B. However, placing your bait at point C on the end of the bar means that as long as the fish doesn't kite you will not need to pressure it too much. Obviously, once in the margins you will have to watch out for the sunken snag to your left, but at least as you know it is there you have a chance of leading the carp away from it.

Moving on to Fig. 88, your main problem here is weed. However, with a little thought and sensible choice of tackle you will catch carp. Initially, the Cold Hole looks a good bet as you have a nice easy walk and lots of places to fish to. The trouble is, however, that if you fish from this swim you will always have to bring the carp through the huge sunken weedbed in front of you. Instead of pulling a carp away from the weed, you will be

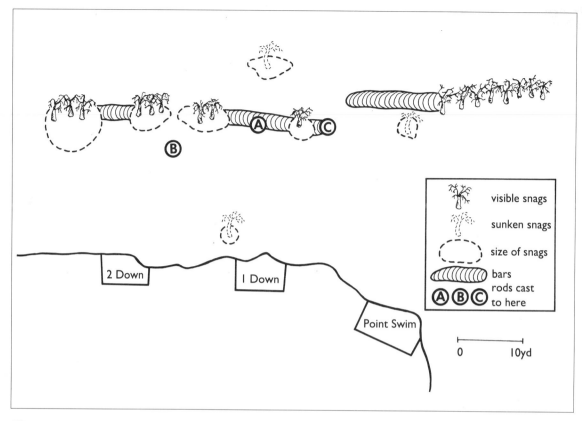

Fig. 87 Snag Swim 1.

pulling it into the weed. It is far better to walk a little further to Thomo's Point and cast to those same spots – as long as you prevent the carp from kiting to the left you should be in with a good chance of landing them.

So, in both situations you may need to spend half an hour with your leading rod, but it *will* benefit you in the long run.

The Correct Tackle to Land the Carp
In an ideal world we would all possess long-range rods, floater rods, snag rods and so on. However, this is a book on practical carp fishing so I realize that most will have to make do with what they have and make sure it can do the job required. If the tackle you have is not up to hooking and holding carp away from the snags, do not even entertain the idea of fishing to them; it's a totally pointless exercise. It is far better to put your time

in where you have a reasonable chance of landing the carp than losing fish after fish. I know that some will ignore this, but I can assure you that if your tackle is not up to it then the carp will tell you even if you don't know it yourself. By the time you've lost half a dozen in the snags you will have had enough!

Rods
Clearly, your rod needs to be strong enough to cast at least 2oz to the snags and also be strong enough once the carp is hooked to draw it away from potential disaster areas. I tend not to fish to snags once they are over 60yd away, as the further out you are the more chance the carp has of getting into them before you stop it. Most rods will cast 2–3oz, so it is just a question of whether they have the backbone to pull the carp away. Don't think that because your rod is soft it is an

A big-water success in ideal feeding conditions.

Opposite: *the ultimate prize from a well-known big water.*

Left: *an ample reward for sticking at it all winter long.*

Below: *torrential rain, yet still the carp fed.*

Despite the bankside conditions some waters are worth persisting with.

A night-time specimen taken at very long range.

Three feet of fighting machine.

A large bed of hemp attracted this whacker.

A single bait to a clear spot on the bar produced this lovely carp.

A change in hook pattern stopped the run of lost fish for me.

Once on the bank they are totally in your hands.

At 30lb 12oz, this was the lake record for me.

One of four weighing over 20lb taken in a day.

Three mid-twenties taken in six hours – good bait does produce dividends.

Bottom left: *one of a number of doubles taken on floater tackle one memorable afternoon.*

Bottom right: *moving off the fishmeals and on to the birdseed produced instant success.*

Twenty twenty-pounders – ambition achieved!

A nice double in the snow at Willow Park.

Twenty minutes later the lake froze over.

A special moment on a weekend grueller.

Brace shots – my last one over four years ago. Perhaps something to think about?

Large or small – do you need to photograph them all?

Keep still, will you!

It doesn't just have to be trophy shots.

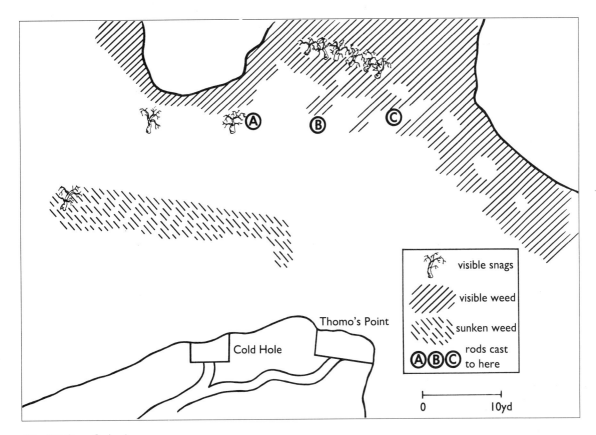

Fig. 88 *Snag Swim 2.*

ideal tool – it may actually be too soft to utilize the line strength. No matter how strong your line is, if your rod is too sloppy the carp you hook will be in snags before you can stop them. Also, don't think that fast-taper rods are too tippy – because I have found that they work, providing that you do take care once the carp is in the margin. To be fair, most rods of 11–13ft with a 2lb test curve or more will do the job; if they are not up to it you will soon find out!

Reels

When the initial take and hooking takes place, your rod and reel will be subjected to an almighty surge of power. Consequently, any deficiencies in them will be shown up immediately and the carp may reach the snags. Most reels will do, providing you can load sufficiently strong line on to them and still be able to cast the required

distance. Never set your reels to backwind as you will be scrambling to grab that flying reel handle as the carp is through the snags and away, or buried deep in the weed. You need a reel which also allows you to fish either off the clutch or off the baitrunner. I know baitrunner systems are very popular at the moment, but personally I prefer to fish with a slackened clutch. Using a baitrunner you have to engage the handle in order to click in the preset clutch. This takes a valuable second which could cost you fish, and I fear that the strain imposed on that 'flick-over point' could damage your reel gearing system. In my opinion, it is far better to slacken your clutch off a little so that the carp can only just take line and, once you get a run, simply cup the front of the spool with one hand whilst striking and screw the rear clutch tighter with the other. Don't just be a fashion follower; use your brain and you will

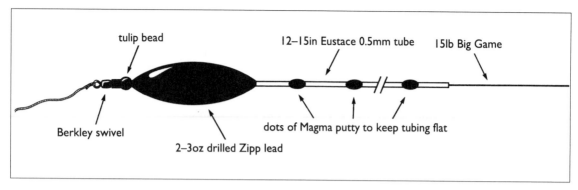

Fig. 89 *In-line end tackle.*

be surprised just what a difference this can make. Front-clutch reels have no place in your set-up when snag fishing because by the time you've got your fingers round that drag at the front of the reel you may have missed your chance!

Line

Your line clearly needs to be sufficiently strong to allow you to hook the carp and pull it away from its natural haven of weed or tree snags. Stretch in the line is necessary to cushion this harnessing of power, but it should not be so great that the power of the rod is lost in the give of the line. Prestretched lines such as Drennan Double Strength have no place in this type of situation. Also, your line will be placed in areas of high abrasion so it does need to have a high degree of abrasion resistance, even if you change it regularly. My favourite is 15lb Berkley Big Game for most snag and weed fishing, and I feel that this is as good a choice as any. However,

even though it is a very good line I would not hesitate to change it at least once a month as constant snag fishing exerts pressures on it and just one nick or flat spot in it will weaken it. It is far better to have less bait that weekend than a line which will let you down.

Rigs

The two 'lead' rigs I favour when fishing to snags are illustrated in Figs 89 and 90. Both have their plus and minus points, but I must emphasize that they must only be used when you are not using a shock leader. Because the tube is fine it will not pass over a leader knot, so that if you do break off at the leader knot a carp may end up towing a 30ft piece of heavy line around. This could result in tethering, which at best causes distress and injury to carp, and at worst causes death. I don't recommend snag fishing at range, so straight-through main line should not cause problems.

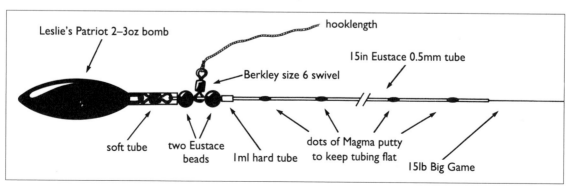

Fig. 90 *Helicopter end tackle.*

Presentations

In Chapter 5 I covered all the main hook and hooklength set-ups I would advise you to try. Most of those will work in snag-fishing situations. All I would say is that you should keep your set-up as simple as possible – do remember that the more complex your set-up is, the more chance you have of snagging up.

Whilst it is always vital that you tie good knots and check hooklengths in all carp fishing situations, it is even more vital when you fish snags. This type of fishing can test your tackle to the limit because of the initial surge of power, and a knot which isn't quite right, a hook which is a bit rusty or a hooklength which is somewhat frayed will come to grief in such situations. Do not risk it.

In snag fishing you may need to hook and hold, or at least need to be in a position in which you can put pressure on the carp. You may need to increase your hooklength strength to, say, 15lb Merlin or 25lb Silkworm, and perhaps your hook size to, say, a 2, 4 or 6. Hooks do need to be strong, so I would look towards a proven strong pattern like Partridge Z2 or Z.15, Drennan Boily Hook, Drennan Super Specimen or Terry Eustace Gaper Carp. It has been my experience that you can increase your hook size and hooklength ratings in such circumstances and get away with it, even if you couldn't in open water. Clearly, if you are not getting the chances you may need to think again. Always start heavy and *possibly* scale down, rather than starting light and losing fish.

Buzzers and Indicators

Unless you are fishing the confidence set-up as described on page 134, you will be fishing a bolt-rig presentation. I am sure in theory that it would be nice to fish confidence set-ups and have a carp moving about steadily, not realizing it is hooked, but other than on one or two occasions I'm not sure I can guarantee that. As you will generally be fishing self-hooking set-ups, the hard work will be done as soon as that line tightens. So you need to know as soon as possible that the fish has been hooked before it gets into its sanctuary. There is absolutely no point at all in fishing brilliant baits on great presentations in perfect spots if you allow the carp to reach its sanctuary before you can stop it because of poor bite indication.

Generally, you will be fishing at close to medium range (0–60yd), so you should be able to fine-tune your set-up for minimum movement and maximum indication. The diagram in Fig. 91 shows my ideal set-up – if conditions allow it. Unless I am convinced carp are line-shy I fish my line as tight as possible with the rod tip as low as possible and angled to the snags. The line is

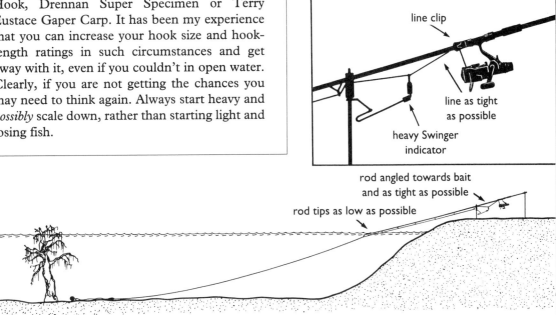

Fig. 91 Indication set-up.

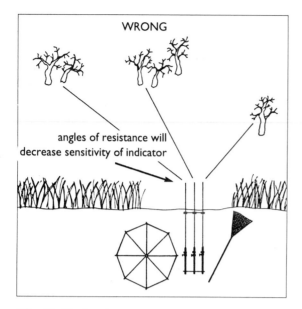

Fig. 92 Single rod rests.

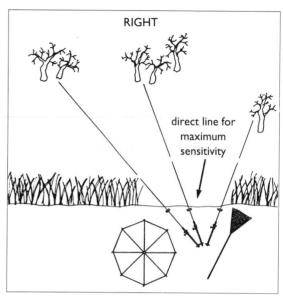

Fig. 93 Buzzer bar problems.

clipped on to a back clip as tight as possible, and I use as heavy a Swinger as possible so that the slightest flicker of movement shows. Buzzers are set as loud as possible and if I am using Optonic type models I make sure I have in an eight-paddle vane.

Remember that you want your indicator to sound at the slightest movement so you can strike, hit, hold and land that carp. Whilst I know it isn't the done thing, use single front rod rests so each rod is pointing directly at the hookbait (*see* Fig. 92). As you can see from the diagram, having a fixed front rod rest causes resistance, more line out in the water and more chance of the carp making his sanctuary before you stop him – compare the correct set-up to that in Fig. 93. Whilst it may seem such a little thing, it is these fine-tunings that separate the successes from the 'nearlies'. For that reason I tend not to use back-leads as, due to the angle between lead, backlead and indicator, these ruin your sensitivity. Unless you really feel you need to use them, then try to do without them.

The Correct Approach to Land the Carp
Whilst it's necessary to have the correct tackle to hook and land carp, it's just as important to have

the correct approach to snag fishing; chucking a rig in the general direction of a snag and hoping is going to cost you carp. You must be positive and make sure all the advantages that you can possibly think of are in your court and not in the carp's. After all, the carp has an advantage over you anyway – it can choose when, where and how to feed, it is a master of its own environment, and whilst your incentive is 'photographed fish', its incentive is survival.

By now you will hopefully have mapped the place out and picked the tackle to do the job 'in all the circumstances' – now you have to decide where to put the hookbait. The first thing you will probably do is to cast as near as possible to that weedbed or snag tree. This is almost a nat-ural reaction – the closer you are the more con-fident you feel. Unfortunately, the closer you are the more likely you are to lose that fish. When fishing to snags such as trees and thicket bushes, a bait too close to such a feature will cost you fish. Instead, start by fishing your baits at least 6–12ft away and gradually move them closer if you feel you are obviously missing out on convertible chances. You may be saying to yourself that on your water the only way to get a chance is to fish next to the snag. Well, unless it's a hard-fished water, I doubt this. I agree that it's a good way to get a lot of runs, but it is far better to have two runs and land them both than to have ten runs and lose all ten!

When fishing to weed or up to lilies you can get a little closer as weed doesn't snap or fray lines as tree stumps and the like do. I've found weeded fish are extractable but I like to keep them out of it in the first place. In soft weed you can pull them out gently, but in heavy weed you may either need to lead them out or con them out!

One thing I wouldn't advise you to do, even though many people seem to, is to make lines of bait between the centre of the snags and your hookbait. My personal experience is that when I am fishing, the least amount of bait I have out there the better. I believe that if they want a bait it should have a hook in it. After all, you don't need to entice fish into the area as they are hopefully already there. Your bait should be an instantly acceptable one and, as carp are inquisitive

creatures, I believe they will venture out to pick it up. With large amounts of bait all over the place you are decreasing your chances of a pick-up on the law of averages alone, and I don't feel it's necessary in such circumstances. By all means bait up when you leave, but do make sure that you bait all over the place so that the carp get used to finding baits away from the very worst of the snags. Obviously, if carp are not leaving the central snag or weed areas you may need to entice them with trails of bait for a while, but there will come a time when they will have it and you want to be sure you at least have a convertible chance.

Having sorted all that out, it is vital that you formulate some sort of plan on how to land the carp once they have been hooked. It is pointless leaving this decision until you get a take – you may panic, the fish will be in the weed and you will have wasted a convertible chance. So decide what to do in advance. My usual plan of action is as follows:

The inflatable boat – cheating or just an edge?

1. As lines are so low and tight I hit any bleeps or line movements.

2. In order to strike them I cup my right hand over the spool cover and, using my left hand, I screw up the clutch. If I have overscrewed the clutch it is compensated for by line stretch.

3. When the rod hits something firm I move backwards, so taking up all the slack and moving the fish away from the snags.

4. Until I am sure the fish is out of the danger zone I remain the 'bully'.

Once you have formulated your plan, stick to it.

Following it Through

Having done all the hard work you must follow your game plan through. Whether it's dawn, dusk or midday you have to follow exactly the same procedure of hooking and landing those carp. Unless it's a day-only water you will inevitably hook carp at night as well. Does your plan of action take this into account? Should your baits be a little further from the snags than you first decided? Can you find your landing net easily in the dark? Do you need to put wellies or waders on to net the fish? With this type of fishing there is no time to mess about putting coats on or doing shoes up. You've got to be on your

rods and master of the situation from first bleep. When I am fishing close to weed or snags I don't bother with shoes at all and prefer to wade out in stocking feet or keep a pair of unlaced trainers next to my rods that I can slip on just prior to netting. I always keep a torch next to the landing net and have the landing net mesh taped to the handle to avoid tugs of war with bramble bushes, needle tops, reel handles and so on. Be prepared and you will be successful!

So there you have it, a guide to fishing up to snags. I'm sure some of you won't agree with what I've had to say, but these are specifically my findings and do not repeat those of other carp anglers. One point I haven't mentioned is that of fishing confidence rigs next to snags – until very recently this had not worked for me at all. The theory is that the carp picks the bait up but does not panic, allowing you to hook him, surprise him and gain the upper hand immediately (*see* Fig. 94). Whilst this is not a tactic I have found to work with any degree of consistency, I have used it as a last resort and occasionally it has worked. Whether it has worked because of the confidence aspect or in spite of it I don't know; as in all carp fishing only the carp really know the answer.

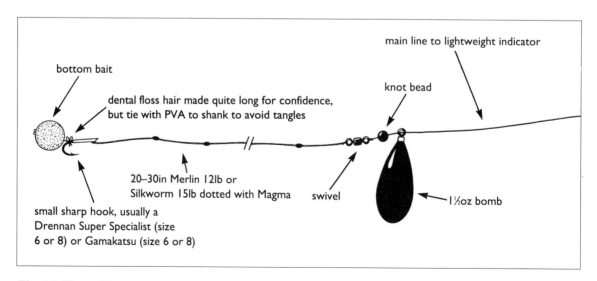

Fig. 94 *The confidence presentation.*

9 WINTER CARP FISHING

As pictures of carp appear in the angling press so regularly, it is tempting to think that carp are easy to catch. Unfortunately, the truth is a little different – many carp anglers don't catch as many carp as they could do, relying instead on the defence mechanism of 'talking carp' rather than actually getting out on the bank and fishing. Winter carp fishing is merely an extension of this problem, and for some it's a case of a lot of hot air with not much in the way of actual doing and catching. Time and time again I hear anglers claim that 'this winter I'm going to go carping', but come November or December it's all over for most and very few struggle along in this quarter.

I am sure there are many anglers who have never fished for carp in winter purely and simply because they don't feel they are in with a realistic chance of catching them – this simply is not so! There is not a single angler who, providing they can master the basics and accept that they *may* have to travel a bit, cannot catch a carp or two in winter. In fact, I guarantee that after you've read this chapter you will catch carp in winter if you do follow the advice I've included and pick the correct venue.

Winter carp fishing can be a hard slog at times and, providing you can accept that it is a different ball game from summer carp fishing, you are half-way there. The people who fail to catch in winter are generally the people who come·up with no new ideas for winter carp fishing and who keep to the same plan year in year out, despite its obvious shortcomings. If you do want to catch carp all year round then you will catch, but only if you are prepared to change venue, bait and presentation as necessary. After a few winters you will probably start to wonder what all the fuss was about!

WHAT IS WINTER CARP FISHING?

As there is no textbook definition of the season we call winter, it's very difficult to actually define winter carp fishing. Some writers believe it's the period following the first frosts, but does that therefore mean that it starts in October if you have an overnight ground frost then? Others believe that the true definition of winter carping is when the water temperature drops below 37°C. However, as far as I'm concerned, winter carp fishing is the period starting on 1 November and ending on 1 March. If I can catch carp, between those two dates I'm happy to call them winter carp, no matter what other people may say. During some years you will be lucky and may not have the cold snap until December, but during other years you may see snow on the ground in October. It's up to you to choose your own definition. but you've caught a winter carp as far as I'm concerned if it is after 1 November. After all, it's what matters to you and not others that counts.

WHY FISH FOR CARP IN WINTER?

One thing you must be sure of straight away is that you really want to fish for carp in winter. You should never fish for carp during the season just because you feel you have to. By its very nature, winter can bring snow, rain, ice, twelve hours of darkness and not many fish. If you are not convinced that you really want to go then you will soon be fed up. A fed-up angler does not fish well in summer, never mind during the winter. Accurate casting and rebaiting will become a chore, and watching a dormant water even more so. Unless you really want to be there you won't make that final effort to put the carp on the bank – this can become such a waste of time that it has even broken some carp anglers to the extent that they actually stop fishing altogether. You might not believe this, but I can assure you that it's true; I've seen it happen and I'm sure I will continue to do so. However, providing you do want to fish for carp in winter and can accept that it is usually going to be slower than fishing in summer, you should also be aware that winter carp fishing does have some advantages over summer carp fishing. These are listed below:

1. There are fewer anglers on the bank. I have heard it said that although there may be 150,000 carp anglers in the UK, in winter this decreases to no more than 2,000. I don't find this hard to believe. In summer some waters are teeming with anglers and getting a swim at all, never mind a going swim, is difficult. If you go to the same venue in October or November, however, you will sometimes be hard pressed to find another angler. Although Darenth, Yateley and so on can be packed all year round, these are the exception rather than the rule. So if you want to fish a swim of your choice, then any time from November onwards is the ideal time to be down at the lake.

2. Bumper weights – I would say that at least ninety per cent of carp I've caught in winter have weighed more than their normal summer weights. I'm not quite sure why this is so, but it appears that some carp are not caught in summer and simply build up weight on the huge food stocks available to them (boilies, particles and the water's natural food). If you catch that fish in November or December it could well be up in weight.

3. Certain carp are more catchable – on anything but the most productive waters it has become apparent that after the initial feeding frenzy in May and June some carp seem to disappear all summer. As with bumper weights, I can't state the reason for this other than the fact that in the summer you are competing with the huge natural food stocks which reduce your chances. However, once the first ground frosts knock back these food stocks, *and* providing you are able to find the carp, you are always in with a chance of catching carp that eluded you in summer.

Hopefully, these three reasons will be enough to inspire you on to the banks in winter, but don't go just because I have stated that it is a good time to go; go because you want to.

PLANS, PLANS AND MORE PLANS!

You must plan out your winter carp fishing in advance. It may be too late if you leave it until November before you decide where, how and when you are going to fish – you may find that your choice of winter venue is unavailable (booked up and so on), your bait is an unproven one in which you have no confidence in winter, or 101 other reasons which may make your fishing a wash-out that winter. Each year I see lots of people in tackle shops thinking about winter carp fishing, but when it actually boils down to it, they never do so because they haven't planned it out in advance. Please, if you are seriously thinking about winter carp fishing at a particular venue then plan it out now. Ring up the owners, book your sessions in advance or at least make sure it will be available then. Don't leave it until November – it may be too late! If you are reading this in the warmer months, you should start planning now. If not, don't say I didn't warn you!

WINTER CONSIDERATIONS

For as long as I have fished seriously for carp, it has been apparent to me that to succeed on a regular basis I must plan my fishing out in advance and, if possible, not leave anything to chance. Whilst some people may feel this is stereotyped or makes fishing too mechanical or preplanned, as far as I'm concerned, the more you put into your fishing the more you will get out of it. This particularly applies to winter carp fishing where you cannot afford to go just on the off chance, hoping that your summer fishmeal bait and warm-water presentation will do the trick. Now and again you may get lucky, but I can say with confidence that unless you are a fortunate angler on a particularly productive water, you will *not* catch carp with any sort of regularity. Assuming that you want to catch carp regularly, I advise you to follow these considerations:

correct choice of venue; correct choice of swim; correct choice of bait; correct choice of presentation; and staying the course. All five of these considerations are subject to you having the correct attitude and approach to carp fishing in winter. I look in detail at each consideration throughout this chapter, but to justify each I will open with an example to emphasize the points.

Venue

I had been fishing Drax all summer and had taken some marvellous fish to over 20lb on a heavily-baited birdseed bait. Unfortunately, no one had ever fished Drax in winter before and when I continued to fish on all winter I didn't even have a single run between 3 November and 20 February. Whilst it would be easy to blame the fish, it was all down to the fact that I had picked an unproven winter venue, and had failed accordingly!

At −1°C is this dedication or just stupidity?

Swim

I had fished Willow Park half a dozen times in the summer and, if the previous winter was anything to go by, I expected to catch at least ten to twelve fish each weekend throughout the winter. However, four weekend sessions in the previous year's hot spots failed to produce the goods for me, even though others continued to catch odd fish round the lake. I knew I had a good bait and that my presentation at least matched those who were catching, but because I was not in the correct swim all that was in vain until I managed to get on the fish in early March.

Bait

The fishmeal bait I was using had been very successful all summer and, with eighteen carp over 20lb under my belt by August, I was determined to stick with it all winter, despite a niggling doubt at the back of my mind telling me that I should move on to protein or birdseed. However, it wasn't until I moved on to a birdseed bait that I managed to get action again, proving that even on a water you do know well, you do need a bait the carp will be prepared to eat.

Presentation

Andy Little had invited me down to what he termed an 'easy' singles water to break the winter boredom. Whilst we both fished identical baits in almost the same swim, I kept to my weedy water gear of 12lb hooklength, size 8 hook, 3oz lead and 11lb main line. Andy knew better and stuck with 8lb hooklength, size 12 hooks, 1¼oz leads and 8lb main line. Needless to say, he had thirty-odd fish in a day to my half-dozen. So, even on an easy water you do need to get your presentation spot-on – imagine how important it may be on a water with more wily fish.

Staying the Course

I had battled away all winter at the local lake, but all I had to show for my efforts was one upper double. By late December I was fed up and decided to call it a day. Needless to say, one or two other anglers did stick with it and when I returned to the lake in early April they had taken sixteen fish between them once they had found them. Had I stayed the course and accepted those blanks more philosophically, I may well have had a share of those feeding carp!

So, there you have an example of each consideration where I failed to solve the problems and ended up paying the price. Hopefully, you will learn by my mistakes and let my experience help you along in the long term. I shall now look a little deeper at each factor which may govern your chances of success in winter.

HOW TO CHOOSE A VENUE

I am sure in my own mind that the correct choice of swim, bait and presentation are necessary in winter, but even more important is the correct choice of venue. No matter how good your bait is, no matter how good your presentation is and no matter how good your watercraft may be, it could all go to waste if you pick the wrong venue. All those considerations will definitely improve your chances on even a bad choice of venue, but if you can get all of those right *and* pick a productive winter fishery, you really do stand a good chance of winter action. However, whilst it's very easy to, say, pick a productive water when you know a number, it's far harder if your fishing has been restricted to local waters only. For my first six or seven years I spent winter after winter on unproductive waters, banging my head on what were effectively brick walls. However, as soon as I was put on a productive winter water it all came together, and I now know that 100 doubles between November and March each year is a realistic proposition if I wish to fish for them.

To help you, I list below one or two methods I have used to find productive waters, and I then list ten waters which every angler can visit and be in with a realistic chance of a winter carp. So, how do you go about finding a good winter water? These are the main guidelines many of my friends and I follow:

1. By purchasing either Beekay's *Guide to 1,000 Carp Waters* or my own *Guide to 750 Carp Waters* (Angling Publications). In both publications you will find dozens (if not hundreds) of waters within travelling distance of your home. Both guides also rate some waters as good in winter when they are proven winter waters.

2. By purchasing the regular monthly magazines such as *Carpworld*, *Coarse Fisherman* and *Coarse Fishing*. Certainly in my series of articles in 1992 for *Coarse Fisherman*, I named at least a dozen waters on which I knew anybody would be in with a chance of catching a winter carp. *Carpworld*, being an up-to-date magazine devoted solely to carp, often covers winter carp fishing in detail, so have a look at issues between September and March for pieces devoted to the subject. Providing an author backs up his claims with pictures, you can be pretty sure you are on to a winner, especially when he gives details of the lake. Another good thing about these articles is that they will probably detail the bait and rigs used – if they do, then you are on to a winner. Certainly don't go with pre-fixed ideas in your mind, but don't turn down advice on baits and rigs by successful anglers either.

3. By looking at the water reports published in *Carpworld* and *Big Carp*, and at the list of carp caught from various locations in *Angler's Mail*. This is a particularly useful and usually accurate way of finding out good winter waters, because if you've saved a year or so's copies of *Big Carp*, *Carpworld* or *Angler's Mail* you can see if that year's productive winter carp waters are the same as those of the previous year. If they are, then you won't need to waste your time checking them out. Willow Park, Farlows and Cuttle Mill come up far too often in these water reports to be wind-ups, so keep those magazines if you want to find the best venue.

4. By asking in local tackle shops. Carp anglers are not so secretive nowadays, and an angler who is doing well may want everyone to know about it. By visiting your local tackle shop, providing it is a specialist shop, you will usually be given some good advice on where to and where not to fish in winter. After all, it's in the tackle dealer's interest to make sure you do catch – while you are catching you will keep buying bait and tackle, and that's what keeps those cash tills rattling! Look at the carp pictures on the wall of the shop – some will have been caught in winter and I'm sure that the tackle-shop employees will be only too eager to tell you who caught them, and why and when they were caught.

5. By spending some time on the bank. Spend some of your free time walking round your local waters – although you don't have to ask obvious questions such as 'Is it a good winter water?', you should be able to assess its potential as a winter carp fishery. Most carp anglers are only too willing to help if you are polite and, if the same anglers are there week in, week out from November onwards and have caught fish, it's a fair bet that you could as well. However, when you are walking round waters please use your common sense as some anglers do wish to keep things to themselves – this is their right and it should be respected. A little politeness goes a long way and could save you a lot of wasted hours this winter.

6. By going to regional Carp Society meetings. Between November and May every year, each regional branch of the Carp Society in the UK holds at least two, and sometimes three meetings for members and non-members. As these regions stretch from Scotland to Cornwall, I'm sure your local area is covered. Whilst the speaker may be an out-of-town guest speaker giving a slide show on Yateley, Darenth or the like, you can rest assured that anglers who have fished or are fishing your local waters in winter will be present at the meetings. No doubt some will talk shop and, even if they don't specifically name every single lake, I'm sure you will come away with some knowledge of which lakes do and which don't fish well in winter.

These six main pointers should help you when finding out which venues produce in winter. However, because some anglers are notorious exaggerators, you do have to be careful with what is said. Whilst I don't think that many will deliberately mislead you, some automatically forget to mention all those blanks, preferring instead to concentrate on the fish captures. Do not accept everything as the gospel truth, but use your common sense. Personally, I have been lead up too many false avenues ever to accept something on winter fishing that I couldn't prove for myself. So don't book ten sessions on a water just because someone has told you that it's dead easy and is full of twenty-pounders which just give themselves up in winter. Play it by ear.

Should You Stick with Your Local Water?

I'm sure that whilst some anglers will take my word for it and try the named waters, there will be at least as many who, due to personal choice, lack of transport and so on, will decide to stick to their local waters instead. Personally, however, unless I was 110 per cent confident in my local water producing carp in winter and was also satisfied that I would rather not fish a known winter carp water, I would leave my local venue alone. Whilst I'm sure some anglers will disagree, it has been my experience that some waters just don't produce in winter and, no matter how good a summer water they may be, come November they die a death. I really wish that this wasn't true, but it is – if it wasn't then I certainly wouldn't spend all the money I do on travelling here, there and everywhere each year.

In my local area alone I can name four waters from which I have taken large numbers of fish between May and October, yet by November they are completely dead. It would be nice to think that this was just due to my own inability to locate the carp, but when you have upwards of ten anglers who catch one fish every month or two from a water no more than 3 acres in size, that water could hardly be classified as productive. My personal opinion is that some waters do fish well in winter and some don't.

If you want to amass a good working knowledge of winter carping, do try to make a trip to a good winter venue unless your water is a proven one. I can assure you that you won't regret it. In years to come you can return to your local water to put your experience to the test – who knows, you may be able to unlock the key to cracking it in winter.

Hard 'Name' Waters

There is a temptation when you read books like *Tiger Bay* and *Fox Pool*, and articles in *Big Carp* and *Carpworld* about Savay, Harefield and Yateley to say to yourself 'I am going to have some of that this winter'. Talk of very big thirty-pounders and low forty-pounders will have anybody's adrenalin pumping, and when many of these fish are caught between November and March it is easy to think that these months are the time to get down to those venues for the chance of such a fish. However, although in theory you do have a chance, I have to be brutally honest and say that this chance is actually very slim indeed. Remember that these 'name' venues are fished by very competent anglers indeed, and when anglers who are as talented as Rob Maylin and Kevin Maddocks feel they are banging their heads against a brick wall, what chance do the rest of us have? Between November and March these venues become packed with anglers all hoping for a big carp and, to be fair, if you are a weekend angler you will be lucky if you can even get a swim, let alone a take. Some anglers on Yateley set up in December and don't even go home until the season ends!

All that pressure, all that bait and all those lines in the water makes the job of catching even harder, and until you have done it all or want to blank like the rest, I suggest you leave these waters alone. However, if you do feel you are able to stand the blanks and pressure, I take my hat off to you and wish you well. At the same time, remember that it's a long time between November and March, and come June when we are all raring to go, you may have had enough – wouldn't that be a shame?

Proven Winter Fisheries

Just to prove that you needn't go to a big 'name' fishery, I list below ten fisheries from which most anglers could catch carp during the winter. Hopefully there will be one within travelling distance of your house – now all you need to do is go out and prove me right! Even if these ten are not to your liking, the two *Carp Water* books listed on page 185 detail many more.

Willow Park, Aldershot, Hampshire
This 12-acre gravel pit is very shallow and has a carp stock of 750–1,000 fish. These range from 7–28lb and are easily caught. However, because it is such a prolific fishery you do need to book in advance. For details, telephone John Raison on (0252) 543470.

Cuttle Mill, Sutton Coldfield,
West Midlands
This 5-acre lake is probably the UK's best winter water – providing you can get a place on it. A huge stock of carp of 9–32lb means it is very busy all year round. For details, telephone Tony Higgins on (0827) 872253.

Anglers' Paradise, Beaworthy, Devon
This is a holiday complex of five lakes, with carp present to well over 30lb and averaging upper doubles. This is fishable on season and day tickets, and having produced a thirty-pounder it will be very popular with carp anglers in winter. For details, telephone Zyg Gregorek on (0409) 221559.

Horseshoe Lake, Lechlade, Gloucestershire
This is now a Carp Society water with carp to just below 30lb, but it is still open to other carp anglers via a day-ticket operation. Day tickets are available, but I do advise you to ring Vic Cranfield on (081) 551 8250 for details.

Fish Trade's Pond, Newport, Humberside
This is a prolific little water of 1¼ acres with carp present to nearly 30lb. The stock is limited, but all are mid- to upper doubles and it is an excellent winter water. Day tickets are available on the bank.

Broadlands, Romsey, Hampshire
A very prolific carp water of around 20 acres, Broadlands has a huge head of carp which are still catchable in cold-water conditions. The carp range in size from 12–30lb and it's an excellent water to learn all about winter carping. Bookings are in advance only: telephone Mark Simmonds on (0703) 733167.

College Lake, Falmouth, Cornwall
This lovely looking water of 38 acres has been often written about in the press and is well worth a visit in winter. It has large numbers of carp which, although quite well educated, are still relatively easy to catch in winter. Day tickets are available on the bank.

Old Bury Hill, Dorking, Surrey
This 12-acre estate lake has a number of natural features and a good head of carp. It is productive in winter with fish to upper twenty-pounders being present. Bookings are required in advance: telephone Mike Ewin on (0306) 883621.

Emmotland Fishery, North Frodingham,
Humberside
Whilst Number 1 Lake is now a private syndicate water, Number 2 Lake is still a day-ticket water and holds a good number of carp to around 30lb. This is a gravel pit which is not easy, but fish do get caught quite regularly in winter. Day tickets are available on the bank.

Farlows Lake, Iver, Buckinghamshire
This large gravel pit has a sizeable stocking of carp and is a very popular fishery for anglers of all abilities who fish carp in winter. If you don't mind company and want to catch a carp in winter this is a good bet. Bookings are required in advance: telephone Ben Tucker on (0753) 630302.

There are actually many more waters good for winter carping other than these ten, and once you really do get into the swing of it I'm sure you will be able to find your own water which is both quiet and productive.

CORRECT CHOICE OF SWIM

I am convinced that the correct choice of venue is your number one priority for a successful winter, but even then your success or failure will be very much dependent on choosing the right swim. In the summer months carp can be highly mobile and may move all over the lake in search of food. Whilst they may be only caught in certain recognized hot spots it is fair to say that many places in the lake will see some form of carp activity during the day. However, with the onset of colder weather the carp can become more limited in their travels, and as the winter approaches they may become extremely localized, sticking to just one or two areas. I am not sure whether this is because of the temperature change and the need to conserve energy, but you can be fairly sure that on most waters the situation in December will be far removed from that in June. While you could be in with a chance no matter where you set up in June, it is vital to be in the right swim in December. Quite simply, if you end up in the wrong swim in winter you may never even have carp in front of you, never mind carp that are feeding.

Having convinced you that carp in winter can be a completely different prospect from those in summer, how can you try to make sure that you do choose the right swim and place your end tackle to the correct part of the swim? Unfortunately, there are no hard-and-fast rules and it's a case of experimenting. However, having spent many years fishing for carp in winter and having had numerous discussions with successful carp anglers, I think I can narrow the options down somewhat. Below are listed the considerations I would look to when choosing my winter swim.

Proven Winter Hot Spots

If you have already fished a particular water in winter and caught consistently from one spot, then that is as good a spot as any at which to start the following winter. It may be that you didn't catch every time, but if you were catching fairly well in comparison to other anglers on the lake then you should certainly look at that area first. However, this does not mean that you should continue to ignore fish which show or are caught in other areas. Even if you believe that the hot spot is dead, fish it on a couple of sessions at least just to make sure, and do move your rods around because the fish may have changed position slightly from the previous year or (more likely) you are not casting in exactly the same spot as you were the previous year. However, previously productive hot spots do blow or 'fade away' as I'm only too well aware. The secret is knowing when to move – something, I'm afraid, that only comes with experience!

As well as proven hot spots you know of, it's also worth looking at hot spots you have been told of. Note that I dropped 'proven' out of the equation here, because until you catch from it then it's not proven, is it? As I said earlier most anglers won't deliberately mislead you, but always take advice with a certain degree of cynicism or you may waste a lot of time. That said, some advice is better than no advice at all, so at least think about it.

You can catch carp in the snow, I assure you.

Proven Summer Hot Spots

These are not usually as productive as proven winter hot spots, but they are still worth looking at unless it's apparent that the carp have left them altogether. I have known carp to feed in what I would term summer spots for most of the year, and even when they did move they stayed in the general area (although it took some fishing about with roving rods to find them). If one spot is continuing to produce the fish week in week out then don't automatically go dashing into deeper water just because it's November. For as long as possible keep to those areas which produce – it's only when they dry up that you need to look elsewhere.

Places with Catches the Previous Year

Another good place to start, particularly when you are allowed to fish in the so-called close season, is to places where the first fish was caught in the previous year. Sometimes carp will have been laid up in such spots for weeks on end, only picking up a bait and being caught because of a temperature rise. It has been my experience that when visiting a new fishery it's always worth asking which areas produce fish consistently in April and May, because it's a fair bet that those fish were in those areas in November and December as well.

Places with Most Recent Catches

If nobody is catching fish with any consistency on your water in winter it is always worth fishing the area where the last carp was caught before that area went dead. Carp will sometimes leave an area completely, but more often than not some fish will be resident and providing you can put a bait in an acceptable position, you are in with a chance. Your best choice for such an area would be one in which a number of fish had been caught, rather than an area where just one had been caught on its travels!

Places with Signs of Fish

Although this is an obvious point, unfortunately it is so obvious that people seem to ignore it at times. I can't stress this facet too much – if you see a carp roll, head and shoulder, or whatever, then get a bait to it. I have not found carp to move much in winter, so a fish showing in one spot could be showing you a potential carp-catching area. If you do find such a spot you could end up with a number of carp and not just one. When you do see a carp, cast a single bait at it and leave it at that. At the end of your session spend some time plumbing that area, feeling around with a lead to see why a carp may be in it. It could be a nice gravel patch, a hard area in an area of silt or a small snag, but whatever it is, mark it down on paper and mark your line with liquid paper to be sure you can hit the exact spot next time. I know that when you are midway through another long blank session and see a fish roll it's all too easy to say you yourself 'I can't be bothered, I'll move there next week'. However, it may be too late and somebody else will probably be in the spot. Don't let that happen!

Places where You Have Seen Carp Catches

This is a bit of a difficult one as I personally don't approve of moving into somebody else's swim just to fish off their hard work. Whilst some anglers have the motto 'If a swim's free then fish it'; mine has been 'Do unto others as you would wish done unto yourself'. However, you don't have to fish exactly the same spot to learn something from their successes. Ask yourself why they are catching and you are not. Could it be down to location? If so, what are they doing that is different from you? Are you fishing to snags, fishing to weed, pulling back to find clear spots or fishing in the margins? Even if you don't fish the same spot you can still learn something. Of course, if that angler doesn't intend to fish the venue again, you have an open invitation to get in there next time!

These six points are the more obvious aids to location, but what do you do if it's a brand new water that you know nothing about or if it's a local water you've decided to try and crack? There are no carp showing, there is nobody on the fishery and there is nothing to go on, so what do you do? It's all down to watercraft. Watercraft cannot be bought or even explained, but it's a way of looking at a water and picking certain spots that you feel could hold carp in winter. Don't be worried as these signs are actually quite obvious. I have listed eight such spots – I'm sure they will be just as obvious to you.

Snags

Of all the possible features to fish to in winter, this has to be one of the best. On a number of waters I have fished in winter you don't seem to get any action at all unless you fish next to snags. These may be as large as full-sized trees or as small as a submerged branch. Indeed, in winter some friends of mine found a whole stack of carp round a tree stump no bigger than 1ft x 6in. The carp were almost head to tail over this stump, yet the surrounding 4–5 acres of water was devoid of fish.

Unfortunately, fishing close to snags does cause problems when actually trying to land the fish – if you are ever lucky enough to hook one. I have covered snag fishing in detail in Chapter 8, so if you find some snags in your water, it's a good bet that carp are holed up round them. Providing you can find a way of extracting these carp, you could be in for action.

Dead Weedbeds

I am not convinced by the theory that carp automatically go into deeper water in winter as I have plenty of experience that they look for natural food and shelter in winter rather than *just* deep water. Probably one of the best areas for food and shelter are any of the lake's remaining weedbeds. With the mild winters of recent years in the UK some areas of weed never die back, even if they do change colour and appearance somewhat. I've actually recorded temperatures in the centre of such weedbeds, and have found that they are always higher than those of the surrounding water. Could it be that the weed acts as a thermal blanket for the carp, and by laying up in it they have an area of warmer water than would be normally found?

Even though the weed may smell rotten, I have found that it contains vast quantities of natural food which just has to be appealing to carp – in winter they seem to work on a minimum effort for maximum food intake theory. However, if the weed is so stagnant as to put carp off even when they lay up in it, you may have to fish well away from such areas.

Having accepted that weed is a good area in which to find carp in winter, where should you place your baits – in the thick of the weed or as close to it as possible? Well, I have caught a lot of carp both in and out of the weed, but always when the weed has not affected my presentation. You may, and I stress *may*, catch carp by chucking your bait in the middle of a weedbed, but I can't believe you will not catch more if you place it in fairly clear areas – even if they are surrounded by weed. Do remember that if your hook, hair and bait are all snarled up in weed, the fish is unlikely to hook itself anyway – this makes even fishing near the right spot a waste of time. I covered this information in Chapters 2 and 5; comparing the ideas in those chapters with the discussion on presentation in winter and amalgamating the two should ensure that you get it right.

Unlike summer fishing when a bait placed between two weedbeds may intercept travelling carp, I have found that winter carp do not move as much and you are better off fishing your bait in holes in the weed or as tight to the weed as you dare. Of course, if there are signs of fish travelling between weedbeds don't miss out and put a bait to them straight away. In summer you can have real problems trying to get fish out of thick weedbeds, but in winter I've found that gentle pressure on a tight line will move even the most stubborn of fish in the thickest of weed. The weed tends to break off far more easily and you do have a realistic chance of landing the fish.

Dead Lily Pads

Whilst lily pads are a good summer hot spot, they are certainly are a good winter one as well – providing you can find them. On two or three waters I have fished, areas which hold lily pads in the summer are also brilliant little hot spots in winter. If you've fished the water in summer you will be aware in winter of where the lily pads were. However, if you don't know exactly their location it can be a problem. Sometimes they are close to the bank so that a little careful tree-top observation on bright winter days should show you their whereabouts. Gaps in otherwise thick weedbeds are occasionally a sign that a dead lily pad or two is there. Broadwater fishery in Surrey has extensive lily pads, and I know that when I have fished it in even the coldest of months all my runs came whilst fishing over these dead pads. In terms of rigs, either use a straightforward balanced pop-up or sometimes, if the pads are quite extensive, a pop-up directly off the lead. Both set-ups are illustrated in Chapter 5. One good point about fishing over dead pads in winter is that fish do not snag up in them as they do in summer, and applying gentle pressure will cut through the dead stems and free the carp.

Overhanging Trees or Bushes

Another place well worth placing a bait to is under an overhanging tree or bush, or to a reed area. For some reason carp seem to like foliage or cover over their heads – perhaps for shelter – and I have had a number of fish from such spots. If the water is quite deep (say, 6–12ft) then all the better, but even if it is shallower than this you should still be successful as the carp can lay up or move into such areas. Providing the bankside disturbance has not moved the carp away from the area, you should at least think of placing a bait under them. If the area is at range and you can place a bait there accurately, then this is all the better.

Island Margins

Again, providing you are accurate with your cast, a bait tight to island margins is worth a try – I have found that carp tend to hug island margins, providing the cold winds have not lowered water temperatures too much. However, do be aware of the fact that margins may be steep and a bait apparently cast close to an island can actually roll many yards away from it by the time it has come to rest.

Bars and Shallow Areas

Whilst I wouldn't constantly fish all three rods to shallow areas, I have had a surprising number of takes in water no more than 2–4ft deep in even the coldest of weather. Such areas can produce carp if a strong wind coupled with a winter sun is on them. The water becomes well oxygenated, and with the wave movement stirring up the bottom, food items may be moved about, so encouraging carp to feed. However, a cold winter wind can kill such areas stone dead and should be avoided. Do be aware that such areas are not usually holding areas for carp so for odd sessions or if you are using roving rods they may be worth a look.

Gullies Between Gravel Bars

On gravel pits with gravel bars good places to try are the areas of silt between the bars, especially where they act as a funnel (*see* Fig. 95). I have found that carp which have become almost dormant in winter do lay up in such areas, remaining perfectly still to conserve energy. However, whilst the carp may be in such areas, it can be difficult to tempt them to pick baits up even when these are placed close to the carp.

Areas of Deeper Water

If you pick up a traditional book on carp fishing you will see that many carp anglers advocate placing a bait in deeper water for success. Whilst I would agree that this is a good idea when you have a limited area of deeper water in otherwise shallow water, it is a totally different ball game if most of your lake is 8ft or so deep. In such a lake an area 10ft deep won't automatically hold greater numbers of carp than other areas because they will certainly be able to survive in areas that are 8ft deep in winter. Obviously, if your water was subject to extreme weather conditions (in other words, was frozen) the carp *may* move to the deepest water as this has the most constant temperature, but I can assure you that they will be hard to catch anyway! Personally, I wouldn't fish a bait in deep water just because it was deep water – however, if people are catching in deep water on your lake then get on those carp now!

MOVING YOUR ROD AROUND

If you are able to use a number of rods it is always worth fishing one of them on a 'roving rod' basis. Clearly, if you are having action from a particular spot, keep to it and don't waiver, but if you are not, then use one rod as a rover. Every hour or so recast that rod to a new spot – if you drop a bait on a carp's head you will hopefully incite the carp to take it. Usually, I recast every two hours but I know some experienced carp anglers advocate recasting after one hour or less. Do experiment and use a system that suits you best. Also, if possible, use hookbaits only – with possibly a two-bait stringer at the most – or you will be left with piles of bait all over the swim.

Finally, do make sure you keep a note of where you have cast or you may not be able to find *the* spot again!

ACCURACY AND OBSERVATION

Accuracy and observation are always important, but this is even more true in winter. Looking at observation first, carp tend to be more active in summer than in winter and may show themselves many times in one area in the summer. Obviously, the more times a carp shows the more chance you have of seeing it and putting a bait to it. However, in winter it may just break surface once, and if you sit in the bivvy reading you may miss it and your chance. You must therefore be particularly observant in winter as it may be your only chance of a fish!

Again, accuracy may be important in summer but in winter, when carp can be very localized, the need to have your bait in *the* spot is even more accentuated. In summer the carp may tend to move all around the lake so that even a bait which is not spot-on has a chance of being picked up –

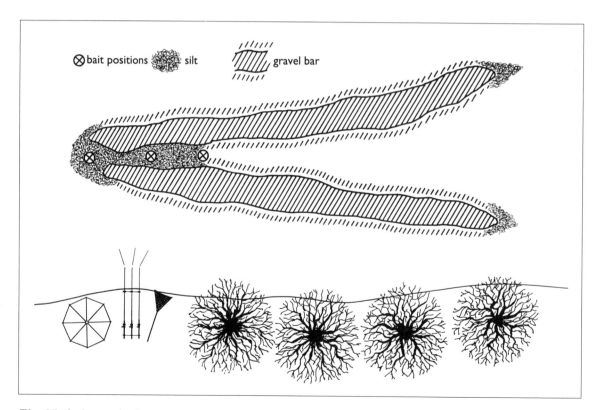

Fig. 95 *An intersection hot spot.*

however, in winter you will have little luck on 'chuck it and chance it' tactics. If a cast is not spot-on then recast it; if you feel you could be a little nearer the weed, then do it again. Your bait may be out there for hours so it might as well be spot-on. Mark your lines with liquid paper or stop knots to ensure that you are able to hit the same spot each time and, if at all possible, keep a note of sight lines and so on. These are all the little edges that can make that vital difference between blanking and actually catching fish in winter!

EFFECTS OF THE ELEMENTS

If you are keen then the elements won't put you off in winter, but it is fair to say that certain weather conditions do have a marked effect on whether carp are prepared to feed in winter or not. Personally, I continue to fish through the period anyway, but if you have a restricted amount of time available it is well worth thinking about the effect that the weather has on the carp and whether it is really worth fishing for them. For those who do have only a limited amount of time, here are my findings on how conditions can influence the carp.

Snow

As an element in itself snow is no bad thing. I have caught carp in the snow and so have many other people. However, it is what accompanies the snow that is the problem as far as feeding fish are concerned. If you are fishing during a cold snap, in sleet or in bitterly cold winds then you are really going to struggle. However, if a warm westerly or south-westerly moves in, or even just a period of calm weather, it's certainly worth staying – if your bait is in the right place then you certainly are in with a chance.

Sleet

It is absolutely hopeless fishing in sleet and it is very uncomfortable as well. Usually sleet will cause a recordable temperature drop and it can be the kiss of death on many waters.

Marked Temperature Drop

The waters I have fished have really been turned off by a sudden cold spell in a period of otherwise mild weather. I know that some anglers have said that the period just before this can be absolutely dynamite, but I have never been able to hit it just right to find out! Unless I had to I would avoid going fishing during this period until the fish acclimatized after a week or two.

Marked Temperature Rise

Whilst this certainly doesn't seem to put the carp off, unless it is accompanied by very warm winds and spring-like weather, I haven't found it to send them wild either. Your chances should improve, but don't expect record catches on this change alone.

Rain

I do not like to fish in rain between November and March as it usually causes a marked drop in water temperature and this can put carp off. A very fine drizzle is no problem, but heavy and prolonged downpours can prove to be the kiss of death on some waters.

Constant Warm or Cold Spell

Once the temperature levels out after a drop or rise I have found very little difference between constant warmer or colder weather. Probably out of the two you will fare better in constant warm weather, but I certainly wouldn't be worried about constant cool weather. Providing the change in temperature was some time ago you should keep at it.

Ice

Solid ice is, of course, impossible for fishing, but cat ice is still fishable. Obviously, a temperature drop which causes ice to form can cause a drop in action but if it has been cold recently anyway the decrease in takes shouldn't be too appreciable. However, if the ice has formed due to a marked temperature drop then you may struggle.

These are the conditions you may meet in winter, but my advice is that unless it is detrimental to your health you should give winter carping a go. Without a bait in the water you can't catch anyway!

CORRECT CHOICE OF TACKLE

Unlike snag fishing or long-range fishing, where you sometimes need specialist items of tackle to catch carp, with carp fishing in winter any additional items you may need to purchase are generally concerned with the comfort side of fishing rather than the actual catching of carp. This means that they can be discretionary rather than obligatory in the purchasing sense. However, if you do decide to fish all winter or even part of it, and especially if this involves night fishing, the better prepared you are the more likely you are to fish effectively and therefore catch carp. However, I will not discuss this side of tackle to start with, but instead concentrate on the carp catching side of winter tackle.

Rods

There is no need to change your rod for winter fishing providing it is up to the job in hand. Most rods will be able to cast as far out as you need, and as long as you have a rod that is good enough then stick with it!

Reels

Again, there is no need to change your reel, providing it is up to the job. I have used Shimanos in winter and haven't found the cold weather to affect their clutches. If you are happy with your current choice then you should have no problems.

Line

I try to use as light a main line as possible in winter for reasons that I outline a little later (*see* page 152), so I try to stick to as reliable a brand as possible. Usually this is Sylcast 7lb or 9lb either straight through or sometimes with a 15lb Berkley leader. If fishing to weedy or snaggy areas I up that to 12lb or 15lb Berkley Big Game, but I always only use tackle that I am confident will land carp.

Buzzbars and Rod Rests

It has been my experience that in winter carp sometimes don't go tearing off, but instead (possibly because of the low temperatures) merely hook themselves lightly and waddle about. Now I'm not saying that this always happens or that it happens more often than not, but it is something of which you should be aware as every little edge counts. There is nothing lost in having the most sensitive set-up possible and this should include, if practical, your rods pointing in a direct line to your baits. As I said in Chapter 7, the greater the angle between the rod tip and bait, the less sensitive is your set-up. The ideal situation is to have everything in line which is about as sensitive as you can get it. If I can, I fish the buzzers on single rod rests directly in line with my hookbaits and keep the rod tips as low as possible. With the new Delkim buzzers you can put the sensitivity control on full, and the less line there is out of the water, the less chance there is of line movement due to wind.

Buzzers

Out of all the buzzers I have ever used, it is fair to say that for sensitivity alone Delkim's 1992 model is hard to beat. I'm not saying that you should run out and buy one, but if you are in the market for a buzzer and you are looking to fish into winter as well then a Delkim is well worth looking at. Mind you, buzzers are only as sensitive as you make them, and it is absolutely essential that you do keep them in good working order and properly set up. I know that it is very trendy to fish with your rod tips high in the air, but unless you are trying to avoid being cut off on close in gravel bars, it's all pose and of little real use. Keep those rod tips down and in line as detailed in Chapter 7.

One tip with buzzers is that in very cold conditions when moisture freezes (so stopping your buzzer working), cover them with an old hessian sack or towel to keep them damp rather than frozen. Try it – it does work well! As you may be fishing some distance from your rods and a take may register as a single bleep, it's absolutely vital that you don't miss any audible indications on your buzzer. A real advantage is an extension box direct from buzzer to bivvy – I can honestly say that the two minutes it takes to set one up will be more than amply rewarded by its fish-catching value. On rain-drenched nights you may have to shut your bivvy door and, with a wind howling outside, it is very easy to miss that single bleep which could be the carp you have waited for all season. Don't miss out on it.

Swingers and Bobbins

I did take a good look at when to use and when not to use Swingers, bobbins and the like in Chapter 4, so I don't intend to duplicate all that information again. However, I should add that if possible I do try to fish as close in as possible so that I can obtain maximum indication from minimum movement. For ninety per cent of the time I do stick to Swingers, only reverting back to bobbins at extreme range. One trick I have found is that with a very strong cross-wind your Swingers

can jangle about when set as neutral as possible so that you may encounter false indications. I do like to hit any bleeps at all in winter so I sometimes use a 'sideboard' (*see* Fig. 96) to protect the Swingers from wind interference. All this comprises is a piece of thin board (or sheet metal) some 2 x 2ft, which has two loops at the top and bottom through which you push your rod rests. It is very easy to pop it in your bedchair when in transit, and does cut down on *all* false movement, providing your rod tips are low and sunk if possible.

End Tackle and Presentation

I mentioned earlier that on many waters I have encountered the carp tend not to be as voracious in their feeding habits in winter as they might be in summer, and even when hooked they sometimes don't go tearing off with the bait. It is therefore up to you to make your end tackle as responsive as possible, bearing in mind where you are fishing.

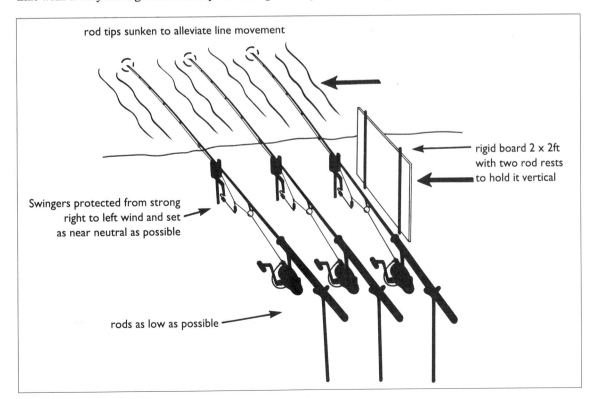

rod tips sunken to alleviate line movement

rigid board 2 x 2ft
with two rod rests
to hold it vertical

Swingers protected from strong
right to left wind and set
as near neutral as possible

rods as low as possible

Fig. 96 *The advantages of using a 'sideboard'.*

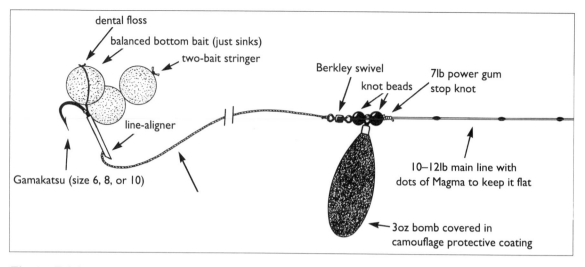

Fig. 97 *Tubeless presentation.*

Generally, I fish a set-up as illustrated in Fig. 97 – a tubeless set-up utilizing a stringer tied to the hook in order to stop tangles. This suffices as a good starting point on most waters, but I'm sure you may have to change each and every component to some degree to arrive at the correct presentation for your water. This change could relate to the following.

Hooks

My normal carp hook in winter is generally a lot smaller than I would use in summer, purely and simply because a smaller hook is a sharper and lighter hook, and is therefore more likely to nick into a carp's mouth in cold-water feeding conditions. Normally the hook is a Gamakatzu 6318 (Black Carp Hook) in size 6, 8 or 10, but if I feel results could be improved by a smaller hook, I would choose a Drennan Super Specimen in size 10, 12 or 14, or a Middlesex Angling Centre pre-bent hook in size 8 or 10. Please do remember that the smaller the hook the weaker it is, so do not fish small hooks in situations where a degree of pressure is required. I know that the Super Specimen hooks are brilliant little hooks, but a size 10 won't stand hooking and holding in snags. With both Drennans and Gamakatzus I used to bend the eye over slightly to achieve a 'flick over' effect, but now I stick firmly to the

line aligner which does the trick equally as well. I shouldn't, of course, need to tell you that it is very important to keep hooks extremely sharp in winter!

Hooklengths

More often than not I use Kryston's excellent Merlin in 10lb or 12lb, or Supersilk in 14lb which I dot with Magma putty to ensure that it sits tight on the bottom, so avoiding false indications from pelvic fins, tails and so on. Remember that if you do have a liner, strike at it and miss, that carp will have had a 2oz or more bomb whistling past its face – not something that will tempt it to stay around long. The only indications you get should be from a hooked fish.

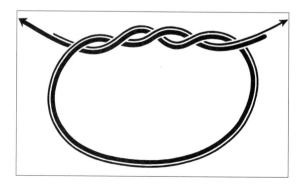

Fig. 98 *The Combi Link knot.*

I have done very well with Kryston's Silkworm in 8lb or 10lb – it is very supple indeed but definitely does need dotting with putty to keep it flat. This stuff does float up, and although it may not put the carp off I can't believe it attracts them either. However, do choose what you are confident with!

One form of presentation I have played about with and which has turned out to be very effective indeed is Harry Haskell's famous Combi Link set-up – 3in Multistrand plus 7in Merlin (*see* Fig. 98). It lays tight to the lake bed, allows very free bait movement and I'm very happy with it. One point, though, is that you should avoid using it with pop-ups or on weedy waters. The weed can get in between the strands to cause all sorts of problems, and pop-ups tend to tie themselves in knots. However, for straightforward bottom baits on gravel pits it's very good. For most situations I tend to stick to a 12in hooklength and vary it up or down depending on where I am fishing. Sometimes I have gone as short as 3in in winter and had some well hooked fish, but I do feel that in scratching periods it is worth leaving one hooklength nearer 2ft than 1ft. This will give that bait lots of free movement and may catch carp which have seen tethered 12in hookbaits all summer.

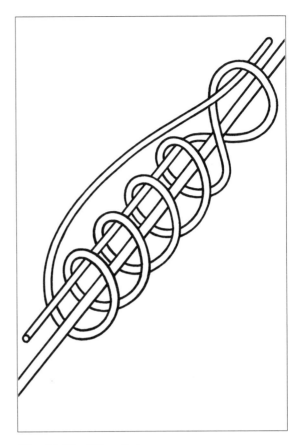

Fig. 99 *The sliding slip knot.*

Bomb Size (Fixed or Non-Fixed)

When fishing bolt-lead style you really want to fish as heavy a lead as possible as it is this which pulls the hook home. For that reason I usually use a 3oz lead which is also fixed with a power gum stop knot (*see* Fig. 99), providing I am not using a leader. However, on occasions I have decided to fish unfixed leads (no back stop) and have dropped the lead size to 1oz or 1¼oz. This is very rare, but there have been occasions when I had at least five times as many runs by using this running lead method. I wouldn't recommend you use it everywhere, but as carp can be contrary creatures keep it tucked away just in case.

Tubing or Not?

If I can, I try to do away with tubing, especially on shallow gravel pits where it stands out rather prominently. In summer, feeding carp stir up all sorts of debris, so covering the tubing up. However, in winter one or two lethargic carp can move around and hardly even disturb the silt, so do try to keep your end tackle as unobtrusive as possible. By using a stringer off the hook you can do away with tubing, but if you fancy fishing single hookbaits popped-up you may need to fish a helicopter rig or tubing to give yourself peace of mind. Twelve hours of darkness is a long time to sit and worry whether you've got a tangle or not.

If I am fishing in weedy waters where the bottom is covered with all sorts of dead leaves, weed and the like, I personally wouldn't hesitate to use tubing and a set-up as illustrated in Fig. 100.

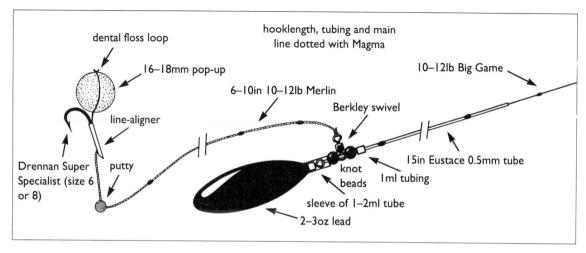

Fig. 100 *Tubed winter presentation.*

Main Line Strength

The finer your main line is, the less visual it is and the more likely that any movement on it will be registered at the buzzer end of your tackle. So, if possible, fish as light a main line as your lead *and* the swim allows. Don't fish 7lb in weed, but at the same time don't use straight-through 15lb Big Game in clear, open gravel pits where it may stand out. Use your common sense at all times.

I like my main line to be as tight to the indicator as possible. That way any movement at all will be registered. A fine main line can be pulled a lot tighter than a thick one, but make sure that your line clip does not flatten and damage it.

SURVIVING THE ELEMENTS

Having found yourself a good venue, have picked the correct swim and put the right presentation on your end tackle, it is important that you are there long enough and fish effectively enough to give a fish the chance to pick the bait up, and for you to strike and land it. Whilst it is an obvious point, if you have packed up when you are cold, wet, dejected and bored, you are not going to catch a carp that starts to feed whilst you are making your way home! You must spend as much time as possible getting to know the water, and there is absolutely nothing wrong in spend-

ing it in luxury if you want to. For that reason, in winter I do like to be well prepared as regards comfort and the like, and whilst I hardly bother at all with my own comfort in summer, nothing is too much trouble to take with me in winter. Obviously, if you are restricted to short day sessions you want to fish as soon as daylight breaks, so you will not need half of the gear I detail below.

Umbrella

I have always fished in winter with an umbrella and bivvy set up, and as I explained in Chapter 4 I'm more than happy with my Steadefast Wavelock 50in umbrella with a screw-in pole.

Bivvy

I have a Kevin Nash 50in Canvas as detailed in Chapter 4 because it keeps the warmth in, allows me to have lights, a television and cooker on full blast without light shining on the water, it tightens up and doesn't slacken in wet weather, doesn't flap around in high winds and it has kept going strong since I bought it in 1986! I use at least four storm rods to make sure that it is completely stable, and the Kingfisher pegs at all sixteen pegging points keep it tight to the ground so that I do not get hit by cold winds where it hurts. The best storm poles I have seen are Steadefast which, when coupled with Kevin Nash's screw-in storm bolts, stop slippage and buffeting. Do remember that a canvas bivvy which is covered in rain or snow will increase in weight and is likely to push down heavily on those storm poles. Unless these poles are decent ones they will bend or your storm bolts will ride up your umbrella frame.

Groundsheet

You must have a groundsheet or any damp on the ground will start to rise and you may end up catching cold. I can't stress the need for a groundsheet too much as it really will keep out the cold and wet and will keep your gear dry as well. Kevin Nash produces a custom-made groundsheet for 50in umbrellas, and as I have had mine for four years now they must be well made.

Bivvy Pegs

The best bivvy pegs I have seen are Kingfisher 10in ones or the new ones by Fox which are almost identical in appearance. As I have stitched on an extra set of peg holders to allow me to really nail my bivvy down I use two sets. Always take one or two spare because it's amazing how they disappear even whilst in transit.

Bedchair

Use one you feel comfortable sleeping on and not automatically what the experts direct you towards. I personally find a five-legged Lafuma a joy to sleep on but hard to get off. Some people prefer the Cliff Fox version and I must admit that his new one looks comfortable. If you only have a sunlounger don't worry about it at all because that won't stop you catching the fish. If you put a second cover on it for strength and a foam mat which you can purchase from most camping stores, you will have a lovely bed for a cheap price. Such foam mats or blankets stop the damp from rising to the bits you like to keep warm and provide an extra degree of comfort.

Sleeping Bag

Again, the choice is very much down to personal preference and what suits you and your pocket best. I have used a Coleman Long Mummy Sleeping Bag for years, and I really rated it until the zip went. However, now with Fox, Nash, Leslie's and the Middlesex Angling Centre all selling their own pukka versions, it is better to try one out and see if one of these is your size in terms of length and width. If you don't want to spend a lot of money on a sleeping bag then simply buy two common or garden ones and put one inside the other; for most conditions in which you will fish and have a chance of catching carp this is more than sufficient. As a tip, to keep your feet really warm push an old jersey down to the bottom of the bag and push your feet into it; for a really good night's sleep take a pillow as well. Fox's new pillow is good, but if you don't want to spend money buying one then take a normal pillow and cover it with a towel.

Clothing

Hopefully you won't be in your bivvy all day, and if you are in and out landing fish or just fishing day sessions then it is vital that you are protected against wind, rain and the cold. A scarf around your neck keeps out the chills and a bobble hat keeps in the heat. Gloves are vital if you are standing around for any length of time, and if you've any sense you will keep a spare set of socks, jeans, jersey and so on in your car for emergencies.

Boots

The best boots I have seen are Skeetex – these are ideal if you are fishing day sessions and don't need to take them off. However, for bivvy anglers a good pair of waterproof wellingtons will do, along with a couple of pairs of good commando socks to keep in the warmth. Mind you, if you do suffer from cold feet then Skeetex boots may well be essential.

Undersuits

I am still extremely pleased with my Leslie's undersuit which has served me well for many years now. For day sessions I would choose a one piece suit such as this, but for overnighter sessions I prefer a Stalker jacket and quality thermal jogging pants.

Oversuits

These are not really necessary unless you are fishing for several days and are out in the cold all the time. I have a nice Dartex jacket which fits over my Stalker, but for really foul weather I use Kevin Nash's Titan Oversuit which keeps everything out. With oversuits and undersuits it's usually a case that you only get what you pay for, so if you really do fish for several days you may need to pick quality gear if you are to survive. Don't pick suits which are too tight as you will find that your casting is restricted and the next time you give it the 'big one' you might hear an ominous ripping sound under one arm!

Cooking Equipment

There is really only one choice – the Coleman Multi-Fuel which runs on unleaded petrol. I won't go into its advantages as I covered them in Chapter 4, suffice it to say it does a superb job on even icy days and a gallon of fuel will last you all winter. Gas stoves are awful in winter; they refuse to light, have to be cuddled to warm them up, and Triangas stoves take ages and make you smell of meths. Colemans are definitely the thing to get.

Food and Drink

It goes without saying that plenty of hot food and drink are vital if you are going to be able to stick winter fishing week in and week out. Buy one of Twilight Tackle's thermal cups for your coffee, and take plenty of tea, coffee and milk and a guest cup.

Other Items

I wouldn't be without my television, which makes a long session in winter more bearable. However, do make sure that if you do take one you are not disturbing other anglers and that your extension box will give you advance warning of a take. I don't watch it in the day as I keep an eye on the water, and even at night I keep the volume low so I can hear fish. Portable televisions which run off a standard car battery can be bought easily, and the battery will last all winter. Ones which run off normal batteries will give you

about an hour's use so avoid them. Take plenty of books to pass the time as at times you will have to contend with sixteen hours of darkness. Remember that you don't get any prizes for blanking and feeling miserable – you are supposed to enjoy it, you know!

CORRECT CHOICE OF BAIT

Although I have left this consideration to last, it does not mean that I think bait choice is unimportant in winter and that you can sling out any old rubbish and catch. As far as I am concerned, the correct choice of bait can be just as vital a consideration as location, presentation and so on. You may well have limited success with one bait in the right place at the right time, but if you put the correct bait in the right place at the right time your chances must be considerably increased. We are not stuck in the 1960s, 1970s or even 1980s, so there is no real excuse for not having a good winter bait out there, and you must spend some time on it. However, it's probably easy for me to sit and say that, but it is a lot harder to actually find the bait that does work – or is it? How do you choose a bait to use in winter?

Use the 'Going' Bait

On some fisheries a 'going' bait will be all that is necessary to give you a good chance of regular winter action. A 'going' bait is a bait that is catching well on that fishery and because many people are using it and catching, it is *the* bait to use. A going bait is not, and I repeat not, a bait which has received popularity on waters such as Yateley and Darenth but which has yet to prove itself on your lake. That is a bait which might work, or which might not work! If you are able to find out what *the* bait on your water is and, providing you feel it is producing fish on a basis which is acceptable to you, then by all means choose this bait. However, do remember that a large number of fish may already have been caught on it and your chance will therefore be reduced in proportion to whatever will be caught on that bait. Not every fish will want to feed on it, and if you are only fishing for, say, a hundred feeding fish and thirty of you are on that bait, you only have a one in thirty chance of a pick-up on your rod unless you have a better presentation, better swim or spend more time there. Mind you, the going bait may be a better bet than using an unproven bait.

Use a Bait in which You Have Confidence

Winter carp fishing is all about confidence, and if you are not confident in winter you will struggle to catch. If you have a bait with which you are happy then it's definitely worth while sticking with it, providing you are not turning your nose up at the obvious. Your choice of bait may be a fishmeal, but if everybody else is catching fish on Richworth's Strawberry Yoghurt readymades then you are a fool if you keep persevering for nothing. This observation does not take anything away from those who wish to work things out for themselves, it's just common sense. I must admit that I would have to take a lot of fish on my bait if I was to ignore one which was catching fish. I have made this mistake once or twice and it won't happen again – don't be as stupid as I was.

Use a Proven Winter Carp Bait

If you have not been able to find out what the going bait is, or if there isn't one and you don't have a winter bait of your own, then what do you do? Well, as we have all done in the past, you have to put your faith in other people's advice. So, if you are unsure then it's worth looking at the winter baits I describe below. I list two that I have complete confidence in and, providing a water is not being 'turned over' on a particular type of bait, these are the two I am prepared to use with confidence anywhere.

Birdseed Winter Recipe

This first bait is one I use at any venue in the UK which I don't intend to fish on a very regular basis, or any water where I want to use an instant attractor bait. I have used it as far afield as Surrey, Humberside and Kent and it has not failed

me yet. Having given the recipe to friends, I know it has also worked well on other waters all over the UK, so give it a try. If I'm fishing a gravel pit I do like to fish straightforward bottom baits or semi-balanced baits (polyballs), but if I fish weedy waters or waters where I need to leave the bait out for up to twenty-four hours at a time, I use the microwaved pop-ups as they work a treat.

16oz Nutrabaits Enervite Gold
5 Size 2 eggs
10ml Nutrabaits Multimino
3ml SBS Cornish Ice Cream EA Flavour
1½ml SBS Strawberry Jam EA Flavour
2 level teaspoons of Cotswold Baits Milk 'B' Enhancer
Colour: yellow, orange or red

Boil for two minutes. The size is somewhat variable.

Microwaved Pop-Ups
They are made from the same base mix as used in the recipe above.

8oz Enervite Gold
2 Size 2 eggs
3ml SBS Cornish Ice Cream EA Flavour
1½ml SBS Strawberry Jam EA Flavour
1 level teaspoon Cotswold Baits Milk 'B' Enhancer
Colour

Roll into boilies no greater than 14–16mm. Boil for two minutes and allow them to dry for three hours. Place them in a microwave in batches of ten to twelve and use level 9, and cook for two minutes. Allow them to cool for three to five minutes. Place them in the microwave for a second time in batches of ten at level 9, and cook for a further two minutes. Allow the baits to cool for three minutes

Place the baits in a freezer bag which contains 1ml Cornish Cream and ½ml Strawberry Jam Flavours. Give the freezer bag a good shake to allow the flavour to coat the baits. Place baits in a new freezer bag and allow them to absorb the flavour and dry for eight hours. Freeze and use as required.

Balanced Pop-Ups
Again, these are made from the same base mix as used above.

6oz Nutrabaits Enervite Gold
2–3oz egg albumin
2 Size 2 eggs
2ml SBS Cornish Ice Cream EA Flavour
1ml SBS Strawberry Jam EA Flavour
1 level teaspoon Cotswold Baits Milk 'B' Enhancer Colour

Roll round ¼in or ½in Cotswold polyballs. Boil for two minutes, then allow them to cool for four to six hours. Freeze and use as required.

Protein Bait Winter Recipe
This recipe, which has a higher food rating and which is therefore a better quality bait is one I use if I am intending to fish a water on a regular week in, week out basis. As this is my usual way of fishing in winter, this is the bait I use for a lot of my winter carping. Whilst I am not saying that a higher protein bait will catch you more fish than a lower protein bait on its own, I am convinced that over a period of time it will catch at least as many fish and probably more! This type of quality bait could provide you with that edge which we all seek to find in winter, so on that point alone it has to be worth thinking about. I will not discuss the high protein versus low protein debate here as I covered it in Chapter 6, suffice it to say that it could give you that edge. Although this is the reason why I use protein, you decide what you think is best. After all, this book offers ideas only – go out and prove me wrong.

16oz Nutrabaits Hi-Nu-Val
6 Size 2 eggs
20ml Nutrabaits Complete Food Oil
2ml SBS Cornish Ice Cream EA Flavour
1ml SBS Strawberry Jam EA Flavour
6 drops Nutrabaits Bergamot Essential Oil
1 level teaspoon Cotswold Baits Milk 'B' Enhancer

Boil for seventy-five seconds. The size is somewhat variable.

Balanced Pop-Ups
These are made from the same base mix as the recipe above.

6oz Nutrabaits Hi-Nu-Val
2oz egg albumin
3 Size 2 eggs
1½ml SBS Cornish Ice Cream EA Flavour
1ml SBS Strawberry Jam EA Flavour
3 drops Nutrabaits Bergamot Essential Oil
1 level teaspoon Cotswold Baits Milk 'B' Enhancer

Roll round Cotswold ¼in or ½in polyballs. Boil for ninety seconds. Freeze and use as required.

These two excellent winter baits should allow you to catch in winter on most waters which are not being saturated or turned over by another type of bait. However, just choosing a good bait is not the complete answer to success as it does also depend on how you apply that bait.

BAITING LEVELS

Whilst baiting levels are always important in carp fishing (*see* Chapter 6), it is vital in winter to get it right. You must use enough to attract and tempt the carp but not too much so that you overfill them. As I discussed in Chapter 1 on the carp's physical make-up, cold water decreases a carp's appetite and its ability to convert that food is greatly reduced. For that reason alone, I keep bait to a minimum when fishing in winter as I want to catch those carp rather than feed them. A carp may well be able to eat 100 to 200 boilies in July, but the same carp may find six too many in December! If you put too many freebies out there you may fill the carp up before they even encounter your hookbait, and this can ruin your chances in cold-water carping conditions.

Personally, my tactic on most waters is to fish no more than four to eight 16–18 mm freebies around each hookbait. These are no more than

1–3in away from the hookbait, and definitely within 12in if possible. In my experience on the waters I've fished, that number is enough to attract the carp and still give you the chance of a pick-up. I hardly ever increase the level, but on some occasions I will drop it to a stringer only (or even just single hookbaits) if I feel I am in the correct spot. Remember the carp fisher's maxim: 'You can always put some more out but you can never take it back'. Therefore, if in doubt, keep it low. Obviously, if other people are doing far better by using more bait, then don't ignore this and get on that method immediately. However, my bet is that you would be better sticking to a low level of bait, building it up only if you are sure it's necessary. If you are used to piling in baits, or even just fishing over fifty or so, it does take some getting used to – but it's better than blanking!

If you want to educate carp to your bait, it's best that you keep a steady trickle of bait going into the water before and after fishing but not during your session. With a bait such as Hi-Nu-Val and an average stock of fish, I use 3lb or so a week trickled into an area in which I am confident carp feed. Unless you know where the carp are, it's a waste of good bait piling it in all over the place, and because you are using such limited quantities of pre-bait it is vital to put it in the correct spot. The carp won't go looking for it, so put it where they can't miss it.

ADDITIONAL BAIT THOUGHTS

Colour

Whilst it may be that I just fish easy gravel pits and the like in winter, I have found that the more visual the hookbait has been the better my results. Although I do accept that this may not be the case on hard waters, the waters I've fished, and advocate you to fish, seem to respond to bright baits. Both Cotswold Baits and Nutrabaits

Some of my favourite cold-water smells.

do ranges of colours and I can thoroughly recommend both firms' products in that respect.

Size

I have tended to stick to a fairly middle-of-the-road 18mm boily over the last few years, but I can see a case for using both smaller and larger baits. Larger baits can be catapulted out more accurately, but by their very size you can't put too many out without the danger of overfeeding the carp. Smaller baits don't go out half as well but tend to rest on silt and weed better, and you can spread quite a few about without being worried about filling up the carp.

Weight

If possible, I like to use as light a mix as possible so that any baits I do put out are where the carp can find them and not buried in the silt. Hi-Nu-Val is an excellent bait for this and because it is so light it rests on the lake bottom.

Crumb baits

I did look at this in Chapter 6, but it is such a good idea to use it in winter that it would be unfair not to mention it here. The crumb has all the attraction of boilies but with nothing for the carp to really feed on except your single hookbait. However, unless you are fishing close in, can get to grips with PVA bags or have a boat, it is difficult to put out.

Bait soaks

Again, this was covered briefly in Chapter 6, but it is something you should look to in winter. Crumb soaked in cream or boilies soaked in Multimino and the like provide a good source of attraction and can draw the carp in easier than straightforward boilies.

Paste

A good trick when winter fishing is not to boil all your boily mix but to keep a little to use as paste. For close-range fishing paste is brilliant – I mould it around the hookbait, swivels, bomb and so on to provide added attraction and minimal feed to the carp. Because it is not boiled it does 'leak off'

easier, but its uses are limited unless you are fishing close in.

Stringers

A super little trick which many anglers use in winter is a two- or three-bait stringer which has either two or three times the potential attraction of a single hookbait. However, because it is in such close proximity to your hookbait that attraction is very concentrated, there are perhaps times when you would be better off catapulting out two freebies near your hookbait to spread the attraction. Do remember also that if you are using a roving rod, every time you change its position there is a two- or three-bait stringer somewhere out there to no purpose at all. Roving rods should perhaps be fished as single hookbaits.

Flavour capsules

These have now been introduced commercially by Streamselect. You inject your neat flavour, dip or whatever into them, place them in the lead recess and when cast out you have a nice cloud of attractor which attracts but does not feed the carp. They are a very good idea when fishing a roving rod or single hookbait set-up.

Natural baits

Never neglect natural or traditional baits such as sweetcorn, maggots and worms because cold-water conditions are when these baits can come into their own. This could be due to the natural movement of the worms or maggots, but whatever the reason it is at 'scratching times' that these baits are well worth trying if you have the confidence to do so (*see* Chapter 6).

Hopefully, the information in this chapter will give you a good chance of catching carp in winter. However, no matter how good your choice of venue has been, no matter how good your choice of swim has been, no matter what your bait or presentation is, and no matter what your tackle is, you will only be successful if you work at it. Without confidence and perseverance in winter you will never succeed; I'm sure you can, so go out and do it.

10 STRIKING, PLAYING AND NETTING YOUR CARP

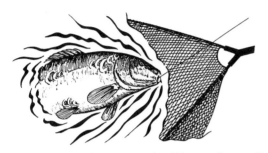

Having managed to get a take, I know that striking and actually managing to land the carp is another thing. Like everybody else I have missed my share of takes, have pulled out of carp and have dropped them at the net. At those times, all that hard work went to waste just because I didn't get my striking, playing or netting techniques quite right. In this chapter I will take you through how I strike, play and net carp, and hopefully the information will help you if you are doing the hard work but are not reaping the results. It is very easy to sit back and believe that you've got it down to a fine art, but unless you manage to hit every take and net every fish you can always improve your technique.

TYPES OF TAKE

Not all takes are screaming ones where the fish goes belting off from you, pulling line from the clutch, self-hooking itself and allowing you all the time in the world to get out of your bedchair to strike and net it. Some takes (especially at range or in winter) are slow movements on your Swinger which you have to decide whether to strike or ignore. Generally, I strike all indications unless I feel it's due to carp touching my line. Providing the line falls or rises at least 1in then

you should strike. In winter I hit every single movement (*see* Fig. 101) because although I will miss some takes, it has been my experience that anglers who ignore anything but screamers miss out on a number of fish. However, waters vary and if your water is one which has a high stocking level of carp or nuisance fish which give false indications, you will need to use your common sense as to when to strike and when to sit on your hands. If in doubt, strike at it – if you miss then recast.

STRIKING

If you are fishing with a baitrunner device on your reel or are fishing as I do with your clutch slackened off, you have to make sure that when

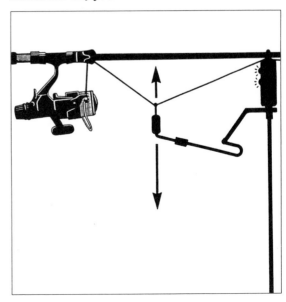

Fig. 101 *Should you strike?*

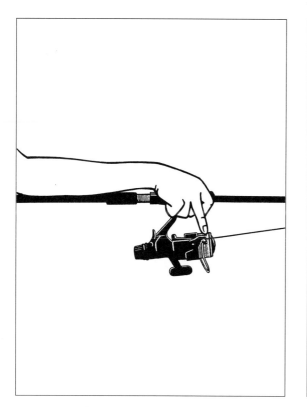

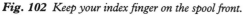

Fig. 102 Keep your index finger on the spool front.

Fig. 103 Success?

you strike you keep the tension up between rod and hook. Whilst on some occasions the carp will be well hooked anyway, there is nothing lost by striking. However, before you even manage to lift the rod up to strike into the carp, it is important that you make the line between reel and hook as tight as possible. My usual way is to reach down with my right hand and place my thumb on top of the reel stem, my index finger on the spool front and my next three fingers round the area where the reel stem meets the rod (*see* Fig. 102). The purpose of putting my index finger on the spool front (or side) is that when I come to strike I can keep the pressure on between reel and hook. One little tip is to keep your hands as clean as possible – hands which are covered in fish oils and bacon fat don't grip well.

Having placed your hand around the reel stem you now have to strike into the fish (*see* Fig. 103). Before you strike, however, use your brain and think where you are fishing to. If you are fishing

close in there will be little line out in front of you and, as that line can be the stretch factor which stops you pulling hooks out of fish, you have to be careful. With fish hooked in the margin which are not shooting off, I only strike moderately hard to avoid pulling hooks out. If you are fishing at close range and the water is deep, all a hard strike will do is pull the hook upwards, perhaps straight out of the carp's mouth. For normal carp fishing I strike quite hard as lines such as Big Game and Sylcast have a lot of stretch in them and it is important to take up as much slack as soon as possible with the strike. Do remember that the sooner you have a tight line to the carp the sooner you can exert pressure on it to stop it kiting into snags, weedbeds or your other lines. At long range the job is even harder – 120yd of stretch takes far more tightening than 60yd. Before you strike fully at range you may have to wind your reel handle a couple of times so that you have some contact with the carp.

Drop-Backs

Drop-backs are more difficult to strike into because the fish is coming towards you and you will have to pick up a slack line. Gentle drop-backs of 1–3in are usually not a problem as a good, hard strike should hook the fish. However, a drop-back where the Swinger hangs straight down and your line drops slack can be a real problem. As with long-range carping, you may have to wind until you make contact with the fish and then strike. This must be done quickly, so don't sit there thinking whether you should hit it or not: be positive.

PLAYING THE FISH

Having hopefully made some contact with the carp via your strike, it is vital that you increase the level of contact and control that you have over your hooked fish. With a baitrunner system in use you engage your preset clutch by turning the handle and in comes the clutch. However, I'm no big fan of the baitrunner and do prefer to fish straight off the clutch. The clutch is set as I feel necessary, and this usually means that it does take a degree of pull to take line from it. A very loosely set clutch may cause problems as some reels have such infinitely adjustable clutches that it can take you seconds to tighten

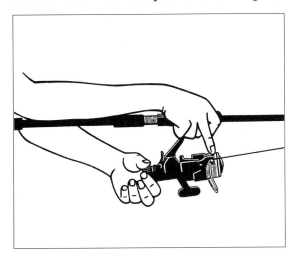

Fig. 104 *The advantages of a rear clutch.*

them up. In that period the carp could be in the snags. However, by having your clutch set fairly tightly (but not so tight that the rod is pulled in), you only need to twist the clutch adjuster at the back once at the most (*see* Fig. 104). This is the main reason why I favour a rear clutch – one in front of your reel can be very difficult to adjust.

Once you have made contact with the carp you need to bring it closer to you and stop it from making its way further out into the lake. Clearly, the further out the fish gets, the more difficult it will be to retrieve and the more likely it is to find a snag or weedbed, or to cut you off on a gravel bar. Obviously, line has to be retrieved on to your reel, but if you merely wind with your reel you will exert no real pressure on the carp, may ruin your reel and may lose the fish. Your main ally is your rod which is not only a casting tool but is a lever for exerting pressure on the carp and allowing your reel to take up line gained. The stronger your rod is the more leverage it will have, which in turn can allow you to stop a fish in its tracks.

When I strike into a fish I tighten up to it as described above and then I have to decide how to use my lever to best advantage. If I am fishing to snags, if possible I walk backwards to take up all the stretch and pull the carp from the danger. However, for normal carp fishing situations, you should be able to stop the carp from running if you hold your rod vertical, apply finger pressure on your spool and set your clutch correctly. Do not lower your rod tip to start pumping until the fish has stopped its run. That could be disastrous as it allows a decrease in tension causing the hook to fall out. Sometimes the carp will really go wild and keep on running. If this is the case it is up to you to increase tension via your clutch and not let it get away. Do not attempt to wind line on to a reel when the clutch is spinning away; all you will do is twist your line and possibly weaken it. At some stage you will have to stop the fish and you may have to use more force than you want to at times, but with more fish under your belt the process does become easier.

Fig. 105 *Pumping.*

Fig. 106 *Applying side-strain.*

Pumping

Once the carp has stopped running you can use the rod as a lever via a lifting and lowering technique which is known as pumping (*see* Fig. 105). When your rod is vertical the line is at its tightest and no line should be taken, and hopefully you will be exerting enough pressure to pull the carp towards you. As you lower your rod, wind with your reel handle to take in the gained line so that you stop the carp moving out again. Many fights are dour affairs where, once a carp is prevented from running, the next two or three minutes are taken up with pumping it in. However, if it does fly off again, lift the rod up and use your clutch to its best advantage. Never let the line go slack when you lower your rod tip and keep a tight line by winding your reel handle. Don't let the rod tip drop too much – usually I don't let it drop below a ten- to twenty-degree level. Also, don't be too vigorous with this raising and lowering of the rod or you may

bounce or pull the hook out of the carp's mouth. Again, practice will improve your technique. All movements should be smooth and controlled to ensure maximum strain on the fish with minimum risk of a hook pull.

Applying Sidestrain

So, you have the carp under control and it's getting closer to the bank, but what do you do if it suddenly starts to power away to your left or right? You may be able to let it take line – providing it is not heading for snags or weed. If you have been pumping for quite some time your clutch will probably be firm, so if there is any danger of the hook pulling out then slacken off a bit. Remember, as the carp gets closer in, the amount of line out decreases and so does the safety effect that the stretch gives. The closer the carp is to you, the more you will have to rely on your own skill and not hope that a stretchy line will see you through.

By placing your rod to the right or left as in Fig. 106, you can usually persuade the carp to stop. This is called sidestrain. Do be careful when angling your rod to the left or right that the tip does not become caught in overhead foliage. A line which gets caught round a branch or twig is a line which may jam, resulting in the fish coming off. Similarly, when playing fish don't lift your rod so high that it catches in tree branches. It can spell disaster and if you think it won't happen to you, then you are wrong. In the heat of the moment when your adrenalin is pumping it is very easy to make mistakes, and these kind of mistakes will cost you fish!

Position when Playing a Fish

If there is one mistake which anglers of all experience tend to make it is standing up to play fish when they are in the final throes of being played out. Providing you don't need to stand up, don't do so when the carp is within 10yd of the bank. Take a look back to Chapter 1 and remember how a carp can see out of the water with its unique set of eyes. Now think how an angler standing up close to the bank may appear to that carp. Whilst a tree or somebody standing still may not scare it, a person standing up waving a rod almost certainly will (*see* Fig. 107). A frightened carp is a carp which is likely to bolt at the last minute. If it does bolt and you are not expecting it you may lose the fish, and this is stupid if you have worked hard trying to catch it. To avoid this, kneel down instead and move the rod round smoothly, rather than as if you were waving a bull whip or magician's wand. The lower you are the less the angle through which the carp can possibly view you (*see* Fig. 108), and hopefully the more chance you have of leading it in rather than pulling it in.

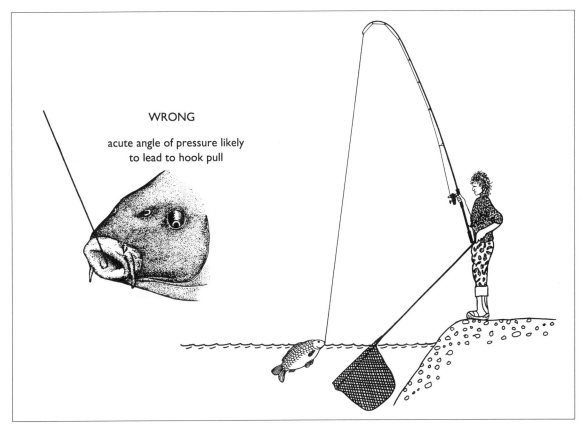

WRONG

acute angle of pressure likely to lead to hook pull

Fig. 107 *An incorrect netting stance.*

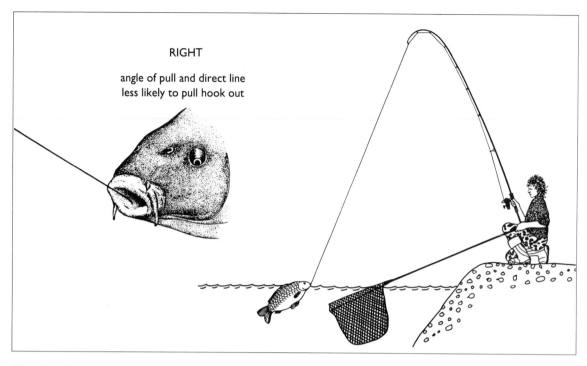

RIGHT

angle of pull and direct line
less likely to pull hook out

Fig. 108 *The correct netting stance.*

Obviously, if there is a canopy of reeds in front of you or you have to remain standing in order to draw the fish over a gravel bar then do so. However, if you don't have to then keep low.

NETTING THE FISH

Having drawn the carp in close and having knelt down to avoid scaring it, it's vital that you don't chase it around with your landing net – this is bound to result in your carp tearing around in the margins. Your landing net should be within easy reach (*see* Fig. 109), and once the carp is within range and you are on your knees you should not have to stand up again to get the net. Push the net gently out into the water in front of you, making sure the mesh sinks and does not float. Also, make sure it doesn't snag up in the marginal reeds because you won't have any free hands to untangle it at that stage.

If your fishery is a popular carp fishery where even a single bleep brings the crowds running,

then some people may want to come to give you advice on how to net your carp. Tell them politely to keep well back, to keep quiet and to kneel down as well (*see* Fig. 110). The last thing you want is for someone to jump up and down waving his arms and shouting just before the hook pulls out in front of the crowd and the carp bolts away.

You are leading your carp in and not trying to pull its head off, so pressure at this point should be enough to lead it to the net but not so much as to pull the hook out. Often at this stage carp seem to find an extra burst of energy, and power up and down the margin in front of you in an attempt to get free. Don't panic, but simply let the rod tip follow its progress; when the carp wants line then give it, and when you can take line then do so. You have almost won the contest at this stage so, if you take it easy, it is all yours. When the carp has had enough it will probably come to the surface, and its mouth will open and display the hook. Once your carp is on the surface it is a dead weight, and at that stage you can

Fig. 109 Keep your landing net within easy reach.

Fig. 110 Take it easy.

pull the hook out. Simply draw the fish in with minimal pressure, keep that clutch slackened right off and it's yours (*see* Fig. 111). Using no quick movements or lunges, carefully draw it into the net.

Netting Your Own Fish or Not?

If possible, it is advisable to net your own fish and not let other people do it. Most of the time I prefer to net my own fish so that if anything does go wrong it is my fault and no one else can be blamed. Once that carp has fallen off, all the accusations, shouts or whatever won't bring it back, so button your mouth and learn by your mistakes. Obviously, if you have a fishing partner whose netting ability you trust then this is even better. He can hold the net out further than you can and, providing neither of you panics, you should have the job over and done with a lot quicker. However, if you don't have a regular partner then insist that you do the netting your-

self. Even if people claim to have netted hundreds of fish in their time, politely refuse and say that you prefer to do it yourself. If you don't believe me, you certainly will when someone manages to push the carp off with the net!

Netting a Fish at Night

Unless your fishery is permanently lit at night by factory lights or whatever, then in my opinion netting fish at night without light can be a real lottery. In pitch blackness when you have just woken up it is difficult trying to see just how far out the carp is and whether you are netting the weed round the shock leader knot or a carp. Over the years I have lost too many carp by not using a light, so I always use one now. Whilst the purists may jump up and down in horror at this, I can only give advice on what I feel is the most effective way – to be fair, I have used this method for the last three or four years with much success. All I do is switch the torch on whilst I am playing the fish and draw it into the beam of light. I angle the light so it does not point into the water but across it. Once the fish is beaten I draw it into the light and net it with no struggling to see where it is – easy and very effective. Providing you don't move the light, you won't scare the carp and you will find netting it a lot easier. The light I use is a common or garden torch: don't use a Tilley lamp.

The diagrams and information in this chapter should have explained the striking, playing and netting of a fish if you have ever had any trouble with those facets. It really isn't as complicated as it sounds, and in most cases it is poor techniques that cost fish rather than the fish's strength winning out. Be aware what you have to do, keep to a plan and don't panic.

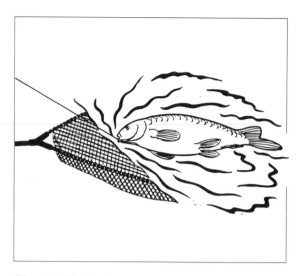

Fig. 111 *The final moments.*

A tiny hook, but a good hookhold helped me to land this carp.

The moment of truth.

11 PHOTOGRAPHY FOR THE CARP ANGLER

I suppose one or two people who buy this book might find it unusual that I have included a full chapter on fish photography as it isn't really a part of catching carp. However, in this day and age where you can spend so much money and so much time trying to catch a carp, it's silly not to have a decent record of it. Many people over the years have said to me that they wish they had bought a decent camera earlier, or had photographed a certain fish properly, so I thought a basic step-by-step guide would be a useful feature to include in this book. The information should not become too dated as although the cameras may get better the principles don't change. If you've ever wondered why other people's pictures are better than yours or how to get your pictures to a printable quality, then this is for you. As with everything I've covered in the book it is plain advice and certainly won't mean that you have to spend a fortune on cameras or hours over photography manuals.

WHICH CAMERA?

If there is one thing that rings true it is that you shouldn't expect professional-looking pictures from a cheap camera. Unlike with rods, reels and bedchairs, you ought to spend as much as you can on a good camera because if you learn how to use it properly and look after it, you should not need to change it for a long time.

Cheap cameras are cheap because they don't have good lenses or powerful flashes. If you purchase a cheap camera you may regret it in the long run. Some of the fish you catch are ones you may never catch again, and if it's a fish of a lifetime and nobody else has a good camera you will kick yourself time and time again. If possible, try not to rely on anybody having a decent camera as there will come a time when they don't and you will regret it. If I still haven't convinced you of the need for a good camera, then I'm sure time will change your mind – I only hope it is before you catch that special carp.

As with fishing rods, there are hundreds of cameras around and the trick is finding one which is suitable for you. To purchase a good camera you may have to spend quite a lot of money, but as it will record your catches over the next several years, it should be a good investment. I'm sure you will have wasted more money on things like bait which didn't work, radical hooks, buzzers and 101 things that I dare not even mention! Do try to purchase a good camera because it will prove its worth many times over, and if you are still concerned over the money aspect just think that *Angler's Mail* pays for every shot printed – take photographs of ten carp and you will have your money back.

What is a Good Camera?

Once you spend a reasonable amount on a camera you will end up, or should end up with something that will produce shots equally as good as those featured in the colour section of this book. These pictures were all taken on a Minolta 5000i

Dynax camera which is still going strong three years after purchase. It has all the features I think you will need in a camera for basic carp fishing photography, and these are discussed below.

Autofocus

Remember that a camera is only as good as the person using it, and in many cases the person behind the lens taking your photograph will not have a working knowledge of your particular camera. This is usually apparent when your photos end up out of focus because he didn't understand the focusing method or couldn't tell whether it was in focus or not. With an autofocus camera all the photographer has to do is make sure you are framed in the picture and make sure the autofocus circle or square is on the fish. Once he presses the shutter knob the camera automatically focuses itself on the fish and your picture should be spot-on. At night this feature is absolutely brilliant as such cameras often have an infra-red autofocus which bounces an infra-red beam off the carp so that the photographer knows he's got it right. I look in detail at how to take good photos later in this chapter, so I won't pursue this any further here.

Built-In Flash

Because some of your carp may be caught in the hours of darkness or in low light conditions, it is essential that your camera has a built-in flash unit to compensate for this lack of light. I used to have various cameras to which I could add flash units, but in my experience it is far too fiddly having to play about slotting these on, setting the correct aperture and so on. With a built-in flash all you do is press your flash button (your camera will tell you if it's necessary or not) and the camera will do the rest – brilliant and foolproof.

Reliability

No matter how many features a camera may have it is only useful if it is reliable. Databanks and multi-zoom lenses are all well and good, but will they continue to perform just as well in three or five years' time? My advice would be to buy as simple a camera as possible because most of the time all you are looking for is a sharp and properly exposed trophy-type shot. However, if you want to experiment with all sorts of trick shots then by all means invest in a 'special', providing it's a proven model and is reliable.

Self-Timer Device

Never contemplate buying a camera which does not have a self-timer built into it. Even if you fish popular waters, sooner or later you are going to catch a good fish when no one is there to do the honours. A self-timer device allows you to press a switch and after a gap of, say, nine to thirteen seconds, the camera will automatically take a photograph of what is in the frame – hopefully this is you with a fish! Most cameras have built-in self-timer devices and they can be operated via a button or a separate bulb release. Never having used a bulb release, I cannot comment on their advantages over normal buttons, but all I would say is that I have never had a problem with my Minolta's twelve-second delay – providing you set up everything properly, you shouldn't have a problem.

These are the four criteria I would look for in a camera and, as I like to provide guidance through my personal usage of an item, I will let you know that my two personal choices are the Minolta 5000i Dynax and the Minolta 7000i Dynax. Both satisfy the criteria and if there was one single item I could guarantee success with in carp fishing, it would have to be either of these two. Personally, I would choose the Minolta 5000i Dynax because it has never let me down and because it's cheaper!

FILM CHOICE

Before you even think of using your camera you will have to decide whether you want your record of capture to be in the form of a photograph or a slide. For most anglers who don't write regularly for fishing magazines or give slide shows, I would advise prints. If you are rich enough, you could have a camera for each format!

Print Film

A print film is a record in photograph form which you can show to your friends and then place in your photograph album. I have used print film quite a lot in the past and have always looked to Fuji to satisfy my requirements. My specific choice of print film is a Fuji HG grade which I use all year round. The reason why I use Fuji film is that it does seem to give a warm tone to pictures – this has the effect of putting a slight tinge of colour in your face, and stops both you and the fish looking washed out and pasty in appearance. Some people swear by Kodacolor film which has an excellent reputation, but I feel that it tends to leave you and the fish looking cold – although this may be truer to how you feel at the time, I would still recommend Fuji print film.

Slide Film

In this case, your record of capture will be on a slide which has to be viewed with a slide projector. For the last two or three years I have used slide film exclusively because I give slide shows and must submit good-quality slides with the articles I write. Whilst I know many prints are good enough for publication, as a features editor I think I can say fairly that colour front covers and full-page shots are usually reproduced from slides. If you intend to write or talk on a regular basis, you should therefore choose a good slide film; if you don't I'm sure a good print film will do for your requirements just as well. My choice of slide film has been Fuji, which again I use all year round. Do also remember that you can have good prints taken from slides.

Film Speed (ASA Rating)

If you have an interest in photography already you will know all about this aspect, but if you don't then it can be quite baffling at times. Most films have an ASA rating of either 60, 100, 200, 400 or 1,000. The smaller the number is, the more light you require to take a good picture; the higher the number, the less light you need to take a picture. However, if it was as simple as that you would surely plumb for a 1,000 speed every time. Unfortunately there is a second leg to the equation. The bigger the number, the poorer the quality (more grainy or blurred) of your picture. At an ASA rating of 60 or 100 the pictures will be very crisp, providing your autofocus has been used properly.

Clearly you can't have the best of both worlds (quality and high speed) so you will have to make your mind up which is most important. If your camera has a good flash unit you would be best choosing a film speed which gives sharp pictures, even if you have to use your flash in low-light conditions. A film speed of 100 is a good choice, and with a good flash unit you should have good, sharp pictures which are also properly exposed.

Quality and Size?

Do not purchase films in quantity because they may end up hanging around in your camera bag for a long time. Also, don't be tempted to buy an out-of-date film or a film from your corner shop that is covered in dust! Films deteriorate in time and an expensive camera can't do anything about that. I like to buy films with twenty-four exposures on them because that number will allow me to cover four fish adequately. Unless it is a prolific water, thirty-six shots is a lot and you will have itchy fingers a long time before you use all the film up.

DEVELOPING PRINTS OR SLIDE FILM

Even if you have a good camera and take a crisp shot on good-quality print film, it can all come to grief if you insist on taking the film to poor developers or to one-hour developers. I know that it is often tempting to have your pictures developed as soon as possible, but if you hold back a little and choose a reputable firm it will be worth it.

If you live in a big city there should be a number of developers around – once you've found a good one stick with it and don't fall into the trap of believing that cheapest is best or that free film with each order is a bargain. Why buy an expensive camera and then cut back on developing costs? With print film I tend to use the professional laboratories or the seven-day service chemists offer. No matter what some places may tell you, a one-hour turn-round gives a one-hour-quality print and usually that is poor. If you really want a good print choose a professional laboratory.

For slides I purchase prepaid Fuji slide film which contains an envelope inside each box so that you can send your film to the Fuji laboratory. I can honestly say that I have never had any quibbles about the quality of these slides, and even if the film does take up to a week to come back the wait is worth it. A good tip here is to send your slide film to Fuji by first class recorded delivery post because they seem to treat it as a priority order and return it as soon as possible.

ADDITIONAL PURCHASES

Camera Bag
There are lots of types to choose from and as a good one is fairly cheap it won't break the bank either. Pick one which will fit into your rucksack and preferably one which will take camera, spare films, batteries, cleaning equipment, binoculars and permits. Pack them all away in one gadget bag so that you know where everything is when you need it.

Spare Batteries and Films
Keep two spare films just in case you do catch a number of fish in a session. I keep at least one spare camera battery as well, because if one does go you will probably not be able to buy another at a service station or newsagent.

Skylight Filter
These are vital if you want to spend little on protecting expensive lenses. All you do is screw one on the front of your lens – as well as keeping the mud off your expensive lens front they also tend to quieten down colours and brightness when taking pictures. Very few people seem to use them, which is very shortsighted indeed and can be very costly in the long run.

Lens Hood
A little push-on rubber hood which fits round the lens is again something I see very few people using. It keeps back any 'spare' light which can cause flare-ups on your picture and, even more obvious, it stops rain finding its way on to your lens.

Cleaning Kits
No matter how clean and tidy you are as an angler, your camera will pick up a certain quantity of dust, moisture and the like. Superficially this may not look much, but if it covers your filter or lens front, or enters your camera body it can spell disaster. Cameras should be kept in their case unless being used, but as they may even pick up dust there a cleaning kit is necessary. Buy a kit rather than separate items, as it works out cheaper that way and you won't forget anything. A blower gets rid of the dust, the solution is used to clean off mud and dirt, and tissues are essential so that you don't scratch your filter cover. Whilst it is certainly acceptable to use a towel or duster on your camera body, don't contemplate using one on your lens.

Tripod
If you wish to use a self-timer then you will need to have some sort of tripod on which to place your camera. Don't be tempted to use a bankstick with a screw-in adaptor because you will be restricted to landscape shots ('sideways' shots taken with the camera in the 'normal' position) as the screw is built into the camera bottom. However, with a tripod you can heighten or lower your camera, take vertical (portrait) shots, and so frame the picture properly. A good tripod which will fit in your rucksack pocket is very reasonably priced and will repay you many times over.

Hopefully these details will give you some idea of just what you are looking for in order to obtain a good-quality picture of your fish. In photography you get what you pay for, and even though you don't need to spend the earth, a quality camera and accessories will be a sound investment. Now, on to your other priority – getting the pictures taken.

CHOOSING A BACKGROUND AND FOREGROUND (FIG. 112)

No matter how good your camera is and no matter how versatile your photographer or self-timer may be, if you've put yourself in a silly position in the first place your photograph will be poor in comparison to what they could be. In order to get a good trophy shot, the area behind you (the background) and the area in front of you (the foreground) need to be chosen carefully.

Background

The ideal backgrounds are a tree, bushes, reeds or similar which will provide a suitable back area for your photograph. What you are looking for is something which will bounce some of the flash-light off to give a scenic effect. If you choose to use a flat stretch of bank with nothing behind you, you will look a little isolated and your picture will be somewhat barren. A tree or bush adds a little character to the picture and allows flash to illuminate it slightly. Do avoid placing housing estates, pylons, motorway signs or other anglers in the background as these stand out like sore thumbs and ruin otherwise good pictures. A final point is that you should make sure when having your photograph taken in front of a tree that its branches don't seem to be growing out of the top of your head.

Foreground

Sometimes even more important than the background is the area between you and the camera. If there are grass stalks, brambles or reeds in this area the camera lens will pick them up and you could end up with a photograph of fish obscured by blurred stalks or stems. If possible, and without ruining the swim, make sure that your foreground is flattened to avoid this. Keep things like landing-net poles, forceps, cups of water and carp sacks out of the foreground as well because these also distract from you holding your fish. A little care and thought goes a long way!

HOLDING A CARP FOR PHOTOGRAPHS

Carp are quite large in comparison with most other fish specimens, but many anglers still seem to want to exaggerate their size by holding them out at arm's length in all sorts of poses. There is no need to do this and I hope that you will follow

Fig. 112 *The background and foreground.*

the easy instructions below for perfect pictures every time.

1. Before you decide to have the photograph taken, make sure that the carp's flank is free of grass, dirt and leaves – these are easy to miss and can spoil a potentially lovely picture. Pick them off carefully or, in the case of dirt, wash it off with water. Do not wipe the fish's flank down with towels, carp sacks or whatever as this removes mucus from the carp and can leave it vulnerable to disease. Always keep your hands nice and wet as well.

2. Make sure that you have taken your watch off and any jackets which have zips, badges or press studs. If the carp starts to flap and you have to hold it tight to your body, you do not want a metal badge or watch strap cutting into its flank.

3. Place one hand under its gills and one hand under its anal area (see Chapter 12 for a description on how to do this). Do not, and I can't stress this too much, hold the carp away from your body because it is both dangerous to the carp and can ruin your pictures as well. As you can see from Fig. 112, the further the carp is away from your body, the more your face is likely to be a blur on the photograph. The autofocus will hopefully lock on to the carp's flank so that the greater the distance between that locking point and your face, the more chance you have of your face being out of focus. Your fingers will look like sausages and whilst the carp will look big, it will also look very silly indeed. It is a mistake we have made, so learn from that. A 15lb-plus carp is a big fish and need not be held out.

4. Tilt the carp's head slightly upwards and make sure that the carp is on a level keel and not leaning into your body. The more it leans towards the captor the more likely it is that your flash will bounce off it and give it a burnt-out look.

5. A panful of water over the fish at this stage gives it a lovely wet look and keeps it nice and moist. Take two to four shots of each flank to make sure you have at least one which is spot-on. Once you have put it back it is too late,

and a roll of film for three or four fish really isn't too much.

6. When holding the carp, hold it firmly but not harshly. Let it know you are boss and you should be okay. However, some fish are frisky so you will have to be prepared for that; always keep them over that unhooking mat.

7. Finally, do try to smile and at least look as if you are happy. Don't scowl or look over the moon either as a camera picture only seems to accentuate such expressions. If you are using a flash which does not have a red-eye device on it, look to the left or right and not directly into the camera if you want to avoid those red-eye shots!

PHOTOGRAPHY WITH ASSISTANCE (FIGS 113–20)

If you have someone to take photographs for you, the following steps should lead to successful pictures.

1. As soon as possible after casting out (and preferably before casting out on very prolific waters), you should make sure everything is ready for photography. I have been amazed at times just how quick action has been even on winter days, so the first job to do once your rods are out is to situate your unhooking mat where you intend to take the photograph (see Fig. 113).

2. Having hopefully landed a fish, it's a question of how to get as good a picture as you can even if your photographer has never handled your type of camera before. The first job is to make sure that the fish is safely unhooked and that your rod is out of the way. Give the carp a minute's breather whilst you arrange the photographic gear. I usually leave the carp in the landing net at the edge while I sort out the camera (see Fig. 114). If it's a particularly energetic fish it may be a good idea to stake down the landing-net handle.

3. Get your photographer to kneel in exactly the position you will be when you are having your photo taken (see Fig. 115). Having an unhooking mat helps because it does give the exact spot over which will hold your fish.

Fig. 113 Position your unhooking mat first.

Fig. 114 Secure the carp.

4. Look through your viewfinder and check that everything is framed correctly (*see* Fig. 116). Normally I tilt the camera on its side for portrait shots – this utilizes all the person and fish rather than the scenery. Is the person you are framing the same size as you? If he is then there will be no problem – providing he and you change places

exactly the result should be the same. However, if he is a lot smaller than you are, you should move a little further back to take this fact into account. Remember the dos and don'ts of backgrounds, and check that everything is as it should be. If it is then you are ready to move on to the next step.

Fig. 115 Focus the camera.

Fig. 116 Frame the shot.

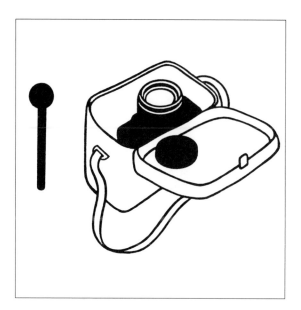

Fig. 117 Insert the marker.

Fig. 118 Change places with your photographer

5. Putting the lens cap in your pocket, mark the exact spot where you and your camera were positioned and put it down on a bait tub, camera bag or whatever. I usually mark the spot with a small peg, but a stick will do (*see* Fig. 117). Make sure this marker is where your camera was held (in other words, a little in front of your body) and not where your feet were. Don't put the camera on the ground as that is just asking for trouble – either moisture or dirt will get in it or someone will put their foot on it!

6. Go back to the water's edge, carry the carp from there to the unhooking mat and position yourself in exactly the same position as your friend was earlier (*see* Fig. 118). Read through Chapter 12 so that you know how to handle the carp correctly – have some water ready to pour on the carp and don't rush the job.

7. Now you are ready to have your photograph taken. Ensure the flank of the carp is not covered in dirt or leaves – a quick douse in water will usually do the trick but individual stems of grass and so on may need picking off. Kneel down and keep the carp 12–24in off the ground at the most. Hold the carp as I have described and you are now ready for action! Do keep a firm grip on the carp.

8. Ensure that your photographer is standing in exactly the same spot as you were and that the camera is held over the marker (*see* Fig. 119). Is he holding the camera in the vertical position? Are any camera straps hanging down? Is his hand over the lens? Have you remembered to take the lens cap off? Does he keep jerking when he takes

Fig. 119 Are you in focus?

Fig. 120 *The final result.*

your photograph? Is he centralizing the autofocus on the carp? As far as the latter goes, he should be – if he isn't, you and your knee will be in focus and not the carp. Keep telling him what to do and watch out for all these little things. If you need or want a flash, make sure it operates each time. Keep talking to your photographer all the time and take him through it (*see* Fig. 120). Once you are satisfied he has taken three or four good shots of each side, return the carp to the water as soon as possible. After you have cleaned your hands, put the lens cap on the camera and then put that camera in the bag out of harm's way.

SELF-TIMER PHOTOGRAPHY

Although having a fellow angler taking the picture is quite easy and self-timer photography is *potentially* quite difficult, with a little thought it can be just as easy and sometimes more effective. However, as with most things it's all down to planning so that if you have carried out just one or two chores in advance it can be easy.

First, you must have a decent tripod as I described earlier (*see* page 170). If it is a good one it will have a device which allows you to

release the camera from tripod quickly without having to unscrew it. All this device consists of is a small base which screws into your camera base and which you then push into the tripod top. A one-touch lever allows you to release it each time without having to disturb the tripod setting – a godsend and vital if you do fish on your own!

Second, look at Figs. 115 and 116, and the accompanying text where I described how to size up a 'framing' area. All you need to do is go through exactly the same steps at home with a friend, and then mark that distance with a piece of rope. Once your friend is correctly framed, simply mark the distance on the rope with a knot or otherwise and also mark on your tripod exactly how high it was set (*see* Fig. 121). All this is done at home and saves you having to mess about on the bank every time you want to set your camera up. Providing you are satisfied it has been correctly set up, you can then put your camera, tripod and rope away until you need them next time.

The following step-by-step guide and accompanying diagrams (Figs 122–7) should ensure success when you are taking photographs of yourself and your carp on the bank.

1. As before, having caught the fish unhook it and make sure it is safely left in the landing net close to the bank. If you have any doubts that it may power off with your net then stake the handle down. Set your tripod up and make sure your unhooking mat is at the end of that premarked piece of rope. The rope should run from the tripod leg to the exact spot where you intend to hold the fish above the unhooking mat (*see* Fig. 122).

2. Having marked the distance out, go to your tripod, jack it up to the required height (your white mark) and make sure your camera is set to take those vertical shots. Look carefully down the viewer (*see* Fig. 123); are there any obstructions in the foreground and what does the background look like?

3. Go back to the water's edge, carry the carp to the unhooking mat and make sure it is ready to

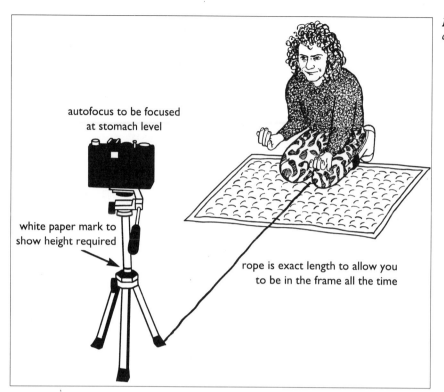

Fig. 121 Pre-set your camera and tripod at home.

autofocus to be focused at stomach level

white paper mark to show height required

rope is exact length to allow you to be in the frame all the time

be photographed. If it is still lively you may have to let it settle for a minute or two whilst it calms down. Check its flank – is there any grass or leaves on it? If it is fine then proceed (*see* Fig. 124).

4. Go back to the tripod, retrieve the rope (*see* Fig. 125) while keeping a watchful eye on the carp all the time and have one last look through the camera lens to make sure it's all set perfectly.

5. Touch the self-timer button (*see* Fig. 126) and you have between nine and thirteen seconds to pose with the carp. Touch the button gently so you don't knock the tripod, and be careful not to knock it over in your haste to get back to the fish.

6. Hold the fish in the correct position, look to the left or right of the camera and say 'Cheese' (*see* Fig. 127). Did the flash go off if necessary? Repeat Steps 5 and 6 for three shots of each flank and you've cracked it.

That's a lot easier than you expected, isn't it? A little planning means that you will never have to worry again about good-quality shots. I usually erect the camera with the prefixed mark and

tripod set properly *before* I catch a fish, and detach the camera and leave it in its case. Then if I do catch a fish I simply clip the camera back on its mount and I'm on my way. If I don't catch one then I pack the tripod away the next morning.

When I originally decided to write a chapter on photography, I wanted to keep it brief and to the point. However, there are so many little tricks I have discovered over the years which can give you brilliant results easily that I have put down everything I know. There is no reason at all why anyone shouldn't be able to reproduce pictures equally as good as mine, and who knows, one day you may be doing the honours for me or I for you.

Fig. 122 Measure the distance with a piece of rope (*top left*).
Fig. 123 Set the height and focus (*top right*).
Fig. 124 Place the carp in the position in which you want it (*centre left*).
Fig. 125 Detach the rope (*centre right*).
Fig. 126 Only twelve seconds to go (*bottom left*).
Fig. 127 Smile (*bottom right*).

12 CARE AND CONSERVATION

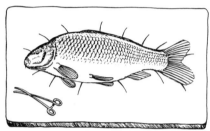

No instructional book on carp fishing would be complete without an in-depth look at how best to care for the carp you have caught. In fact, such a chapter should really be at the start of the book. In these days when we have become so efficient at catching carp, it is vitally important that carp which are sometimes caught as much as ten times a year are returned with as little trauma as possible. It has been my experience that the less stress a carp is placed under, the more likely it is to be caught again within a reasonable period. Carp which are subjected to lengthy sackings, long photo sessions and so on suffer stress. This stress causes a loss of appetite, weight loss and, even if you only think of yourself, it makes them harder to catch next time. Imagine if everybody really made an effort to look after the carp – we would all find them somewhat easier to catch.

As there are a number of ways to improve your care of the carp, in this chapter I look at the whole scenario from netting to finally returning the carp so that you can see just how you can do your bit to look after the carp.

NETTING CARP

Due to the popularity of carp fishing and the availability of good tackle, decent landing nets are not difficult to get hold of and carp anglers are able to purchase a good net from a reputable company. Gardner, Nash and Solar all have good landing nets in their ranges, so choose the one which suits you, your pocket and your fishing best.

However, the safe netting of a carp is just as important to your fishing as purchasing a good net. Once you have drawn the carp into the net don't panic and start trying to pull it up the bank to see which fish it is. What's in the net is in it and you can't do anything about it to change that. Simply take your time and get things done with the minimum of fuss. If you are on your own, leave the carp in the net (providing it's not going to power away with it), put your rod down and ensure that your unhooking mat, forceps, Klinik and tripod are all at the ready. Your unhooking mat and tripod should have been set up in advance, so you have no excuse to start messing about with them at this stage. When everything is done you can get your carp to the unhooking stage.

READY FOR UNHOOKING

In an ideal world it would be nice to be able to unhook the carp in the water, but this can be difficult so I wouldn't advise anybody to try it. You will only end up bending the carp into all sorts of positions, frightening it to death and sometimes transferring the hook from its mouth to your hand. Instead, take a pair of scissors and carefully cut your trace off at the swivel. This allows you to move your rod away – this stops it from being trodden on, keeps the 3oz bomb from hitting the carp in the face each time you move the rod and generally makes things a lot easier. Don't worry that you have to tie on a new trace – surely a carp of *any* size has got to make that worthwhile. Take your rod and place it out of harm's way and not where someone will stand on it.

If you are going to use a self-timer for photography then dry your hands, put your camera on the tripod and get everything set up. Providing the carp is in deep enough water it will be all right, and the short rest will even do it good as you prepare your gear. If somebody else is taking the photo, then do all the framing at this point and have him wait by the mark (*see* page 173). When all this is done, get the carp over to the unhooking mat. Before you lift the carp out of the water, it is vital that you remember that water is a support for carp – once out of water they are a dead weight and are more likely to damage themselves if they thrash about, so once you lift them up they are out of their natural environment and totally in your care. If the carp fought for a long time before being landed it may need a breather of five minutes or so to regain some strength. However, don't give any carp too long or it will fight you on the bank. The last thing you want is a wrestling match over an unhooking mat.

Usually I will disengage the landing net from its handle by pulling both spigots out of the spreader block. This means that when you walk around with a carp in the net, the 6ft or 7ft pole will not catch everything. Locke's new net has a detachable top piece which is a great idea and saves all that messing about. Similarly, Landeasy have the concept of an inner net which means you just pull the velcro tape away and the carp is already in a weigh-bag or sling. Unfortunately, however, because many waters ban weigh-slings, it is difficult to find waters on which you can use this particular brand of net.

Providing your net is deep enough, gather the mesh round the poles and prepare to lift up the carp. My usual method is to lift up each side of the net, and once I can feel where the carp is I put my hands in the water under it and lift it up. This way I am supporting its body with my two hands rather than allowing it to swing about (*see* Fig. 128). Make sure that the hook which is still in the carp isn't likely to catch in your hand and, having got the carp close to your body, cradle it carefully to the unhooking mat.

UNHOOKING THE CARP

Put the carp down carefully on your unhooking mat, and make sure as you do so that its fins are not bent under each other, and that its tail is flat and not likely to catch in the net. Make sure the carp does not flap all over the place – if it does seem frisky, use your body to keep it flat on the mat. As you are using your body as a lever to keep the carp down, it is vital that you don't have any badges or zips dangling as these can penetrate or scar the carp. Now, open your landing net mesh to reveal the carp and locate its mouth. Don't pull and tug the landing net or you may take scales off the carp or frighten it into thrashing about and causing itself damage. If it is somewhat tricky to get the carp out because the mesh has knotted itself up, take your time and don't panic. Finally, when the mouth of the carp is visible put one *wet* hand under its far side and slightly tilt its mouth up to you so that the whole opening is visible. Look for the hook. Is it lightly nicked in or is it well hooked? If the hookhold is a reasonable one, I always use my forceps which I clip to the unhooking mat. Open your forceps and grab the eye of the hook to pull it back through. If you are using large hooks, crush the barb first and then pull the hook through. Sometimes your boily will still be attached, so crush it off to make sure that it doesn't get in the way when you are fiddling about with the forceps. Under no circumstances should you try to push hooks out with your fingers or try to wiggle them out, because this can tear the carp's flesh, elongate the hook and make a real mess of the carp's mouth.

One little point to note is that once you have unhooked the carp and have the hook and hooklength clipped into the forceps, don't just throw the hooklength away, put it in your tackle box. As you saw in Chapter 5, the length of your trace can be vitally important and it's no good discarding a proven trace and forgetting its length!

If a hook is too deeply embedded to pull out with forceps, snip it in half with wire cutters (you can purchase these from any hardware shop). Don't leave hooks in carp, and when you do snip a hook in two get back both halves. Always use

Fig. 128 *Carrying a carp from water's edge to the unhooking mat.*

Kryston's excellent Klinik treatment on hook wounds (no matter how small) as this stops infection and keeps disease and parasites at bay. It has been specially designed for carp and is essential to keep in your tackle box.

Unhooking Mats

Luckily these seem to be more and more popular nowadays, and on most venues I fish they seem to be standard bankside equipment. Hopefully you will have an unhooking mat of some kind because they are vital on all fisheries. Even waters with grass banks should make unhooking mats compulsory to promote the carps' welfare. By having a mat, the carp, if it decides to flap about, has a cushion between itself and the ground. All the force is directed into the mat and hopefully the carp won't cause any major damage to itself. Even on a grassy bank a flapping carp can injure itself – grass is not as absorbent

as foam or air. As carp do not have eyelids either, one placed on grass or dirt can cause itself damage or eye irritation if not shielded from such elements. I always wet my unhooking mats first to stop mucus coming off the carp's body, and always make sure that the mat is on level ground to stop the carp sliding off it. There are a wide variety of mats from which to choose, but some with which I have been particularly impressed are listed below:

Romart Multimat You can inflate these with your mouth, and they provide a 1–2in cushion of air between the carp and the ground. Probably the best one available.

Andy Little Unhooking Mat Again inflatable with side walls to stop carp sliding about and ending up on the ground.

Kevin Nash/ET Mats These standard mats do a good job, but need j183 supplementing with foam or extra padding to stop a carp knocking itself against the ground. **Fox Mat** A more robust, compact version of Romart's which has been well thought out and which has served me well during the initial trial period. Well recommended.

WEIGHING FISH

Your first and most important question here is do you really need to weigh that carp? We should be fishing for carp as fish and not just as weights so please do ask yourself if it matters if the carp is 12lb or 13lb. Obviously, in your formative years you will naturally want to weigh everything, and I certainly wouldn't criticize that. However, when you've caught numbers of singles and doubles do you really need to weigh it rather than just photograph it? I hope not.

Weighing with a Conventional Weigh-Sling
This is the easiest of the two options and is also the most accurate. With your carp unhooked and safely on its unhooking mat (preferably covered by the landing net), take out your carp weigh-sling and wet it thoroughly in the water. Never contemplate using a dry sling because this can take off protective mucus. Having got the sling wet, hang it from your scales and zero them exactly on this wet sling. When all is set correctly put your scales down somewhere safe and take the sling over to the carp. Open the sling out next to the unhooked carp and, after cradling the carp in your hands as shown in Fig. 128, place it on top of the open sling. Do not try to push a sling under a carp or slide the carp about over the sling – you may break its fins and more likely than not will make a mess of it. Simply lift the carp up slightly and place it on the open sling. Make sure its fins are all lined up correctly, close up the sling and clip your hook on to the scales. Do remember again that as you lift the carp up it will be a dead weight and may start to flap about. Holding the T-bar which you should have on your scales, lift the carp up and over the unhooking mat. Don't lift it too high, but just

high enough to get an accurate reading. If the carp is flapping all over the place, put it down for a second on the mat and try again. Do not keep a carp suspended for minutes trying to see if it's 19lb 15oz or 20lb 0oz because you can cause it stress.

Weighing in a Landing Net
Some waters have a complete ban on carp sacks and weigh-slings, so if you want to weigh a fish you have to use your landing net. Whilst I can see problems in having to do this, if it stops people sacking fish for hours on end just to satisfy their egos with brace shots or daylight photography, I am all in favour of it. Again, with a little thought you shouldn't have a problem, and as many of the waters I fish have this ban I have had to find a way to do it properly.

All you need to do is take a 14in piece of rope and tie each end together so you have a continuous loop of rope. Do make sure this knot is secure as you have to rely on it when you are lifting up that carp. To weigh your carp, first zero your scales, and then place this loop round the mesh (*see* Fig. 129) and clip the hook into it. The arms of the net will act as a stop, so lift gently until the loop meets the arms and then lift it up to weigh your fish. This is very easy and, providing your carp is laid properly in the net, it causes no problem to the fish either. One point to note if you are an 'exact weight' man is that once the carp has been weighed you will have to subtract the weight of the landing net as well. Don't wring the net out though – you weighed the carp in a wet net so you subtract the weight of the wet net.

SHOULD YOU SACK FISH?

I have tried not to be too controversial in this book, but I may have to be in this section on sacking fish. It is my opinion that in the majority of cases the use of sacks is totally unnecessary, and if all that they are being used for is to get a good daylight shot or a brace shot, then you really have to ask yourself why you are fishing for carp. Brace shots are not necessary in carp fishing, and whilst

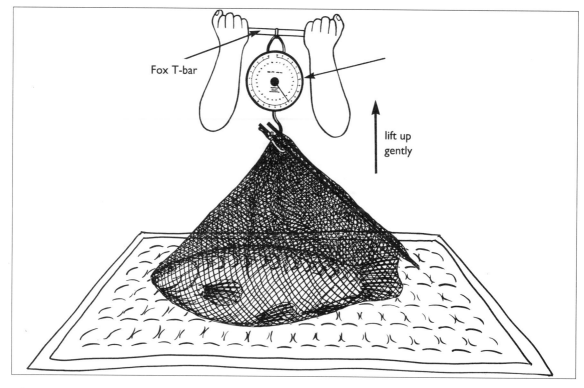

Fox T-bar

lift up
gently

Fig. 129 *Weigh-slings banned? This solves your problem of how to weigh your catch.*

we have all been guilty of this I hope we can learn from our mistakes and not do it again. As regards getting good photographs, even a fairly cheap camera has a good enough flash for night shots, and with self-timers on most you have no excuse to put a fish's welfare after your need for a trophy shot. Time and time again I see sackers using the old 'good photos' argument for sacks – as far as I am concerned, this is very irresponsible.

In my opinion you should only need to sack a fish on four occasions:

1. If you catch a record carp and need to have it verified by a member of the committee.

2. If a fish is obviously exhausted after a long fight and no amount of time in the landing net is helping it to recover. Even then, however, I believe you would be better off keeping it in a landing net where you can observe its progress rather than a sack where you have to 'guess' its progress.

3. Where fishery rules state that all carp must be

sacked so that they can be shown to the owner for whatever reasons. Even then I would have to ask myself how much I want to fish such a water.

4. Where a fish is diseased or ill and needs to be kept so that it can be shown to a person who is qualified to diagnose the complaint or who can take it away. After that, you must destroy your sack in order to stop transfer of disease.

As fishing is all about free choice, however, it is up to an individual angler to choose whether he sacks a fish or not.

HOW TO SACK FISH

If it is necessary to sack a fish, then please follow the guide-lines below:

1. Make sure that the sack you use is a good one. I used to use Kevin Nash's Standard or Monster

Carp Sacks until I stopped sacking carp and I found them to be excellent.

2. Only ever put one carp in a sack. This may sound obvious, but I once saw an angler put three in at one time.

3. Before a carp is put in a sack, the sack should be completely wet through to ensure that the carp does not lose mucus when inside.

4. Place the carp in an open sack and don't slide it in. As with weighing fish, place the carp on the open sack so it is in the bottom of the sack and doesn't slip and slide down it. Make sure its fins are all in line and not folded over so that they are likely to break or split.

5. Lift the carp in the sack as you would carry a carp in a landing net (see Fig. 128), and don't carry it like a dog on a lead. It is a dead weight out of water and may panic.

6. Make sure the sack is safely togged up or zipped up. Don't tie knots in the top of the sack as this can cause delay when you try to undo them, so causing the carp to suffer stress.

7. Secure your sack to an approved sack clip so there is no chance at all of it coming free and a carp being left somewhere in the lake inside a carp sack.

8. Never sack your fish in shallow water – it can be almost devoid of oxygen and so warm that it can cook the carp. Carp can suffer a form of sunstroke or sunburn which will kill them, and a lack of oxygen will also kill them. If you have to sack them then do so in water that is at least 6ft deep. If you can't find deep water then don't sack them, it's as simple as that.

9. If you have to sack a carp, make sure that it is for the minimum period necessary. I can't believe that this will ever exceed two hours. The longer the carp is in the sack the more stressed it will be and the more likely it is to cause damage to itself as it regains its strength and starts a wrestling match with you on the bank. All the time your carp is in the sack, please keep an eye on it. Is it lying properly in the water? Does it appear stressed? How warm is the water? Is it in direct sunlight? Is it being worried by pike and waterfowl? There are so many worries for you and the carp – please avoid them.

10. When you decide to unsack the carp, do remember that it may have regained its strength and will be very lively to say the least. When lifting it out of the water, cradle it and don't suspend it like a dog on a lead. Take it to the unhooking mat and keep a good eye on it. Undo the sack quickly and unravel it to get to the carp. Open your sack out fully and for goodness' sake don't slide the carp out on to your mat. Do keep a watchful eye on the carp because once daylight hits it you could be in for a real wrestling match.

Hopefully I have persuaded you *not* to sack carp except in extreme circumstances. In my opinion, the more venues that ban sacks the better. Whilst they do have their uses and can be used responsibly by responsible anglers, there are so many idiots that it is better for all carp anglers to suffer a ban than the carp to be knocked about.

CARP CARE DURING PHOTOGRAPHY

Chapter 11 looked fully at how to photograph carp for best results, but here I balance those instructions with the need to care for your carp to its best advantage.

Time Out of the Water

Always be aware how long you have had a carp out of water. If you have a plan and have everything to hand you should be able to take the photographs in under ninety seconds. However, if you haven't got a clue what to do you will waste vital minutes – this can cause stress and damage to the carp. The answer then is to plan it all out in advance.

Keep the Carp Wet

Always make sure that your hands are wet when you handle carp, and keep a large bucket of water handy to pour over the carp. Don't pour water down its mouth, but instead over its gills and head area. Don't wipe it down with a cloth to make it shine, but pick grass off and use a wet hand if you must wipe the carp at all.

Do You Need a Photograph?

I must admit that I like to photograph my carp if they are over 20lb or so, or are a pretty fish. However, on waters which are full of singles and low doubles, ask yourself if you really need to photograph each fish.

How Many Photographs?

I usually take three to four photographs of each flank of the fish, and have found that on my own with a self-timer this takes ninety seconds for three only of each side, or sixty seconds at most. Taking twenty or thirty shots of fish is unacceptable.

Brace Shots

Like many other people, I have been guilty of taking brace shots of carp – this, however, is not good for a carp's health. Even with a number of assistants you do end up with carp all over the place and with carp out of water longer than they need to be, so that all sorts of damage can be caused to the carp. Leave such shots out!

Holding Carp

I looked at this in Chapter 11 and also in Chapter 1 on carp's vital organs. Keep a carp low at all times and, unless you are carrying it to the water, always keep it over an unhooking mat. A dropped carp is a seriously damaged carp at least. Support the carp with both hands and don't try to conjure up some ridiculous poses. Please don't bounce carp up and down to get their fins to stand up.

Finally, no matter how well you treat your carp on the bank, there are probably 101 other things which can affect them. If I was going to cover each and every one in any detail, I would need a bigger book, so instead I will list certain things of which you should be aware. I'm sure your way of fishing may in some way encompass some of these topics, so if possible think how you can do your bit to care and conserve the carp.

1. Large hooks can cause holes in flesh.
2. Small hooks can cut through flesh like a knife.
3. Barbed hooks can increase the hole made by a hook.
4. Bent hooks can cause double hooking at times.
5. Modern hooklengths have no stretch and so can cause hooks to tear.
6. Modern shock leaders can act like a knife if they come into contact with a carp's body during a fight.
7. Fishing at range results in more chance of a carp being exhausted or becoming snagged up.
8. Fishing to snags can cause a carp to become tethered or rip its mouth.
9. Fishing in weed can lead to heaving at carp which in turn can cause mouth damage.
10. Particles – have you prepared them properly? What good do they do the carp?.
11. Boiled baits – do you know what quality the ingredients are and how they will affect the carp?
12. Flavours – if these are alcohol-based what levels have what effect on a carp's liver?
13. Fish oils – how much is too much?
14. Flash photography – what does a flash do to a carp's eye?

There are lots more factors which can cause carp harm, but do remember when carp fishing that if you see somebody doing something wrong, try to educate them into doing the right thing in future. Be polite, however, as shouting, bad language and the like cause ill-feeling and a poor attitude which is no good for the carp. Obviously, if people don't learn from their mistakes, you may need to take it further. Old people, young people and the inexperienced angler are all more likely to make mistakes, so if possible help them before this happens. If you sit there smugly waiting for the mistakes to occur and watch while they do occur, you are as guilty yourself. Remember that the carp are our future, so look after them!

FURTHER READING

TACKLE

Gibbinson, Jim, *Big Water Carp*, Chapter 5 (Beekay).

Maddocks, Kevin, *Carp Fever (10th Edition)*, Chapter 2 (Beekay).

Townley, Ken, *Tackle and Tactics – Carp in Depth* (Angling Publications).

Look also at the reviews on tackle news in each edition of *Carpworld*, *Coarse Fisherman* and other angling monthlies.

BAITS

Cottam, Bill and Paisley, Tim, *Carp Baits – Carp in Depth* (Angling Publications).

Look also at any bait catalogues produced by Nutrabaits, Cotswold Baits or Rod Hutchinson.

LONG-RANGE FISHING

Boots, Geoff, *Carpworld 24*, pages 88–91.

Carver, John, *Carp Fisher*.

Gibbinson, Jim, *Big Water Carp*, pages 184–98 (Beekay).

Townley, Ken, *Tackle and Tactics – Carp in Depth*, pages 64–72 (Angling Publications).

SNAG FISHING

Hutchinson, Rod, *Carp Now and Then*, Chapters 12 and 13 (Wonderdog).

Kenyon, Clive, 'Rock Solid 1', *Carp Fisher* (Number 13).

Kenyon, Clive, 'Rock Solid 2', *Carp Fisher* (Number 19).

Maddocks, Kevin, *Carp Fever (10th Edition)*, Chapter 3 (Beekay).

WINTER FISHING

Guide to 1,000 Carp Waters (Beekay).

Cundiff, Julian, *Guide to 750 Carp Waters* (Angling Publications).

Look also at *Carpworld*, *Coarse Fisherman* and *Coarse Fishing* magazines for suitable winter carp waters.

USEFUL ADDRESSES

There are a lot of manufacturers who are connected with carp angling and it seems that each month one or two more spring up. I have included here names, addresses and telephone numbers of reputable manufacturers whose products I can thoroughly recommend. Most of these firms have been in existence for many years and, providing you enclose a stamped addressed envelope or telephone at a sensible time, they will be only too pleased to help you. If you do have a problem with a product, or need help or advice, then get in touch with them and don't sit at home or moan on the bank because you are fishing with ineffective tackle or bait!

I have also included addresses of organizations and publishers connected with carp fishing.

BAIT MANUFACTURERS

Cotswold Baits,
Monts Farm,
Browning Hill,
Baghurst,
Basingstoke,
Hampshire
RG26 5JZ.
(0734) 810875.

Hinders Particles,
Brian Jarrett,
Ermin Street,
Stratton St Margaret,
Swindon,
Wiltshire, SN3 4NJ.
(0793) 828961.

Mainline Baits,
Zenon Bojko,
10 Mygrove Close,
Rainham,
Essex,
RM13 9QS.
(0708) 343165.

Nashbait,
Kevin Nash,
34 Brook Road,
Rayleigh,
Essex, SS6 7XN.
(0268) 770238.

Nutrabaits,
Bill Cottam or Richard
  Skidmore,
25–7 Fife Street,
Wincobank,
Sheffield,
South Yorkshire,
S9 1NN.
(0742) 422611.

Rod Hutchinson Baits,
Rod Hutchinson,
4 Union Street,
Louth,
Lincolnshire.

SBS,
7a Cooper Drive,
Springwood Industrial Estate,
Braintree,
Essex,
CM7 7RF.
(0376) 552333.

Streamselect,
Bob Baker,
Island Farm Avenue,
West Molsey,
Surrey,
KT8 0UZ.

PUBLICATIONS AND PUBLISHERS

Angler's Mail,
Richard Howard,
Kings Reach Tower,
Stamford Street,
London,
SE1 9LS.
(071) 261 5461.

Angling Publications,
Tim Paisley,
1 Grosvenor Square,
Sheffield,
South Yorkshire,
S2 4MS.
(0742) 582728.

Beekay Books,
Kevin Maddocks,
Withy Pool,
Bedford Road,
Henlow Camp,
Bedfordshire,
SG16 6EA.
(0462) 816960.

Big Carp Magazine,
Rob Maylin,
65 The Quantocks,
Flitwick,
Bedfordshire,
MK45 1TG.
(0525) 715728.

Coarse Fisherman,
Simon Roff,
Metrocrest Ltd,
67 Tyrrel Street,
Leicester,
Leicestershire,
LE3 5JB.
(0533) 511277.

The Crowood Press Ltd,
Ken Hathaway,
The Stable Block,
Crowood Lane,
Ramsbury,
Marlborough,
Wiltshire,
SN8 2HR.
(0672) 20320.

TACKLE MANUFACTURERS

Cobra Products,
Nina Sansome,
73 Paines Lane,
Pinner,
Middlesex,
HA5 3BX.

Bi-Tech Viper Ltd,
Bill Thurston,
PO Box 928,
Aylesford,
Kent,
ME20 6XF.
(0732) 872048.

Daiwa Sports Ltd,
John Middleton,
Netherton Industrial Estate,
Wishaw,
Strathclyde,
ML2 0EY.

Delkim Ltd,
Del Romang,
4 Gold Street,
Walgrave,
Northampton,
Northamptonshire,
NN6 9QE.
(0604) 781541.

Drennan Products,
Gary Barclay,
Leopold Street Works,
Oxford,
Oxfordshire,
OX4 1PJ.

Fox International,
Cliff Fox,
Fowler Road,
Hainault Industrial Estate,
Hainault,
Essex, IG6 3UT.
(081) 501 0921.

Gardner Tackle,
Richard Gardner,
2 Pepperbox Lane,
Palmers Cross,
Bramley,
Surrey,
GU5 0LW.
(0483) 66422.

Kevin Nash Tackle,
Kevin Nash,
34 Brook Road,
Rayleigh,
Essex,
SS6 7XN.
(0268) 770238.

Kryston Products,
Dave Chilton,
Bolton Enterprise Centre,
Washington Street,
Bolton,
Greater Manchester,
BL3 5EY.
(0204) 24262.

Partridge Hooks,
Alan Bramley,
Partridge of Redditch,
Redditch,
Hereford and Worcester,
B97 4JE.
(0527) 541380.

Shimano UK Ltd,
John Loftus,
Unit B2,
Lakeside Technology Park,
Phoenix Way,
Swansea Enterprise Park,
Llansamlet,
Swansea,
West Glamorgan,
SA7 9EH.

Solar Tackle,
Martin Locke,
35 Sutherland Road,
Belvedere,
Kent,
DA17 6JR.
(081) 311 3354.

Twilight Tackle,
177 Formans Road,
Sparkhill,
Birmingham,
West Midlands,
B11 3AX.

Zipp Leads,
196–8 Church Street,
Urmston,
Manchester,
Greater Manchester,
M31 1DX.

The following rod builders
will make up rods if you wish
to buy blanks.

Bob Morris Tackle,
1 Lincolnshire Terrace,
Lane End,
Darenth,
Dartford,
Kent,
DA2 7JP.
(0322) 78519.

Bruce Ashby Rods,
233 Maidstone Road,
Rainham,
Gillingham,
Kent,
ME8 0EX.
(0634) 33569.

Simpson's of Turnford,
1–2 Nunsbury Drive,
Turnford,
Hertfordshire,
EN10 6AQ.
(0992) 468799.

**Terry Eustace Fishing
   Tackle**,
370–2 Chester Road,
Sutton Coldfield,
West Midlands.
(021) 373 6627.

ORGANIZATIONS

**Anglers' Cooperative
Association(ACA)**,
Alan Edwards,
Midland Bank Chambers,
Westgate,
Grantham,
Lincolnshire,
NG31 6LE.

BCSG,
Jim Hindle,
c/o Sheila Hindle,
Forest View,
Clunton,
Craven Arms,
Shropshire,
S47 0HT.

Carp Society,
Vic Cranfield,
33 Covert Road,
Hainault,
Ilford,
Essex,
IG6 3AZ.
(081) 551 8250.

INDEX